SO-FJI-179

Development, Sexual Rights and Global Governance

Northwest Vista College
Learning Resource Center
3535 North Ellison Drive
San Antonio, Texas 78251

NORTHWEST
VISTA
COLLEGE
One of the Alamo
Community Colleges

This book addresses how sexual practices and identities are imagined and regulated through development discourses and within institutions of global governance.

The underlying premise of this volume is that the global development industry plays a central role in constructing people's sexual lives, access to citizenship, and struggles for livelihood. Despite the industry's persistent insistence on viewing sexuality as basically outside the realm of economic modernization and anti-poverty programs, this volume brings to the fore heterosexual bias within macroeconomic and human rights development frameworks. The work fills an important gap in understanding how people's intimate lives are governed through heteronormative policies which typically assume that the family is based on blood or property ties rather than on alternative forms of kinship. By placing heteronormativity at the center of analysis, this anthology thus provides a much-needed discussion about the development industry's role in pathologizing sexual deviance yet also, more recently, in helping make visible a sexual rights agenda.

Providing insights valuable to a range of disciplines, this book will be of particular interest to students and scholars of Development Studies, Gender Studies, and International Relations. It will also be highly relevant to development practitioners and international human rights advocates.

Amy Lind is Mary Ellen Heintz Endowed Chair and Associate Professor of Women's, Gender, and Sexuality Studies and faculty affiliate of the Department of Sociology and the School of Planning at the University of Cincinnati.

NORTHWEST VISTA COLLEGE

Development Sexual r

34009001247809

RIPE series in global political economy

Series Editors: Louise Amoore (*University of Durham, UK*), Jacqueline Best (*University of Ottawa, Canada*), Paul Langley (*Northumbria University, UK*), and Leonard Seabrooke (*Copenhagen Business School, Denmark*)

Formerly edited by Randall Germain (*Carleton University, Canada*), Rorden Wilkinson (*University of Manchester, UK*), Otto Holman (*University of Amsterdam*), Marianne Marchand (*Universidad de las Américas-Puebla*), Henk Overbeek (*Free University, Amsterdam*) and Marianne Franklin (*Goldsmiths, University of London, UK*)

The RIPE series editorial board are:

Mathias Albert (*Bielefeld University, Germany*), Mark Beeson (*University of Birmingham, UK*), A. Claire Cutler (*University of Victoria, Canada*), Marianne Franklin (*Goldsmiths, University of London, UK*), Randall Germain (*Carleton University, Canada*), Stephen Gill (*York University, Canada*), Jeffrey Hart (*Indiana University, USA*), Eric Helleiner (*Trent University, Canada*), Otto Holman (*University of Amsterdam, the Netherlands*), Marianne H. Marchand (*Universidad de las Américas-Puebla, Mexico*), Craig N. Murphy (*Wellesley College, USA*), Robert O'Brien (*McMaster University, Canada*), Henk Overbeek (*Vrije Universiteit, the Netherlands*), Anthony Payne (*University of Sheffield, UK*), V. Spike Peterson (*University of Arizona, USA*) and Rorden Wilkinson (*University of Manchester, UK*).

This series, published in association with the *Review of International Political Economy*, provides a forum for current and interdisciplinary debates on international political economy. The series aims to advance understanding of the key issues in the global political economy, and to present innovative analyses of emerging topics. The titles in the series focus on three broad themes:

- the structures, processes and actors of contemporary global transformations
- the changing forms taken by governance, at scales from the local and everyday to the global and systemic
- the inseparability of economic from political, social and cultural questions, including resistance, dissent and social movements.

The series comprises two strands:

The *RIPE Series in Global Political Economy* aims to address the needs of students and teachers, and the titles will be published in hardback and paperback. Titles include

**Transnational Classes and
International Relations**
Kees van der Pijl

Gender and Global Restructuring
Sightings, sites and resistances
*Edited by Marianne H. Marchand
and Anne Sisson Runyan*

Global Political Economy
Contemporary theories
Edited by Ronen Palan

Ideologies of Globalization
Contending visions of a New World
Order
Mark Rupert

The Clash within Civilisations
Coming to terms with cultural
conflicts
Dieter Senghaas

Global Unions?
Theory and strategies of organized
labour in the global political
economy
*Edited by Jeffrey Harrod and Robert
O'Brien*

Political Economy of a Plural World
Critical reflections on power, morals
and civilizations
Robert Cox with Michael Schechter

**A Critical Rewriting of Global
Political Economy**
Integrating reproductive, productive
and virtual economies
V. Spike Peterson

Contesting Globalization
Space and place in the world economy
André C. Drainville

**Global Institutions and
Development**
Framing the world?
*Edited by Morten Bøås and
Desmond McNeill*

**Global Institutions, Marginalization,
and Development**
Craig N. Murphy

**Critical Theories, International
Relations and 'the
Anti-Globalisation Movement'**
The politics of global resistance
*Edited by Catherine Eschle and Bice
Maiguashca*

**Globalization, Governmentality,
and Global Politics**
Regulation for the rest of us?
*Ronnie D. Lipschutz, with James K.
Rowe*

**Critical Perspectives on Global
Governance**
Rights and regulation in governing
regimes
Jean Grugel and Nicola Piper

Beyond States and Markets
The challenges of social
reproduction
*Edited by Isabella Bakker and
Rachel Silvey*

The Industrial Vagina
The political economy of the global
sex trade
Sheila Jeffreys

Capital as Power
A study of order and *creorder*
*Jonathan Nitzan and Shimshon
Bichler*

The Global Political Economy of Intellectual Property Rights
The new enclosures
Second Edition
Christopher May

Corporate Power and Ownership in Contemporary Capitalism
The politics of resistance and domination
Susanne Soederberg

Routledge/RIPE Studies in Global Political Economy is a forum for innovative new research intended for a high-level specialist readership, and the titles will be available in hardback only. Titles include:

* *Also available in paperback*

Development, Sexual Rights and Global Governance

Edited by Amy Lind

Routledge
Taylor & Francis Group

LONDON AND NEW YORK

First published 2010 by Routledge
2 Park Square, Milton Park, Abingdon, Oxon OX14 4RN

Simultaneously published in the USA and Canada
by Routledge
270 Madison Avenue, New York, NY 10016

Routledge is an imprint of the Taylor & Francis Group, an informa business

© 2010 Amy Lind selection and editorial matter; individual contributors,
their contributions

Typeset in Times New Roman by
Pindar NZ, Auckland, New Zealand
Printed and bound in Great Britain by
Antony Rowe Ltd, Chippenham, Wiltshire

All rights reserved. No part of this book may be reprinted or reproduced or
utilised in any form or by any electronic, mechanical, or other means, now
known or hereafter invented, including photocopying and recording, or in
any information storage or retrieval system, without permission in writing
from the publishers.

British Library Cataloguing in Publication Data
A catalogue record for this book is available from the British Library

Library of Congress Cataloging in Publication Data
Development, sexual rights and global governance : resisting global power /
Amy Lind.
    p. cm. — (RIPE series in global political economy ; 29)
    Includes bibliographical references and index.
    1. Gay rights—Economic aspects. 2. Economic development—Social
aspects. 3. Economic development—Political aspects. 4. Globalization—
Social aspects. I. Title.
    HQ76.5.L56 2009
    306.7—dc22   2009015002

ISBN 13: 978-0-415-77607-3 (hbk)
ISBN 13: 978-0-415-59262-8 (pbk)
ISBN 13: 978-0-203-86834-8 (ebk)

This book is dedicated to all those individuals whose identities, forms of expression, and desires fall outside the sexual and gender norms of their societies, yet who believe that another world is possible.

Contents

Contributors

Amy Lind (Ph.D., Cornell University) is Mary Ellen Heintz Associate Professor of Women's, Gender, and Sexuality Studies and a faculty affiliate in the Department of Sociology and the School of Planning at the University of Cincinnati. She is the author of *Gendered Paradoxes: women's movements, state restructuring and global development in Ecuador* (Penn State University Press, 2005). Her current research addresses the transnational governance of intimacy and struggles for sexual rights in post/neoliberal Latin America. She is also an affiliated professor of Gender Studies at FLACSO-Ecuador.

Kate Bedford is a Research Fellow at the AHRC Research Centre for Law, Gender and Sexuality at the University of Kent. She has worked on international development projects in Asia, Europe, and Latin America, and she taught numeracy and literacy skills in England. Her current research focuses on the interactions between sexuality studies, development studies, and international political economy. She has just completed a book entitled *Developing Partnerships: gender, sexuality, and the post-Washington consensus World Bank* (University of Minnesota Press, 2009).

Suzanne Bergeron is Director of Women's Studies and Associate Professor of Women's Studies and Social Sciences at the University of Michigan, Dearborn. She is the author of *Fragments of Development: nation, gender and the space of modernity* (University of Michigan Press, 2004) and various articles on gendered narratives of economic discourse in journals such as *Signs: journal of women in culture and society*, *International Journal of Feminist Politics*, *National Women's Studies Association Journal*, and selected anthologies.

Sangeeta Budhiraja is Program Officer, Building Movements at the Ms. Foundation for Women. She has worked as a consultant on sexuality and human rights issues, and is working to advance the sexual rights framework at the local, national, and international levels. Formerly, she was the Regional Program Coordinator for Asia and the Pacific at the International Gay and Lesbian Human Rights Commission (IGLHRC). Sangeeta holds a J.D. from the CUNY School of Law where she focused on International Women's Human Rights Law.

xiv   *Contributors*

Ashley Currier (Ph.D., University of Pittsburgh) is Assistant Professor of Sociology and Women's Studies at Texas A&M University. She is currently working on a book manuscript, *Becoming Visible: LGBT organizing in Namibia and South Africa*, which explores how Namibian and South African lesbian, gay, bisexual, and transgender (LGBT) organizations work to overcome their political and social invisibility. Her current research examines the origins and persistence of homophobia(s) in southern African political discourse.

Petra Doan (Ph.D., Cornell University) is Associate Professor of Urban and Regional Planning at Florida State University. She has published numerous articles on economic development and planning in the Middle East. Her current research addresses LGBT perceptions of urban space in the United States and the Middle East, with an emphasis on transgender issues. Her article, "Queers in the City: transgendered perceptions of urban spaces" appears in *Gender, Place, and Culture* (2006).

Susana T. Fried (Ph.D., Rutgers University) is Gender Advisor at the HIV/AIDS Group/BDP at the United Nations Development Programme (UNDP). With over 20 years of experience in gender, sexuality, and human rights issues, Susana authored "Show Us the Money: is violence against women and girls on the HIV donor agenda?" as part of the *Women Won't Wait: end HIV and violence against women and girls. Now.* Campaign. She was the Program Director at the International Gay and Lesbian Human Rights Commission and Program Director of International Policy and Advocacy at the Center for Women's Global Leadership. She has consulted with many organizations, including Global Rights, Amnesty International, the Program on International Health and Human Rights at the Harvard School of Public Health, and the Sexual Health and Rights Program (SHARP) of the Open Society Initiative (OSI). She is an Adjunct Assistant Professor at Columbia University's School of International and Public Affairs.

Andil Gosine is Associate Professor of Sociology at York University (Canada). He is currently pursuing research on configurations of "race," gender, and sexualities in "ethnic" sexual health promotion in countries of the North and South. His articles include "Marginalization Myths and the Complexity of 'Men': engaging critical conversations about Irish and Caribbean masculinities," in *Men and Masculinities*, and "Sex for pleasure, rights to participation and alternatives to HIV/AIDS: placing sexual minorities in development," IDS Working Paper #228, Sussex, UK.

Maja Horn (Ph.D., Cornell University) is assistant professor of Spanish and Latin American Cultures at Barnard College. Prior to joining Barnard, she was an Associated Researcher at the Latin American Faculty of Social Sciences (FLACSO-Dominican Republic), where she undertook research for a project on the relation between Dominican public spaces and shame and how it regulates Dominican gender and sexual norms.

Susie Jolly is Convenor of the Sexuality and Development Programme, Institute of Development Studies, UK. Her research focuses on the intersections between sexuality and development. Together with Andrea Cornwall and Sonia Corrêa she co-edited *Development with a Body: sexualities, development and human rights* (London: Zed Books, 2008). She has organized several conferences and events enabling exchanges between sexual rights activists and researchers and sharing their insights with people in the development industry. She previously lived in Beijing for several years, managing poverty alleviation programs for the United Nations Development Programme (UNDP), and joining in local women's rights and LGBT activism.

Susan Paulson is Director of Latin American Studies and professor of anthropology at Miami University. She received her Ph.D. in anthropology at the University of Chicago. She has published numerous articles, in English, Spanish, and Portuguese, in the areas of gender and development, sexuality studies, and political ecology in Latin America (especially Bolivia).

Jyoti Puri (Ph.D., Northeastern University) is associate professor and chair of sociology at Simmons College. She is the author of *Woman, Body, Desire in Post-colonial India: narratives of gender and sexuality* (Routledge, 1999) and *Encountering Nationalism* (Blackwell Publishers, 2003).

Alexandra Teixeira is Philanthropic Partner Officer at the Astraea Foundation. Formerly she was Research and Policy Coordinator for Global Advocacy at the International Gay and Lesbian Human Rights Commission (IGLHRC). Her work at IGLHRC focused on advancing sexual rights protection through United Nations human rights mechanisms and coalition work in other global fora. She holds a Master's Degree in International Affairs from Columbia University.

Ara Wilson is Director of Sexuality Studies and Associate Professor of Women's Studies and Cultural Anthropology at Duke University. She is the author of *The Intimate Economies of Bangkok: tomboys, tycoons and Avon ladies in the global city* (University of California Press, 2004) and is currently working on her new book project, *Sexual Latitudes: the erotic politics of globalization.*

Acknowledgements

Like all anthology projects, this volume is the result of the collective energy and dedication of several individuals. It began with me recognizing the fact that among the small but growing group of scholars, activists, and policy-makers focusing on sexual rights and development in one form or another, there was yet to be a solid collection addressing the multiple issues involved in reframing sex through a non-normative lens. Thus this project began with this aim in mind, and with the goal of contributing to a broader global agenda linking sexual and economic justice. Many people contributed to this emerging vision of change. First and foremost, I thank Suzanne Bergeron for her involvement with this project from the start. Not only did she help me brainstorm at initial stages of the project but she helped in numerous other ways – too many to list here – and provided important editorial feedback and support throughout the process.

These chapters have been presented collectively in four venues: I thank Suzanne Bergeron (as principal organizer) and her colleagues at the University of Michigan at Dearborn and at the Institute for Research on Women and Gender at the University of Michigan at Ann Arbor for supporting a panel in March 2007. Several chapters were presented at the 2006 and 2008 National Women's Studies Association annual conferences and additional chapters were presented at the Rethinking Marxism conference, held at the University of Massachusetts-Amherst in fall 2006.

During this process, I have also had the opportunity to share thoughts and ideas from the evolving manuscript with colleagues in academic and NGO settings in Quito, Caracas, Brighton, Lima, London, Montreal, San Francisco, New York City, and Syracuse, and with students in my courses at the University of Cincinnati and FLACSO-Ecuador. I thank my friends, colleagues, and students for their critical and constructive input, and for their ongoing support for this project. I also thank Suparna Bhaskaran, Kate Bedford, Sonia Corrêa, Susie Jolly, Jane Parpart, and Spike Peterson for their comments on the introduction as I presented it in multiple forms, at various venues. Finally, I thank the University of Cincinnati Friends of Women's Studies and the Department of Women's, Gender, and Sexuality Studies for funding portions of the research and travel for this project.

At Routledge, I thank my editor, Heidi Bagtazo, for her support and encouragement. I also thank Jeni Jenkins for her help compiling the bibliography, and Jill Williams for her research assistance.

Abbreviations

ABC	"Abstain, be faithful, use condoms"
AIDS	Acquired Immune Deficiency Syndrome
ANC	African National Congress
ASA	Amigos Siempre Amigos
BDS	Blue Diamond Society
BtM	Behind the Mask
CD	compact disk
CDC	Centers for Disease Control and Prevention
CLIC	lesbian group in Thailand (see Chapter 5)
CMAC	Centre for Media and Alternative Communication
CONAMU	Consejo Nacional de la Mujer (National Women's Council)
COPRESIDA	Consejo Presidencial del SIDA (Presidential AIDS Council)
CREA	Creating Resources for Empowerment and Action
DAWN	Development Alternatives with Women for a New Era
DC	District of Columbia
DFID	Department for International Development
EOHR	Egyptian Organization for Human Rights
EP	Equality Project
FEW	Forum for the Empowerment of Women
FGM	female genital mutilation
GAD	Gender and Development
GALZ	Gays and Lesbians of Zimbabwe
GL	gay and lesbian
GLB	gay, lesbian and bisexual
GLBT	gay, lesbian, bisexual, and transgender
GLIFFA	Gays and Lesbians in Foreign Affairs Agencies
GLOBE	Gay, Lesbian or Bisexual Employees (of the World Bank Group)
GTZ	Deutsche Gesellschaft für Technische Zusammenarbeit
HIV	Human Immunodeficiency Virus
HR	human resources
IASSCS	International Association for the Study of Sexuality, Culture and Society

IGLHRC	International Gay and Lesbian Human Rights Commission
ILGA	International Lesbian and Gay Association
ILO	International Labour Organization
IMF	International Monetary Fund
LGB	lesbian, gay, and bisexual
LGBT	lesbian, gay, bisexual, and transgender
LGBTI	lesbian, gay, bisexual, transgender, and intersexed
LGBTQ	lesbian, gay, bisexual, transgender, and queer
LGBTQI	lesbian, gay, bisexual, transgender, queer, and intersexed
MNR	Movimiento Nacionalista Revolucionario (Nationalist Revolutionary Movement)
MSM	men who have sex with men
MSMW	men who have sex with men and women
NiZA	Netherlands Institute for Southern Africa
NGO	non-governmental organization
PUCL-K	People's Union for Civil Liberties, Karnataka
SICA	Servicio de Información y Censo Agropecuario (Agricultural Census and Information System Service)
SIDA	Swedish International Development Cooperation Agency
SIGI	Sisterhood is Global International
SIP+	South Indian Positive Network
STI	sexually transmitted infection
TI	transgendered and intersexed
UK	United Kingdom
UN	United Nations
UNAIDS	Joint United Nations Programme on HIV/AIDS
UNGLOBE	United Nations Gay, Lesbian or Bisexual Employees
UNIFEM	United Nations Development Fund for Women
US	United States
USAID	United States Agency for International Development
VCR	videocassette recorder
WB	World Bank
WID	Women in Development
WLUML	Women Living Under Muslim Laws
WSW	women who have sex with women
WWHR	Women for Women's Human Rights – New Ways

Introduction

Development, global governance, and sexual subjectivities

Amy Lind

For too long, people who do not fit within socially prescribed sexual and gender roles in their societies have been seen as irrelevant to or "outside" the project of development. We hear accounts of how globalization affects local, typically impoverished, communities in the global South yet rarely if ever do we see any representations of sexual difference other than the heterosexual and "gender-appropriate" norms; norms typically defined in the global media by Western standards. If anything, queers are seen as "unproductive" to development or as destructive to the imagined national community and its modernization goals, and queer sexual subjectivities are rarely understood outside the purview of medical pathologies or criminal behavior. This is so, despite emergent forms of oppositional queer consciousness and political strategizing that we have witnessed, especially since the early 1990s, in many countries around the world. Lesbian, gay, and bisexual activists, along with gender-variant activists including cross-dressers, transsexuals, and transgendered individuals, have challenged post/neocolonial states and global institutions on a variety of grounds pertaining to their marginalized identities. Scholars have only begun to address how these emergent sexual subjectivities have provided important challenges to heterosexist bias and gender normativity in post/neocolonial state planning traditions and technologies. Queer activists have strategically engaged with the global development industry, most literally by seeking foreign aid for their struggles, yet also necessarily as they work in non-governmental, state, and transnational arenas, as a way to forge their political identities and challenge repressive state apparatuses, often countering imperialist logics as well. Perhaps ironically, queerness on a global scale has come to be known largely in the neoliberal era, an era marked by the globalization of economic and social normativities. On an economic level, privatization, state deregulation, and free-market ideologies have helped shape an institutional context in which non-governmental organizations (NGOs), both for profit and non-profit, have had to pick up where the state left off. This has led among other things to the reprivatization of social welfare, with important consequences for non-normative families and households that do not "count" as the subjects of development aid, even within local grassroots efforts where people (necessarily) take planning for survival into their own hands. Many of the lesbian, gay, bisexual, and transgender (LGBT) groups that emerged during the past two decades have held ambivalent relationships to development, modernization, and modernity as they understand it. To begin with, the establishment of liberal human rights mechanisms and globalization has facilitated the rise of public LGBT identities and cultures, albeit in partial and fragmented ways. And LGBT groups have experienced the contradictory effects of globalization based on their own locations in new public–private relationships between civil society sectors and nation-states, which has affected their organizing strategies, funding opportunities, and political subjectivities in unforeseen ways, sometimes leading to their acquiescence, rather than opposition, to neoliberalism (Fernández-Alemany 2000; Lind 2007; Oswin 2007b). As queer studies continues to influence scholarship, advocacy, and policy-making in the area of development, we must take note of the disciplining and material effects on the most marginalized queers in any society, rather than succumbing to new forms of homonormative imperialism.

This collection of essays arose out of my perception that there is a great need for assessing the contributions of queer studies to the field of development and globalization studies. Likewise, it grew out of my preoccupation with the feminist scholarship on gender and development, which, while useful for examining normative family structures and patterns of gender relations, has rarely turned its attention to the study of heterosexuality as a social institution (Lind and Share 2003). By examining how notions of gender and sexuality are inscribed in development institutions, policies, and frameworks, often through a heteronormative and gender-normative lens, authors in this volume provide a critical querying of "development" itself, and explore the liberatory potential as well as the contradictions of any project that attempts "queer development."

At least four sets of current concerns or issues have inspired this collection. First, some of us have become increasingly preoccupied with the entrenched nature of heteronormativity in development narratives, policies, and practices, particularly in the neoliberal era, where normative family models have been newly integrated into many international aid efforts and where the global governance of intimacy is unfolding in complex and contradictory ways (Buss and Herman 2003; Butler 2006; see also Bedford, this volume). Although many observers have noted the effects of global restructuring on heterosexual families and households and on an imagined heterosexual national community, few have begun to analyze how processes of neoliberal development and globalization themselves lead to new arrangements of heteronormative intimacy and to new classes of heterosexuality, let alone how these iterations of identity converge with new forms of hypermasculinity and hyperfemininity on a global scale.

Second, we are concerned about the increasingly globalized backlash against gays, lesbians, bisexuals, and transgendered people, including the re-inscription of heteronormative power in nationalist ideologies and the outright denial of full citizenship to homosexuals in various countries. As has been observed, this backlash that we are witnessing in several countries around the world is the result of a complex set of factors at play, including ongoing struggles concerning postcolonial nation-building and the debates on the effects of westernization on non-Western and poor countries in the western hemisphere; critiques of the US as empire and the accompanying notion of our world as unipolar (despite the fact that some countries are now shifting away from what was once perceived as a quasi-hegemonic neoliberal model; e.g. Venezuela); historical discourses positing homosexuality (and sometimes transgenderism) as either criminal or pathological;[1] and globalized struggles over the meaning of "the family" in religious doctrine and international law.

At the same time, significant advances have been made in some countries with respect to gay and lesbian rights and/or to gender identity claims, leading some to observe that nation-states sometime have strategic reasons tied up with nationalism or global market allegiances to become "gay-friendly" (Oswin 2007b). Interestingly, gayness and queerness have been used as barometers of national progress and development: some view the addition of gay rights as a sign of progress, as in the cases of neoliberal South Africa and Ecuador (Lind 2007; Oswin 2007b), whereas others view it as a Western imposition and/or as a deteriorating factor in their national identities (see Bhaskaran 2004; Hoad 2007). The inclusion of anti-discrimination clauses on the basis of sexual orientation in the new constitutions of South Africa (1996), Fiji (1997) and Ecuador (1998) offer hope for the possibility of sexual citizenship in the global South;[2] however, these legal accomplishments have been met with opposition, and the introduction of gay rights into formal politics and policy domains also raises important questions about the normalizing risks associated with making universal claims on the basis of the gay/lesbian binary, when still many individuals remain outside the project of global gay rights.

Third, we are motivated by the transnational dialogues among scholars and activists about the globalization of sexuality and the queerness of globalization (Gibson-Graham 1996–7; Altman 2001; Bhaskaran 2004; Wilson 2004; Oswin 2007a and b). In an increasingly globalized, marketized context, heteronormativity as well as homonormativity have played roles in shaping global hegemonic expressions of capitalist power; in exoticizing the so-called Third World and queers within it; and in shaping queer consumer subjects in late capitalism who themselves consume and benefit from (typically racialized) images of queer people in poor and/or non-Western countries; for example, as sex tourists, pink travelers, human rights activists, Peace Corp volunteers, missionaries, or NGO volunteers (Hennessy 2000; Altman 2001; Alexander 2005). Needless to say, the relationships among capitalism, westernization, and emergent queer subjectivities are complex at best, and this project aims to contribute to debates on this topic.

Finally, we are inspired by the increased visibility of sexual rights and gender justice movements in the global South, many of which have provided intersectional critiques of the violence of Western normativities from the start. All of these processes combined have played important roles in shaping what we call the new sexual subjects of development: gay men; men who have sex with men, or MSMs; lesbians; women who have sex with women, or WSWs; transsexuals, and other non-normative identities now targeted as subjects in need of development aid or assistance. Of course, most development frameworks continue to rest on heteronormative imaginings of national progress and identity and, more often than not, non-normative individuals are left out of the picture. However, as recent constitutional, legislative, and market victories attest, some nation-states and public cultures in the global South are increasingly "gay-friendly," creating the possibility of sexual citizenship for some. The emergence of the new sexual subjects of development is also related to the fact that gays and lesbians have "come out" within the development industry and challenged its heteronormative premises, at least for their own benefit, if not for those who are the targets of their development interventions. "Coming out" within the development industry may lead to its queering, yet further queries into the cultural, political, and economic effects of development itself, including development efforts to address the needs of lesbians, gay men, and/ or gender-variant people, have yet to be fully addressed or understood, particularly as they may contribute to producing new forms of homonormativities.

Points of departure

In this volume, authors query development, globalization, and global governance through a range of approaches and on various scales. Some utilize political economy as their primary methodological tool; others draw from ethnography or cultural studies. Most draw from poststructuralist and postmodernist thought to address the historical genealogies of queers in development and sexual rights and gender justice struggles. Genealogies of gayness, queerness, and LGBT rights have, in many ways, informed the geopolitical landscape within which we can (or cannot) imagine queerness and various forms of normativities associated with neoliberal forms of global governance. Given how discrimination against LGBT people has long been justified on the basis of its purported relegation to the private realm of our "intimate" lives, here I propose a notion of "global governance" that captures how intimacy and community are equally regulated and disciplined alongside formal citizenship and state development models. An important aspect of my own understanding of global governance, then, involves how people's intimate lives are tied up with state and neoliberal governmentalities; that is, how axes of "personal life" are organized in such a way in modern nation-states that queers are legally excluded from their full citizenship rights and spatially excluded from public life. Ken Plummer refers to this as the realm of "intimate citizenship," which for him includes "… rights, obligations, recognitions and respect around those most intimate spheres of life – who to live with, how to raise children, how to handle one's body, how to relate as a gendered being, how to be an erotic person." (Plummer 2001: 238). As many observers of development and global restructuring have noted, as non-state institutions have increasingly played interpretive roles in defining citizenship and what constitutes "proper" citizen practices in the neoliberal era, so too have people's subjectivities changed as a result (Ong 2006). Importantly, sometimes people have learned to "speak back" rather than merely absorb the dual effects of this broad set of structural reforms and the scholarly understandings of them as linear, unidirectional, penetrating, and omnipresent (Oswin 2007a; see also Gibson-Graham 1996–7). From my perspective, addressing neoliberal governmentalities in this broader sense captures the layers of institutions that are involved in defining and regulating our intimate lives. Seen through this lens, development policies, practices, and institutions work as instruments of governance and as methods of constructing and legitimizing subjectivities (Shore and Wright 1997; Bondi and Laurie 2005). Thus, struggles for interpretive power over policy definitions are not trivial conversations that take place within governing institutions; rather, they represent broader struggles over cultural representation, or recognition, and access to material resources, or redistribution (Franco 1989; Fraser 1997). It is important to point out, however, that while neoliberalism in its multiple iterations has brought with it these new understandings of governance and citizenship, many queers have long been critical of their literal and figurative relegation to the private realm, well before the Washington consensus neoliberal orthodoxy came into being and well before the global justice movement began to visibly push for a shift away from neoliberal economics and from the identity politics models emanating from the philosophical school of liberalism. Thus, the multiple forms of market-led development that we now see around the world represent new challenges to long-standing forms of discrimination and, paradoxically, potential spaces for a queer liberatory politics, as several contributors point out. Combined, the chapters in this volume query development frameworks, policies, and processes that privilege normative genders and sexualities over all others, including those promoting neoliberal ideals, with the ultimate goal of rethinking heteronormativity and genderism (i.e. hostile readings of gender-ambiguous bodies – see Browne 2004) in development and constructing sexual rights, gender justice, and decolonization strategies in the global South and transnationally.

This project is both normative and anti-normative in nature. Authors query development frameworks as a way to rethink and reprioritize global and national development agendas, with the aim of bringing visibility to and providing citizen rights for people who do not have the same rights as "gender-appropriate" heterosexuals. This includes women who love women, men who love men; self-defined gays, lesbians, and bisexuals; heterosexuals who do not fit prescribed gender roles; cross-dressers; transsexuals; and the many other local and regional iterations of non-normative genders and sexualities that the terms "queer," "genderqueer," and "transgender" aim to include (Morton 1996; Nestle, Howell, and Wilchins 2002; Currah 2006; Stryker and Whittle 2006). At the same time, many contributors point out that they are acutely aware of the limitations of normative politics, particularly when one's identity is defined as deviant, pathological, and criminal from the start, where political reform can only improve their secondary status rather than invert or transform the identity model in any substantive way. While some argue that it is difficult to imagine queer possibilities outside the hegemonic monocultural, uniworld vision of neoliberal discourse, many others are optimistically pointing toward the new instances of transnational social justice movements that we have begun to witness in the post-Washington Consensus era – and for some countries, arguably a "post-neoliberal" moment – in which we live (Vargas 2003; Grimson and Kessler 2005; Fernandes 2007; Lind 2007).[3] Authors in this volume are doing just that: providing alternative readings of global normativities reinforced by development policies and suggesting new ways of thinking about queerness and identity in the context of neoliberal governance and governmentalities. Below I outline three general areas of inquiry that inform this scholarship: views on queerness, querying development, and queers in development.

Views on queerness

"Like size, definitions matter," as International Labour Organization (ILO) economist Guy Standing states in an anthology chapter devoted to the social effects of globalization, leaving the reader to decide if his reference is to the phallus, globalization or both (2004: 111). Indeed, when discussing "queerness" in transnational context, definitions matter. Certainly "queerness" has been interrogated by queer and postcolonial studies scholars for its usefulness (or lack thereof) in understanding genders and sexualities in the global South; and contributors to this volume hold a range of views on its usefulness or lack thereof. Suparna Bhaskaran (2004) offers a useful definition of the strategic usage of queerness. She defines the term in both "a broad and narrow sense," in a "strategic, embodied, very much marked, and inventive manner," recognizing that queerness can "flatten out differences," yet also serve as a coalition-building mechanism to challenge various forms of normativity (Bhaskaran 2004: 8–9).

Just as the term "gay" was introduced in many countries of the global South in the 1970s, a topic historically addressed by LGBT studies scholars (Murray 1995; Fernández-Alemany 2000; Altman 2001), the term "queer" began to circulate among scholars and activists in southern countries in the 1980s and 1990s; this, of course, varies by region and by their geopolitical relationship to English-speaking, colonizing nation-states. The circulation of these terms, which involves complex transnational exchanges rather than mere impositions from North to South, have allowed for new ways of examining "gayness" and "queerness" in Western as well as non-Western countries. Some contributors choose to use the term to connote the multiple forms of sexual and gender identities that exist, although with the understanding that this term, too, needs to be problematized. Drawing from queer theory, we suggest that this framework of sexuality is more appropriate than a dualistic framework of homosexuality/heterosexuality (Butler 1990; Sedgwick 1990). As opposed to definitions of homosexual and bisexual, the notion of "queerness" helps us to rethink dualisms in Western thought and in development discourses, which tend to universalize Western definitions – about "good" versus "bad", "normal" versus "abnormal" genders and sexualities. Volume contributors address a wide range of identities that are non-normative or anti-normative, including men who have sex with men, gay men, lesbians, gender-variant individuals, and heterosexual female single-headed households. While contributors do not claim "queer" to encompass "all that is not normative," as some US-based queer theorists have done (in fact, some choose not to use the term at all), they demonstrate how heteronormativity has negative effects not only for self-defined queers (e.g. individuals who do not fit within culturally prescribed sexual and/or gender norms) but also heterosexual individuals who do not fit within prescribed gender roles and therefore do not benefit from development initiatives as their gender-normative counterparts might.

Queerness can flatten out differences among locally understood identities, such as moffies in South Africa; *desi* dykes and *desi* gay men in India; *tortilleras, trasvestis, chitos*/femmes, or *maricones* in Spanish-speaking Latin America and the Caribbean; or toms in Thailand, to name only a few. Queerness, like gayness, when it tends to flatten out differences, is often associated with westernization, universality, hegemonic knowledge production, or epistemic privilege. If and when queerness is viewed as adequately encompassing the numerous forms in which individuals define themselves in their daily lives throughout the world, then queer studies has failed to grasp how the field itself contributes to normativizing gender and sexual variance. Thus this volume addresses both heteronormativity in development thought and institutional practices, as well as the potential homonor-malizing effects of mainstreaming gayness in the development industry. "Queering development," or the effort to bring sexual rights and gender justice agendas to the forefront of development thought and practice, is necessarily a paradoxical process from the start, one that is imbued with hegemonic as well as oppositional forms of knowledge, consciousness, and experience.

The naming of sexual/gender difference is tied up with processes by which marginalized groups of people name themselves in relation to processes of nation-building, racialization, colonization, or class exploitation. "Queering" our analysis of marginalized sexual and gender identities allows us to "account for a sense of difference that comes with marginality" (Arrizón 2006: 3); in this case, within narratives and practices of development. One of the aims of this volume, then, is to rethink how sexual identity is organized and normalized in development narratives and practices, often through its conflation with racialized gender norms (Gosine 2005a). Contributors use the term "heteronormativity" explicitly to illus-trate how heterosexuality is normalized, naturalized, and privileged in societies of the global South, in the international development field, and in colonial and post/neocolonial narratives of the so-called Third World or global South.

Querying development

Queer studies scholars have interrogated the meaning and making of development in various ways, including through re-readings of scholarship on the role of women and the family in development, where women are typically scripted as asexual, except as reproducers, and as gender normative (e.g. mothers, wives); by challeng-ing heteronormativity in development thought; and by addressing how sexual rights have been introduced into and negotiated in development thought and practice.

Heteronormative constructions of the family have underscored post/neocolonial projects of nation-building and development from the start, although this is often overlooked in mainstream political economy accounts. Ideas about sexual practices within the global development industry stem from earlier orientalist narratives of colonization that drew upon heteronormative accounts of the sexual behaviors of "natives" to justify ideological and material conquest. "Moral judgments about the development of civilization were debated in and through 'scientific' claims about the sexual behaviors of 'native others,'" (Pigg and Adams 2005: 3–4). As newly formed post/neocolonial nations developed their state planning technologies, heteronormative claims inscribed in cultural, racial, and national difference were often central to their modernization projects. The post-World War II development industry emerged through and drew from these heteronormative narratives of progress and modernization. Development theory's focus on the nation as the unit of analysis and on the analytical separation between the nation-state and the economy, a process already under way in Western liberal economic thought (Bergeron 2004), rested upon these assumptions now labeled homophobic or heteronormative by LGBT and queer studies scholars.

The development industry necessarily drew from modernization theories of economic development, healthcare, education, population policy, and citizenship to design their blueprints for providing aid to foreign countries. While clearly there was no single blueprint for such a widespread endeavor, certain Western values about the political and economic system, coupled with values about family life and citizenship, were at the heart of many of the earlier development policies. Sex was always central to that project. "Even since Bretton Woods institutions were created, the regulation of sex has been a critical – if generally unrecognized – component of social and economic development policies" (Gosine 2005a: 3). Reproductive sex was what most interested development economists and planners, as "unfettered reproductive sex ... was understood to create 'overpopulation' ..." and through a colonialist, racialized lens, natives were seen as prone to overpopulation (Gosine 2005a: 3).

Today, efforts at sexual health reform are linked to larger development projects and while many local groups have reclaimed, negotiated, or challenged this narrative of population control, reproductive health continues to be linked to narratives of economic growth, prosperity, and sovereignty in complex and problematic ways. Typically, development planners have addressed sexuality under the rubric of "reproductive health," where reproductive (hetero)sexuality is emphasized, especially maternal and child health (Hartmann 1995; Pigg and Adams 2005). And particularly since the start of the HIV/AIDS crisis, sexuality has been increasingly addressed under the rubric of "sexual health," where the control of disease – in this case, the spread of HIV/AIDS to the broader community and nation – is addressed through the regulation of sexual practices, especially those of men who have sex with men (MSMs) as they are seen as potential carriers of the disease (Wright 2000; Gosine 2005a).[4] Yet while development practitioners may focus on disease intervention and prevention, activists have utilized this discourse in strategic ways as a way to construct a sexual rights agenda.

Whereas heterosexual women's bodies have been central to narratives and practices of national development, as has been widely documented by feminist scholars (for a recent account, see Jaquette and Summerfield 2006), men's and women's queer bodies have been largely absent except when viewed as potential threats to the heteronormative social order. How queer men and women are viewed has led to contrasting and contradictory forms of regulation and visibilization in development frameworks. For example, because lesbians are typically viewed as non-procreative and as "non-mothers"; they are mostly left out of the picture, except when targeted in their reproductive roles (e.g. a pregnant lesbian, a mother who happens to be lesbian). In this case, their queer identity is sidelined and they are viewed primarily as mothers or mothers-to-be. Because of the absence of a male in their lives, symbolically, at least, they pose a perceived threat to state-building projects and to the heteronormative social order. They are seen as not "in need" of development interventions, as they are represented either as unlikely-to-get-pregnant or unlikely-to-get-AIDS. This is so, despite the fact that little, if any, research has been conducted to assess lesbian health issues in poor countries.[5]

Men's queer bodies, in contrast, have been widely subject to development interventions through the lens of public health and disease control, primarily as a result of the HIV/AIDS crisis (Gosine 2005a). Seen as potential carriers of disease, gay men are now seen as an important target for intervention because of their potential HIV status; as such, they are brought into the fold of development through health interventions, often implemented by NGOs, that in theory are predicated on pathologized notions of deviance and/or contamination. Of course, many NGOs have negotiated the terms of development funding and reclaimed the purpose of HIV/AIDS projects in their own terms, thereby transforming this type of disease discourse into one of empowerment or strength. As Timothy Wright has pointed out in his research on the globalization of gay identities in Bolivia, many gay rights groups have utilized this type of funding, much of which originally came from the United States Agency for International Development (USAID), to institutionalize their rights-based struggles for sexual and/or gender diversity, expression, and rights in their home countries (Wright 2000).[6]

What these narratives share are an unintended or conscious complicity with heteronormativity, namely with reproductive heterosexuality and its central place in modernist development conceptions of family life and the nation. As women are seen as reproducers, in studies as varied as women's participation in so-called formal and informal sector employment; women's economic contributions to national development; women's household labor; women's survival strategies; or women's educational or health initiatives, they are linked to the family and private realm, and seen as only secondarily participating in the labor market and public realm. That is, even if women are asked to enter the labor market or must necessarily do so (as is the case for the majority of women in poor countries), their labor is less valued than men's and often invisible, as many feminist economists have pointed out (Jackson and Pearson 1998; Benería 2003). Similarly, men are viewed as linked to the market and public realm, and recent fatherhood initiatives have sought primarily to teach men "how to love better" while women are taught "to work harder," thereby reinforcing, even if inverting, the male-public as female-private dichotomy (see Bedford, this volume).[7] And as Gilles Kleitz warns us, although "[d]evelopment work only delivers safe benign packages of income generation and improved rights for women with the family institution ... the truly liberating revolution of redefining identities outside reproduction and the family remains mostly untouched ..." (Kleitz 2000: 2). In this way, even feminist accounts that seek to make women's labor, lives, and identities visible in development frameworks tend to reinforce this presumed male–female heterosexual contract, whereby men and women continue to play heteronormative gendered roles in every level of analysis: the household, the market economy, a specific industry, the community, the global political economy, etc. This narrative about heterosexual family life powerfully shapes a range of scales and representations of daily life, cultural practice, racial purity, national identity, and global political economy. As such, these accounts of development, including those with the important goal of uncovering male biases in economic development frameworks (Elson 1995), leave untouched heterosexuality as a social institution, and the ways in which institutionalized heterosexuality converges with projects of nation-building, empire, globalization, and development as well as influences on people's daily lives, experiences, and subjectivities.

So long as reproductive heterosexuality is seen as the "only functional form of sex" in development policy frameworks (Kleitz 2000), any discussion of pleasure, desire or sexual identity claims will continue to be left to the wayside. While threats to daily survival in the form of hunger, violence, or physical displacement may supercede certain sets of choices about engaging in pleasurable acts, claims for identity rights, desire, and pleasure, when repressed, erased, or criminalized, are also threatening to daily survival. As Dennis Altman states:

> "[T]he pleasures of the body" cannot be separated from the world outside. People who are undernourished, sick, pregnant, old, or threatened by potential violence will experience their bodies very differently, and only when political and economic conditions allow can we engage in certain "pleasures." Indeed bodily pleasure is often shaped by political and economic conditions …
>
> (Altman 2001: 2)

Thus viewing sexuality as a development issue has become an important part of reforming the development industry from within, whereas critically interrogating development as a set of discourses, representations, and practices involves a more radical undertaking. Indeed, this tension between recognizing the needs and rights of LGBT people in development, on one hand, and challenging development's disciplinary mechanisms on the other, appears throughout the chapters.

Queers in development

Increasingly, development practitioners have "come out" in the workplace and pushed for change concerning their own conditions as workers. Some have also worked to incorporate a queer perspective into development planning. How have development practitioners' own perspectives shaped narratives and practices of development? Most development institutions do not have strong programs (if any) in the areas of sexuality or sexual rights, particularly in regard to lesbian, gay, bisexual, transgender and queer (LGBTQ) sexualities. Yet some development practitioners have found interesting ways to intervene in their institutions, occasionally leading to the queering of development initiatives in the global South. Some lesbian and gay development practitioners have sought to acquire their own rights as workers (e.g. employee benefits) within their institutions, as in the case of the World

Bank's Gay, Lesbian or Bisexual Employees (GLOBE), an employee association examined at length by Andil Gosine in this volume, and the United Nations Gay, Lesbian or Bisexual Employees (UNGLOBE). Both GLOBE and UNGLOBE were formed by lesbian, gay, and bisexual employees to address their social needs, rights, and benefits. Ironically, the World Bank offers among the most extensive set of benefits to gay, lesbian, and bisexual employees in the industry:

> The World Bank in particular has … a "full panoply" of rights for same-sex, unmarried heterosexual or other nontraditional partnerships. Regulations at the bank state clearly that when registered by affidavit proving that certain criteria (such as the length and stability of the relationship) have been met, domestic partners of its gay staff members will get medical coverage. Moreover, a "registered domestic partner" of a bank employee also gets an ID card, travel and relocation allowances, accident insurance, education payments for children, health club membership, immunizations and a host of other benefits.
>
> (Crossette 2003: 4)

The presence of GLOBE and the Bank's support of domestic partner benefits can be attributed to a variety of complex and contradictory factors, including the leadership of key Bank employees; efficiency arguments made by GLOBE members and adopted by Bank leaders concerning how the institutional support of workers leads to overall better efficiency and output; and a series of conjunctural events that led to this set of employee policies (Crossette 2003; Gosine, this volume). While some GLOBE members have played key roles in shaping the Bank's policy frameworks, for the most part GLOBE members have either chosen not to or have been unable to directly influence or challenge the Bank's overall development agenda, thus maintaining the invisibility of queerness in the global South and leaving the Bank's neoliberal project intact, as Gosine eloquently argues.

UNGLOBE has a different institutional history, as not all UN member nations support its existence. It was, however, granted official recognition as an employee advocacy group in 1996 by the UN's Office of Human Resources Management. In contrast to GLOBE, UNGLOBE members have called for "a stronger UN role in protecting the rights of lesbians and gays both inside and outside the world body" from the start. Where GLOBE's focus is more on employee relations and GLOBE members often shy away from influencing Bank policy, UNGLOBE members perhaps necessarily have linked their struggle for employee benefits with broader LGBT struggles from the start. As members of the United Nations system, their employee status is based on the national laws of each staff member in question, as Fred Eckhard, UN spokesman for former UN Secretary-General Kofi Annan (1997–2006), has explained (Deen 2003: 3). Annan himself once stated that "this is not something the organization should get involved in," given the controversial nature of the issue of homosexuality in member countries (Deen 2003: 3–4).[8] Thus while UNGLOBE has been recognized as an employee association, members have received little in the way of support from the United Nations, and their struggle is directly linked to the broader UN human rights agenda and to the worldwide struggle for sexual rights and gender justice. In December 2008, 66 countries signed a joint UN statement for LGBT human rights in which they call for the worldwide decriminalization of homosexuality. While this statement was signed by only a small fraction of UN member nations, it represents a significant open- ing for future change within the UN. As an employee association, UNGLOBE's recognition rests upon this broader process and, as such, they have held a more public platform than GLOBE with respect to their mission.

Elsewhere, queer advocates and policy-makers have worked to address the eco- nomic rights of LGBT people, although thus far few studies have been conducted to address how, for example, restructuring processes affect same-sex households or partnerships, the nature and depth of discrimination against gays and lesbians or transgendered individuals in the workplace, or the effects of a myriad devel- opment projects and policy frameworks on producing new forms of gender and sexual normativities and new classes of heterosexuality. Exceptions include the work of the International Gay and Lesbian Human Rights Commission (IGLHRC), International Lesbian and Gay Association (ILGA), and regional networks funded by small donor agencies to address the local consequences of heterosexist discrimi- nation in relation to other forms of oppression such as racism, class exploitation, and the negative effects of state policies or globalization.

While queering development institutions "from the inside" is an uphill battle, the presence of queers in the development industry clearly has led to some progress for a rethinking of sexual and gender rights. Yet these examples reveal important con- tradictions about the role of queers in development and development practitioners (of all sexual identities) who work in queer development institutions, frame- works, and practices. Questions remain about the liberatory potential of queering development: When bringing LGBT concerns into the analysis, are development practitioners contributing to transforming development frameworks or is their queering of development policies a type of "add queers and stir" approach reminis- cent of earlier Women in Development (WID) "add women and stir" approaches?[9] Will their efforts lead to lesbian and gay mainstreaming (here a play on "gender mainstreaming"),[10] whereby normative notions of sexual rights are merely incor- porated into capitalist, neoliberal development frameworks, or will their presence in the industry lead to a deeper transformation of social relations? Will it challenge heteronormativity or to what extent will LGBT planners simply contribute to new orientalist forms of homonormativity in the global South? These are some of the questions addressed in this book.

Querying neoliberalism

Currently, the liberatory potential of "queering development" is complicated by neoliberal politics, including how some development institutions and nation-states are increasingly embracing gay rights through a neoliberal lens, whereas others continue to view sexual/gender deviance as an added threat to what they view as the already-existing imposition of (Western and/or imperialist) neoliberal agen- das. While queer studies scholars might agree on the fact that the pleasures of the body cannot be separated from the world outside, how we strategically intervene in political, cultural and policy arenas varies greatly and has led to widely divergent views on queer engagements with state and global institutions, particularly in neoliberal contexts. Some sexual rights activists safely frame their claims in the context of hegemonic economic logic, leading to contradictory outcomes at best for the targeted recipients of their political victories. For example, in South Africa, the Equality Project (EP), a lesbian and gay rights organization, successfully acquired same-sex marriage legislation in 2005 by making a neoliberal-inspired argument. An EP pamphlet entitled "Marriage: anything less is not equal – lesbian and gay people demand the right to marry" states:

> Family and community involvement in poverty alleviation is a central objective of welfare public policy. For the vast majority of poor people, marriage allows families and communities to recognize the relationships of their members and provides the framework for mutual assistance. In the absence of a welfare state, extended family and community support is crucial to the survival of single parent families, maintenance of children, young couples and the aged. This is true for lesbian and gay, as well as heterosexual people. Sound welfare public policy would acknowledge the benefits recognition of same-sex marriage would bring to families, communities and the state.
>
> (quoted in Oswin 2007a: 663–4)

Thus as the EP claims to represent "poor, black" South Africans (as examined by Oswin) through its defense of the reprivatization of welfare policy, it gained a benefit for gays and lesbians while adhering to the dominant logic of state neoliberal development planning, which ultimately has led to high levels of economic displacement for black (and other) South Africans even in the purportedly more democratic post-apartheid era.

In contrast to debates on same-sex marriage in industrialized countries, where activists have often been divided along the lines of "gay rights" vs. "queer" platforms (see Duggan 2003), in South Africa the embracing of gay rights was viewed by supporters as necessary in order to forge a post-apartheid nationalism distinct to its anti-Western, explicitly homophobic neighbor, Zimbabwe (Oswin 2007b).

In contrast to earlier scholarship that calls for a "queering" of development or globalization as a radical intervention (e.g. Gibson-Graham 1996–7; Cruz-Malavé and Manalansan 2002), nation-states are increasingly in the business of "queering" these fields as well, making queerness normal and queer strategies reformist more so than revolutionary. "Neoliberalism and gay and lesbian 'lifestyles' now seem to happily co-habitate and nation-states are increasingly willing to engage in a politics of recognition in this new dispensation," geographer Natalie Oswin argues with respect to South Africa (2007b: 106). In contrast, the passage of the anti-discrimination clause in Ecuador's 1997 constitution occurred due to shifts in discourse concerning homosexuality, whereby national assembly members generally sided with the proposal that homosexuality is a mental health issue rather than a crime, and therefore this legally defined "vulnerable" group should be protected from discrimination (Lind 2007). In this case, the constitutional victory rested upon defining gays and lesbians as "vulnerable" and as "in need," even if only for protection from discrimination, rather than for access to material benefits as in the case of South Africa (where queer access to economic dispensation came largely following the passage of same-sex legislation in 2005). Thus an important challenge to our scholarship and advocacy concerns how we frame sexual rights and gender justice struggles, as single-issue or coalitional movements; as market-driven or as anti-neoliberal; in terms of how we use related constructions of community and public/private space in our discursive and political frameworks (Seidman 2001; Joseph 2002); and in terms of defining our goal as struggling *for* or *beyond* a queer politics.

Themes, debates, questions

This book is divided into three parts, reflecting the main themes of the volume: querying/queering development, negotiating heteronormativity in development institutions, and resisting global hegemonies.

Querying/queering development: theories, representations, strategies

In this part, authors query development as a set of discourses and practices and attempt to rethink notions of sexual and gender normativities as represented in the realms of economic discourse, development institutions, and cultural production. Their analyses provide important insights into the relationship between institutional practices, representations of queerness, and the making of non-normative subjectivities. To begin, Susie Jolly (Chapter 1) tackles several myths concerning sex and sexuality in the development industry, including the myth that the development industry is not in the business of sex. She argues that the development industry has always dealt with sexuality-related issues, although usually only implicitly, and negatively, in relation to population control, disease, or violence. Now the need to respond to HIV/AIDS, and the increasing legitimacy of human rights approaches in development, are creating spaces for more open discussion of sexuality, but it is usually still described as a problem, in relation to risk, vulnerability, ill-health and violations of rights. Jolly provides a framework for examining sexual pleasure and development, arguing that we need to move away from examining essentialized identities (e.g. men who have sex with men; cross-dressers; lesbians) to thinking about sexual rights and access to pleasure.

In Chapter 2, Jyoti Puri analyzes representations of hijras/kinnars/arvanis in India as they have been invoked in HIV/AIDS, development, and trans/national academic discourse. She points out that hijras have been glaringly absent from discourses and policies of development but increasingly visible in the past decade through HIV/AIDS discourses and intervention programs. This has meant heightened surveillance and scrutiny of hijras, especially by NGOs with ties to the state as well as international donors and agencies. Along with non-transgendered women, sex workers, and male truck drivers, hijras are becoming the most maligned groups in the HIV/AIDS discourse in India. At the same time, Puri notes, anthropological discourses of hijras as "third gender" circulate widely and have been of particular interest to constructing transnational genealogies of transgender identities. She argues that just as HIV/AIDS discourses make hijras visible as metonyms of sexual transgression, so too have trans/national academic discourses troublingly marked them as metonyms for sexual and cultural difference, pointing out the implications of these representations for frameworks of development and for activist-scholars who have embraced hijras as an expression of liberation from Western dualisms.

Suzanne Bergeron (Chapter 3) then addresses the imagined heterosexual norm in the field of economics. She examines some of the ways that economists' ideas about heterosexual norms are implicated in their definitions of what it means for an economy to develop and a society to become modern, focusing in particular on neoclassical and feminist models of the household that have helped to frame gender-sensitive policy in general and at the World Bank in particular. As Bergeron notes, household models have wielded significant influence on how institutions such as the World Bank make sense of gender and development, as evidenced in the Bank's heavy emphasis on household models to explain the gender division of labor, gender differences in power, and differences of men and women with regard to decision-making about household consumption, saving, and human capital investment. Utilizing Judith Butler's (1990) concept of "a heterosexual matrix," she shows that the representation of gender in these household models take for granted that the unit under discussion is a husband and wife that engage in complementary gender roles with a bounded nuclear family, with the overall task of highlighting the ways that the heterosexuality presumed by economists is artificial and unstable.

Negotiating heteronormativity in development institutions

The second part addresses how individuals negotiate heteronormativity within development institutions such as the World Bank, United Nations agencies, state development agencies, community organizations, and non-governmental organizations. The authors address how development practitioners and advocates themselves necessarily negotiate heteronormative representations of the family, community, nation, and state in development practices and policy frameworks, sometimes reproducing orientalist understandings of sexuality while at other times challenging them. Andil Gosine (Chapter 4) provides an examination of GLOBE, the staff organization for "Gay, Lesbian or Bisexual Employees" at the World Bank. As a catalyst for discussions on sexualities and development at the Bank, key GLOBE members have helped shape the Bank's policies on HIV/AIDS and sexual health in Africa and throughout the global South, and some have also contributed to spearheading an "MSM mainstreaming" program. Gosine utilizes an ethnographic approach to relate GLOBE's story and analyze how conversations about sexualities are being taken up in development organizations, with important implications for World Bank policies that target LGBT populations. GLOBE is an interesting space through which to examine the constitution of discourses on sex/sexualities, Gosine argues, as it brings together queer-identified people from the North and South to negotiate ideas about sexual dissidence and identities, in the context of working at a powerful multilateral institution. Yet despite GLOBE's presence in the Bank and despite the fact that the Bank has one of the strongest sets of policies concerning domestic partner benefits, rarely have GLOBE employees' own demands for their rights translated into the queering – or critical querying – of the Bank's international development agenda.

Next, Ara Wilson (Chapter 5) examines NGOs and argues that these organizations can be read as sites of queer possibilities, even in the context of hegemonic neoliberal development in which the institutionalization of NGOs (or so-called NGOization) sometimes converges with the goals of neoliberal programs. NGO offices provide critical spaces for relations, discussion, and politics outside of commercial publics and (to some extent) remain separate from the state; they also can be considered important sites of labor for women, much like factories are seen as sites of labor for men (and in some cases, women). She argues that NGOs offer important venues for relationships, identity, community, and pleasure among women who love women. This has been particularly important, she argues, for women who have typically lacked spaces available to gay men or male-to-female transgendered individuals.

Kate Bedford (Chapter 6) then presents a case study of World Bank export-promotion policy in Ecuador centered on the flower industry, a key site for women's employment, and discusses how World Bank staff in Ecuador attempt to juggle tensions between market and non-market labor by (re)forging normative arrangements of intimacy. As the Bank has attempted to find a policy solution for the tension between paid and unpaid work, including the fact that women's workloads have increased, rather than decreased, as a result of development policies that aim to "integrate women into development," it has developed a policy that restructures normative heterosexuality to encourage a two-partner model of love and labor wherein women work more and men are taught to love better. Specifically, she examines how Bank gender staff have tried to promote better male loving within the family such that floriculture employees can manage social reproduction privately. She critiques the Bank's sexualized policy interventions, including their newly proposed fatherhood initiatives, and suggest that they warrant contestation, both for their pathologization of poor men and for their (mis)designation of privatized social welfare provision as empowering.

Finally, Susan Paulson (Chapter 7) explores relations between scholarly concepts and social practices surrounding marriage, sexuality, and family in Bolivia, where poverty, political volatility, and US interests have allowed international policies and development programs to make a powerful impact on everyday life. She presents ethnographic material from two groups of individuals who do not fit normative categories: a group of households organized around women's sibling, friendship, and intergenerational ties that are variously labeled "headless," "woman-headed," "incomplete," or "broken" because the patriarchal heterosexual male is missing; and a group of men who are involved in webs of meaningful relations, including sexual intimacy with other men, and who are variously labeled "alone," "detoured," and "half-men" because they have not achieved the role of patriarchal heterosexual head of family. Paulson provides a descriptive account of how exclusion from normative models is experienced in different ways according to gender, sexual orientation, and location in the nation. She also looks at how these different experiences are connected as parts of a Bolivian landscape uniquely shaped by colonialism, inequality, and poverty, a high degree of movement and migration, and a powerful push for modern development by international agencies, the Bolivian government, churches, and NGOs.

Resisting global hegemonies

What can queer scholars and activists do to counter heteronormative narratives and envision and work toward a more equitable future? To what extent is there potential for radical transformation in any queering development project, with mainstreaming as its goal? What kinds of advocacy networks and solidarity communities do we wish to construct? And given the risk of producing orientalist homonormativities, what "critical political stances are required when the oppositional begins to assume the shape of the hegemonic" (to paraphrase Jacqui Alexander 2005: 69), when gayness or queerness defends or reinforces rather than puts into question narratives of neoliberal development, globalization, and empire? Several existing advocacy and scholarly examples point us in the direction of social change. In this third part, authors address these questions as they emerge from the complex relationships among global development institutions, neoliberal governmentalities, the spatial arrangements of capital, and emergent sexual subjectivities.

In Chapter 8, Sangeeta Budhiraja, Susana T. Fried and Alexandra Teixeira address tensions among identity-based organizing and sexual rights advocacy. On one hand, activists around the world have addressed "lesbian and gay," and later, "lesbian, gay and bisexual (LGB)," then "lesbian, gay, bisexual and transgender (LGBT)" or "lesbian, gay, bisexual, transgender and questioning and/or queer" (LGBTQ)" rights, the "alphabet soup" approach, as a way to make sexual and gender minorities visible in national and international political and development arenas. Yet, more recently, scholars and activists have turned toward a sexual rights framework as a way to overcome essentialisms in positing individuals as singular identities that are often homogenized and universalized in development discourse and practice. Drawing upon their former advocacy work at the International Gay and Lesbian Human Rights Commission, the authors demonstrate the difficulties of naming and finding a common ground on a global level as well as the usefulness of utilizing a broad-based sexual rights framework for thinking about sexual identity, gender identity, human rights, and development. They argue that a sexual rights framework allows for greater cross-movement organizing, gives deference to local activists' preferred ways of thinking of and expressing any gender which falls outside of social and cultural norms, and encourages modes of organizing that do not reify gender and sexual binaries. Yet activists must necessarily use, perhaps strategically, normative categories of gender and sexuality in order to achieve their

concrete goals for legal and policy reform, a dilemma that they highlight throughout their chapter.

In Chapter 9, Petra Doan discusses how increasing the visibility of gender-variant
individuals in the Middle East, a region often characterized in development discourse in orientalist terms as patriarchal and oppressive to women, might actually
"queer" the development process and stimulate change on a broader scale. For
Doan, genderqueerness does not begin or end in the West; rather, it has always
been part of Middle Eastern societies, but it has been through powerful modern discourses such as that of development which have problematized these identities as
abnormal or deviant. Despite colonialist legacies, it has been through the strategic
utilization of these modern discourses that gender-variant individuals in the region
have found creative ways to organize collectively and fight for their rights.

Ashley Currier (Chapter 10) then presents an in-depth case study of Behind the
Mask, a largely online LGBT rights organization based in Johannesburg, South
Africa whose aim is to establish a safe space for public sexualities. Launched in
2000 with international development funding, Behind the Mask engages in what it
calls "journalistic advocacy," raising public awareness of African LGBT persons
by telling their stories. Currier's study reveals how and why visibility is an important right and development strategy for LGBT social movements.

Maja Horn (Chapter 11) critiques Eurocentric examinations of LGBT movements in Latin America for their inability to capture the relationship between
public space and queer subjects except in hierarchical terms of "progressiveness"
vs. "backwardness." Horn develops critically needed terms to discuss queer lives,
cultures, and epistemologies in the Dominican Republic that are simply erased by
approaches that look for LBGTQ social movements, public visibility, and political
activism through a Western Eurocentric lens. She thus critiques heteronormativity in development frameworks as well as homonormativity in Eurocentric queer
studies of LGBT movements in the Dominican Republic.

Notes

1 Iran's policy on homosexuality and transsexuality is a case in point: Whereas the Iranian
state has held the position that homosexuality (and specifically sodomy) is a sin and
punishable by law, the same state has held that transsexuals "are sick because they are
not happy with their sexuality, and so they should be treated ..." as Muhammad Mehdi
Kariminia, a mid-ranking cleric and university professor at Kam Khomeini University in
Qum, was quoted as saying (Fathi 2004: 5). This has allowed for transsexuals to receive
support for surgical treatment, although some gay men have also been coerced into having surgery as a way to "cure" their homosexuality. As critics of President Mahmoud
Ahmadinejad have pointed out, "For a country that is said to have no homosexuality
[as President Ahmadinejad notoriously claimed at a September 2007 public lecture at
Columbia University], Iran goes to great lengths to ban it." (Fathi 2004: 5).
2 Portugal also included a similar clause in its 2004 constitution, making it the first
country in the European Union and the fourth country in the world to adopt this type
of language.
3 By "post-neoliberal," I am not implying that neoliberal policies no longer exist but
rather that they have lost their "quasi-hegemonic position" in some countries, as new

forms of collective action and articulations of economic and social policy have gained salience (Grimson and Kessler 2005; Fernandes 2007). This is nowhere more true than in Latin America, the region that first underwent structural adjustment measures in the early 1980s and where many countries are now attempting to shift away from the neoliberal model (e.g. Argentina, Bolivia, Brazil, Chile, Ecuador, Nicaragua, Venezuela).

4 Andil Gosine (2005) has pointed out that when studies show that MSM "also have sex with female partners (who may also in turn have sex with exclusively heterosexual male partners)," governments and other institutions can thus argue that "HIV/AIDS in sexual minority/dissident communities may in fact infect the whole society with the disease," thereby causing the perceived threat to national security.

5 Very few development institutions have addressed lesbian health or "development issues." For example, little research has been conducted on how lesbian individuals and households negotiate economic crisis; how lesbians develop survival strategies and experience discrimination in the workplace; or how lesbians experience long-term partnerships or parenting, to name only three examples. I know of one published study on discrimination against lesbians in the workplace in Bolivia, Brazil, Colombia, Honduras, and Mexico (ADEIM-Simbiosis, *et al.* 2006), and while there are studies on lesbians and sexual citizenship in the global South, little research has been done to understand the relationship between sexuality and the economy, and to document how lesbians and queers survive socioeconomic injustices.

6 This, however, has had important, even violent, implications for local activists. According to Dennis Altman, four years after helping to found the visible gay (male) rights movements in Bolivia, Timothy Wright himself was found badly beaten and amnesiac (Altman 2001: 95).

7 Interestingly, global fatherhood initiatives such as those proposed by the World Bank share some similarities with models proposed by US governments in the 1990s and 2000s, especially by the governments of William J. Clinton (1992–2000) and George W. Bush (2000–09; see Gavanas 2004), although the extent to which there is a direct relationship among these policy processes remains unexplored in the scholarship.

8 According to this same report, "more than 70 of the United Nations' 191 member-states have a total ban on homosexuality," and some state leaders have "made a career out of attacking gays and lesbians, calling them "less than humans and dogs," as in the case of Zimbabwean and Namibian leaders (Deen 2003: 2).

9 For a recent review of the literature on liberal-oriented "women in development" or WID approaches and materialist/postmodernist-oriented "gender and development" approaches to development, see Jaquette and Staudt 2006. Earlier articles on this topic include Rathgeber 1990; Kabeer 1994; Goetz 1997.

10 For a review of the debates on gender mainstreaming, see Porter and Sweetman 2005; see also Prügl and Lustgarten 2006.

Part I

Querying/queering development

Theories, representations, strategies

1 Why the development industry should get over its obsession with bad sex and start to think about pleasure

Susie Jolly

Wanted sex, good sex and right to enjoy sex is not something that is covered in many intervention programmes. All I can say is that sexual reproductive health activities concentrate on ABC and family planning, in other words, more of the shock tactics type of education. How do we expect young women to understand the importance of consensual sex and negotiating skills if education is only limited to prevention of pregnancy, STIs, and sex being a no go area in many societies?

(Namibian participant, Young Women's Dialogue, in International Community of Women Living with HIV/AIDS, April 13, 2004)

[W]hen we go beyond conventional research paradigms on African sexuality (which primarily focus on reproduction, violence and disease) to explore the area of desire and pleasure, we gain deeper insights into this complex subject matter. I believe that in the long run, by broadening the scope of our research on sexuality, we can offer fresh perspectives that support more astute strategic interventions on critical areas such as sexual rights, health education, HIV/AIDS and development.

(Tamale 2005: 18)

There is a myth that the development industry[1] is not engaged with sexuality – and some fears that if it does engage with these intimate areas of our lives, it will do harm. In fact, the development industry has always dealt with sexuality-related issues, although usually only implicitly, and negatively, in relation to population control, disease, or violence. More recently, the need to respond to HIV/AIDS, and the increasing legitimacy of human rights approaches in development, have created spaces for more open discussion of sexuality. Huge progress has been made, such as in the Cairo Convention (1994) which understands reproductive health to include that "people are able to have a satisfying and safe sex life" and the Beijing Platform for Action (1995) which asserts women's rights to "have control over and decide freely and responsibly on matters related to their sexuality". However, the focus is still usually on sex as a problem, in relation to risk, vulnerability, ill-health, and violations of rights, and on how to say "no" to risky sex, rather than how to say "yes" or even ask for a broader range of safer sex options (Klugman 2000, Corrêa 2002, Petchesky 2005).

This chapter starts with a look at how development representations of the dangers of sexuality have been combined with stereotypical representations of gender with very problematic results. It then moves on to examine the realities of the imbrications of pleasure and danger in peoples lives, looking at how gender combines with other power dynamics to play out in a variety of sexual cultures. Lastly, the chapter considers why and how development should promote the good sides of sexuality.

Development representations: bad sex and gender stereotypes

The development industry has emphasized the dangers of sex and sexuality. This negative approach to sex has been filtered through a view of gender which stereotypes men as predators, women as victims, and fails to recognize the existence of transgender people.

Women as victims of bad sex ...

Within the development discourses of sex as a problem, women are positioned as victims of bad sex, in line with Chandra Talpade Mohanty's analysis of victim representations of "third world women" in her now renowned piece, "Under Western Eyes: feminist scholarship and colonial discourses" (Mohanty 1991), which, sadly, is still relevant. In her publication, Mohanty considers a series of writings by "first world" feminists on subjects such as female genital mutilation and women in development. The texts she considers consistently define women as objects of what is done to them, and as victims of either "male violence," "the colonial process," "the Arab familial system," "the economic development process," or "the Islamic code." An image is constructed of a homogeneous and victimized population of Third World women. Mohanty recognizes that this homogenizing includes sexuality, erasing "all marginal and resistant modes and experiences. It is significant that none of the texts I reviewed in the ... series focuses on lesbian politics or the politics of ethnic and religious marginal organizations in third world women's groups" (Mohanty 1991: 73).

A powerful current version of this discourse of women as victims is about women's absolute vulnerability to HIV/AIDS due to male violence and economic coercion. For example, at the time of writing, the most frequently downloaded news story on the UNIFEM HIV/AIDS portal reports that the HIV/AIDS pandemic:

> ... has killed more people (mostly women) than World Wars I and II and the Gulf War combined. Some of the reasons identified as the causes of the high prevalence of HIV infections in women include the cultural practice, which gave men the exclusive right to decide when, how and why to have sex with women in or out of marriage. Indeed these cultural practices are reinforced by the dependence of women on men for their needs, both financial and material. Women in this kind of situation, mostly in the developing countries, are subjected to sexual violence in the event they decide to

postpone sexual intercourse for a moment for reasons of health, safety, or tiredness.

(Dowuona 2005)

This piece does reflect important aspects of reality. It is true that many women are pressured into unsafe sex by violence or economic dependency. I do not in any way want to undermine the hugely important work against this violence and coercion. However, the emphasis on violence and gender inequality as the causes of unsafe sex only presents half the picture. There's an underlying idea here that men have total power in sex while women are just trying to impose damage limitation while we "lie back and think of England"[2] or some other appropriate patriotic love object (and that women only ever have unsafe sex because we lack power to negotiate with male partners, never due to our own desires). Do women really have no desire, agency or room for maneuver? Do women have no pleasure or hope of pleasure in sex?

Sylvia Tamale (2005) has challenged portrayals of African women as simply victims of sexual oppression through her research on the *Ssenga* – a tradition among the Baganda people in Uganda where the paternal aunt takes on the task of educating her nieces about sex. Tamale's research shows that while the institution of *Ssenga* can reinforce patriarchal power over women's bodies, it can also present new opportunities for women to challenge control of their sexualities. Many *Ssenga*s in their contemporary form promote messages about women's autonomy and economic independence, and some instruction includes lessons in oral sex, masturbation, and female ejaculation. Tamale also notes the pleasure-enhancing effects for both women and men of the extension of the labia minora,[3] which the World Health Organization has lumped together with harmful forms of female genital mutilation (Tamale 2005).

The danger of the discourse of "women as victims of bad sex" is not just the crushing of any space for discussion of or mobilization around women's pleasure. Dangerous convergences take place between certain feminist positions aiming to protect women from sexual violence and conservative forces concerned with women's chastity. This has already been observed in several instances: feminist anti-pornography activists making alliances with right-wing groups in the West in the 1980s (Rubin 1984); some Indian feminists' images of Indian women as chaste and vulnerable to sexual exploitation echoing the Hindu right's portrayal of virtuous Indian womanhood (Kapur 2002); and the "unholy alliance" between some feminist groups and the Bush administration in the mobilization against prostitution and trafficking (Crago 2003). Such discourses around protecting women from exploitation – sexual and otherwise – have also been drawn upon by the US right to justify the invasion of Afghanistan and Iraq (Petchesky 2005).

Men as perpetrators of bad sex ...

The flipside of the "women as victims of bad sex" discourse is the "men as sexual predator" one. Both the global feminist and the neocolonialist enterprise become white women saving brown women from brown men.[4] Just as Third World women are portrayed as homogeneous, Third World men are portrayed as monolithic, heterosexual, and as perpetrators of sexual oppression of women. The multiple and diverse forms of masculinity, and differentials in men's power, are ignored. Ouzgane and Morrell (2005) argue that in much of the existing literature on gender in Africa, men have tended to be overlooked, taken for granted, or treated as a unified, homogeneous category.

In 2003, the US congress passed the Global Emergency AIDS Act. Gary Barker describes how:

> ... some lawmakers in the United States decided that African men were the problem behind HIV/AIDS and included language in the bill that called for changing how African men treat women, with funding provided for "assistance for the purpose of encouraging men to be responsible in their sexual behaviour, child rearing and to respect women." While many persons would likely agree with the sentiment of this statement, it is important we avoid blaming individual men and instead examine more closely how it is that social constructions of gender and manhood lead to HIV-related vulnerability.
>
> (Barker 2005: 4)

Some men do fit the stereotypes of sexual predator. However, where men diverge from this image, their experiences are erased. Men have been victims of sexual violence in large numbers, and sexual violence against men has been used as a weapon of war and intimidation – for example in the wars in former Yugoslavia in the 1990s, and in the anti-Muslim pogroms in Gujarat, India in 2002, yet these incidents have been under-reported and did not make the media (Petchesky 2005).

This silence on men's sexual victimization has been dramatically broken with stories of the US military's sexual torture of prisoners in Abu Ghraib prison in Iraq. Now added to the relentless images we see of men attacking women are photos of men being tortured, sexually and otherwise, by women as well as men. Petchesky (2005) argues that the reason sexual violence inflicted on men and by women became visible at this point was not only because of the availability of new technologies (digital cameras, e-mail, and Internet), but because US intelligence interpreted sexual violence, and treating men as feminized and homosexualized, as particularly humiliating – both in their own American patriarchal and homophobic frame of reference, and also in their understanding of Muslim and Arab cultures. As such, publicizing such images multiplied the humiliation around the world. Thus while men became visible as victims, this portrayal emerged *precisely* because it served a deliberate function of showing these men as "less than" men. Where men retain their masculinity they remain predators, not victims.

Transgender people ignored

While women are positioned as victims, and men as predators, those who do not fit neatly into the male–female categorizations usually remain invisible in development discourses on sexuality or other issues. I will label these people very loosely as "transgender"[5] by which I include a whole range of self-identifications such as tommy boys and lesbian men in Africa, hijras in South Asia, travestis[6] in Latin America, ladyboys in Thailand, third spirit among native American Indians, the globalized identities of queer, trans, female to male transsexuals and male to female transsexuals, and all those who are intersex, as well as any others who identify as neither male nor female. By transgender, I refer to a gender identity, or anti-identity – a not fitting into the male/female categorizations.

The reality is that many people do not fit into the "male–female" sex categories. Numbers are not small. In his briefing to the United Nations Commission on Human Rights in 2002, Bondyopadhay records an estimate of between half to one million hijras in India. An article in *The New Scientist* declares that up to one in every 500 babies are born "intersex" with chromosomes at odds with their anatomy (Phillips 2001: 31), but this is usually hushed up. In the West one in 2000 babies have surgery because their bodies do not fit the accepted categories of "female" or "male" (Phillips 2001: 39).

Yet such diversity is erased in development discourses, including in gender and development discourses. In our insistence that gender comes from nurture rather than nature, we[7] have been willing to leave sex, and the categorizations of male and female, uncontested in the domain of biology. See, for example, these current unexceptional definitions from the One World Action Glossary:

> Sex marks the distinction between women and men as a result of their biological, physical and genetic differences.
>   Gender roles are the different roles that women and men, girls and boys have that often determine who does what within a society. Gender roles are set by convention and other social, economic, political and cultural forces.
>   (One World Action 2005)

Such definitions, and policies and programs based on this limited understanding of sex, erase the experiences of transgender people worldwide. Campuzano (2008) argues that development and colonialism have suppressed possibilities to identify outside the male–female categories. He gives the example of Peru where historically among indigenous people the distinctions between male and female were more flexible than they are today. A traditional travesti or transgender/transvestite identity and culture existed and persists in spite of the colonial and subsequently development influences which imposed a more restrictive order on gender identity and behavior (2006).

Currently, transgendered people are likely to face particular sexuality-related issues; for example, how to negotiate their own sexual interactions in societies which refuse to recognize their gender identities, high levels of rape and sexual violence from police and others, discrimination by sexual health services, as well as the fact that for certain transgender populations, labor market discrimination means that sex work is virtually the only way to generate income (IGLHRC 2004; Monro 2005). However, development policy and programming is unlikely to support transgendered people in these or other areas.

An important exception is the opportunity to challenge this exclusion created by the response to HIV/AIDS. For example, in the National HIV/AIDS Program in Pakistan, on which I worked as a consultant in 2004, the interventions targeted at "MSM" (men who have sex with men) then focused largely on hijras because this population was most visible to those implementing the program. Men who had sex with men but did not dress in saris were apparently invisible to those implementing the program, even though a gay member of our consultancy team spotted several without going beyond the hotel lobby. On the positive side, the program did endeavor to provide some information, health services, and peer education for hijras. However, the opposite has been reported in Kenya where HIV/AIDS policies have made progress in including MSM, but transgendered, intersexed, and women who have sex with women remain excluded (Urgent Action Fund 2006).

Pleasure and danger: bifurcations and imbrications

So development has largely focused on the downsides of sex, with women seen as victims, men as perpetrators, and transgendered individuals largely ignored. While development focuses on the risks, in many contexts a parallel current runs through popular and commercial culture, focusing only on pleasures, with glamorous sexual images in advertising, media obsession with love and romance, and pornography widely available.

In reality, pleasure and danger are often entwined – not least because, for many, seeking pleasure entails breaking social rules. In the landmark 1984 publication, *Pleasure and Danger*, Carole Vance points out how male sexual violence and the institutions and ideologies that justify it make it dangerous for women to pursue their own sexual pleasures. While she is talking about America, this is arguably common worldwide, although which sanctions are in place to prevent or punish women from such a pursuit vary according to context – ranging from female genital mutilation (FGM) and honor killings to restrictions on mobility, and social exclusion.

However, the oppressive frameworks which forbid pursuit of pleasure are not the only dangers associated with sexuality. Vance reminds us, "The threat of male violence is ... not the only source of sexual danger" (Vance 1984: 4–5). She adds that there are other fears to do with sex such as anxieties about loss of control, merging with another, intense sensation, triggering emotions, invoking of previous experiences, and of not being satisfied. I would add a few more fears such as losing our object of love or lust, and catching a sexually transmitted infection or a cold.

> Without a better language to excavate and delineate these other sources of danger, everything is attributed to men, thereby inflating male power and impoverishing ourselves ... The truth is that the rich brew of our experience contains elements of pleasure and oppression, happiness and humiliation.

Rather than regard this ambiguity as confusion or false consciousness, we should use it as a source-book to examine how women experience sexual desire, fantasy and action.

(Vance 1984: 5–6)

I would argue that this ambiguity is just as relevant for men and for transgendered individuals, all of whom have their sexualities and pleasures constructed by the same power dynamics that women do, even though they are positioned differently in relation to them. In this section, I will discuss a few examples of imbrications of pleasure and danger in constructions of heterosexuality, in the sexual cultures of some travesti populations, and in relation to public sex between men. I will look at how gender and other power dynamics interact with sexual practices to produce these imbrications of pleasure and danger.

Sheila Jeffreys has argued that heterosexuality is the eroticization of gender inequality:

> Heterosexual desire is eroticised power difference ... So heterosexual desire for men is based on eroticising the otherness of women, an otherness which is based on a difference in power. Similarly, in the twentieth century, when women have been required to show sexual enthusiasm for men, they have been trained to eroticise the otherness of men, i.e. men's power and their own subordination ... Women's subordination is sexy for men and for women too ... Women ... are not born into equality and we do not have equality to eroticise. We are not born into power and we do not have power to eroticise. We are born into subordination and it is in subordination that we learn our sexual and emotional responses ... From the discriminating behaviour of her mother while she is still in the cradle, through a training in how to sit and move without taking up space or showing her knickers, how to speak when spoken to and avert her gaze from men, a girl learns subordination ...

(Jeffreys 1991: 299–302)

This argument contains a convincing logic – a huge factor in relations between women and men is inequality. Unless you are a 100 percent sex essentialist who believes biology determines it all, if you accept that sexual desires are even partly constructed by our contexts, then what else would construct heterosexuality, seeing as inequality is such a huge part of relations with the "opposite" sex?

Heterosexual desires can only be constructed in relation to gender inequalities – they can hardly ignore them. Although how our desires are constructed will vary, desires may either mimic or react against inequalities or a combination of the two. For example, in the London sadomasochist club scene men seeking dominant women outnumber women seeking subordinate men.[8] Is this because more men react against the pressure to assume responsibility and power in their lives than the number of women reacting against submission? Or is it to do with how masculinities have been constructed in the British context, perhaps to do with traditional education systems of discipline and hierarchy in all-boy schools? To find any answers would require further research. What this example does tell us is that how desire interacts with gender inequalities varies, and we shouldn't be surprised if a few women enjoy rape fantasies[9] while others abhor them, given the world we live in.

Likewise, the pleasures and desires of transgender people are constructed in relation to gender inequalities and power dynamics. Kulick describes a culture in a travesti community he researched in Brazil of having gender rather than having sex. In a study of travestis and their boyfriends, Kulick finds that although travestis may orgasm at work (sex work) when they penetrate clients, they prefer to play a stereotypical "feminine" role of being passive and penetrated with their boyfriends, which they feel affirms their femininity (Kulick 1997). The travestis Kulick interviewed are categorical that they do not allow their boyfriends to touch their genitals, and that they do not wish to penetrate their boyfriends. They say sex with boyfriends should consist of their boyfriends penetrating them. This kind of sex does not generally bring them orgasms, but it makes them feel like women, which is what they want. This sentiment is echoed in this quote by a "tommy boy" (male-identified lesbian) in Uganda:

> I have to be the dominant partner. When we are having fun I want to be dominant just because I am the one who comes and cons you. So I have to make sure I satisfy you. For me, I don't care if I get satisfied or not because if I make you happy that's good.
>
> (Marci, quoted in Morgan and Wieringa 2005: 75)

Alan Sinfield cites Amnesty International's documentation in "Crimes of Hate" of extensive police and prison guard sexual violence and rape of gay men worldwide. While such torture may have the aim to humiliate, punish, destroy, it also implicates police in same-sex desire and action. At the same time "… a prominent scenario in gay male pornography and chat lines dwells upon police violence and military uniforms, punishment, bondage and assault" (Sinfield 2006: 316). Similar to heterosexual desire, same-sex desire is constructed in relation to inequalities and oppressions.

Of course the power relations that construct desire include a whole range of domains – not just gender, but also state regulation, class struggles, globalization, and neocolonialism, to name just a few. Race is one axis of power which constructs sexuality. Kopano Ratele (2004) coins the term "kinky politics" to describe how race is a fetish that becomes sexualized. This fetishization is part of what constitutes racism – attributing a particular importance and reality to the idea of "race," which is connected with fear and desire:

> Kinky politics follows the fetish of, and refetishises, "race." There can be no racism without this constant re-fetishisation … Racism, together with (hetero) sexism, then, is what keeps us in awe, or in fear, or ignorance of black and white, male and female bodies and sexualities in this society.
>
> (Ratele 2004: 142)

The practice of men having sex with men in public cruising spaces is an illustrative example of the imbrication of desire and danger. Due to exclusion and stigma, there are often no sanctioned spaces for sex between people of the same sex, unlike heterosexual sex which does have a place, albeit constrained. For example, it may be supposed to take place in the marital bed, at the man's initiative, when the woman is not menstruating, etc. – although these rules will vary according to context.

While there is generally no openly sanctioned space for sex between people of the same sex, due to their relative freedom to occupy public spaces, men, and to some degree transgender, may manage to have sex in public areas. This may be quick, guilty and unsafe sex in locations such as parks and toilets, where they risk both sexually transmitted infections and violence from police or others if discovered.

The World Bank sponsored a "mapping" of men who have sex with men in Lahore, Pakistan, which involved interviews with over 200 MSM (Khan and Khilji 2002). The study reported that while women's contact with men is controlled and socially policed, expressions of affection between people of the same sex are easily accepted. Many men have sexual relations with each other, and finding male sexual partners is easy. Sex between men takes place frequently in particular cruising areas in shrines, parks, under bridges, in public toilets, or in empty buses and train carriages around stations. At the same time, such relations are highly stigmatized by society, particularly for partners who may be penetrated rather than penetrate, or who dress in a more feminine manner.

The study found negative health effects of this exclusion:

> … much of male to male sex takes place in public environments such as parks, alleyways, building sites etc. since private spaces are not readily available. This means that time is of the essence to reduce the risks of discovery. Taking time to put on a condom increases the risk of being seen by others.
>
> (Khan and Khilji 2002: 31)

The time constraints also encourage quick aggressive sex. A majority of interviewees report penetration usually taking place within "3 to 5 minutes," with no foreplay, no lubricant other than saliva, and rapid violent movements, the combination of which would have high risk for anal tissue damage, and indeed 10 percent of interviewees reported anal bleeding and discharge.

The above study gives the downside in graphic form. Due to exclusion from private spaces, men have sex in public spaces. Due to stigma and shame, sex is quick and dangerous, causing ill-health. Multiple inequalities contribute to constructing the stigma which underlies these dynamics, one of which is Article 377, put in place by former British Colonial administrations, which criminalizes "carnal intercourse against the order of nature" usually interpreted as anal sex between men. This law is still on the books today in India, Pakistan, and several other former British colonies.

However, while public sex has obvious risks, it can also be experienced as highly erotic and affirming. Zachie Achmat describes how he enjoyed sex in toilets in Cape Town from the age of ten:

I had sex at the toilets every day, sometimes twice or three times a day. I would go to the library to get books, which I would read in the toilet, so that when something happened I would be there. Almost all the men were scared to touch me because of my age, but once they discovered I was into it, they enjoyed themselves. I had sex with anyone who wanted to: old, young, black or white, fat or thin, it did not matter. The sex and tenderness mattered, and there was lots of both.

(Achmat 1995: 333)

Another South African activist, Vasu Reddy, sees public cruising grounds as revolutionary spaces:

As a concept, space may … highlight cultural practices, such as the use of "cottage" (public lavatory), parks as pick-up grounds, and clubs, bars and other negotiated spaces, such as cruising grounds. These homoerotic … spaces in which gay and lesbian subcultures are directed towards sexual release, amusement and sexual pleasure are equally imbued with meanings in a political and politicised sense.

(Reddy 2005: 2)

Achmat also identifies toilets as potentially revolutionary spaces, not just for expression of stigmatized desires – both same-sex and intergenerational – but also for a momentary breakdown of apartheid racial divisions. Although "whites only," the toilet he frequented was used by all ethnicities: "apartheid was destroyed in those toilets. By men who had sex with men, regardless of race or class" (Achmat 1995: 334).

Men in very empowered positions, with long-term male partners and plenty of private space to have sex in, may still want to engage in this kind of sex – most famously the British pop star George Michael, arrested for cruising in a toilet in Los Angeles in 1998. He managed to turn the stigma around into celebration (and profit) with his subsequent single "Let's Go Outside." The lyrics could be interpreted as suggesting having sex outside, and the video featured policemen kissing and was partially shot in a studio set constructed using mirror-tiled urinals and walls. The police officer who had arrested him took the message personally, sued for slander and lost.

Anupam Hazra, a sexual rights activist, HIV/AIDS worker, and former masseur/sex worker, carried out interviews with MSM involved in the sex industry in Calcutta. Recommendations emerging from his study included the need for both the repeal of article 377, and for safe spaces for sex, open houses specifically for the purpose, non-judgmental and welcoming hourly room rental services, as well as making public toilets a better environment for sex:

Some of the respondents to the study suggested promoting public toilets/saunas as pick up joints. It was proposed that maybe these toilets can charge more and allow a couple or more people to use the lavatory (which can be locked from inside) as sex sites. These places can also display safer sex messages and distribute condoms and lubes. But the toilets should be kept clean to make the experience pleasurable.

(Hazra 2005: 3)

Is all this a problem or not? If sexual desire and actions are constructed by oppressions, is sexual practice itself perpetuating these oppressions, providing yet another arena to practice accepting and eroticizing those power relations? On the other hand, if sex acts are consensual, are the playful and horny re-enactments or reversals of the power dynamics of society a form of coping mechanism, resistance or reclaiming, a jolly way to let off steam? A way to play with or against oppressive structures, using our agency to find pleasures within the constraints in which we live?

Kulick describes the travestis' "having gender" rather than "having sex" as fulfilling an important need and desire to live out gender identities denied them by mainstream society. However, Campuzano sees travestis' sexual cultures as more problematic. He argues that with their attraction to macho and sometimes violent men, and passivity in sex, they adopt the position of the "hystericized" woman. Travestis need a new kind of feminism to enable them to no longer deny themselves pleasure (1997).

Can an oppressor be undermined by putting them in the position of lust object – as George Michael succeeded in doing with the police officer who arrested him? And what are the implications for women attracted to macho men? Are we being hysterical? Are we asserting our desires? Can we disarm these men by making them objects of our lust?

Whether the imbrication of pleasure and danger is a problem or not is the subject of much theoretically sophisticated debate arguing from all sides (Vance 1984; Sinfield 2004, 2006; Jeffreys 1991). I will not attempt to add to the theoretical debate here. Instead, I note that explorations of how people experience these imbrications throw up a diverse range of feelings and stories, as shown by the tales of sex in toilets cited in this section. Certain people at certain moments experience the imbrications of pleasure and danger as a problem, and at other moments or for other people these imbrications are felt to be joys or opportunities. Starting from this understanding of pleasure and danger as interrelated in multiple and diverse ways, I proceed to consider the practical question of what to do.

How should development negotiate the imbricated pleasures and dangers of sexuality?

If violence is not an aberration of desire, but, often, integral to it, and the good guys are involved in similar fantasy scenarios to the bad guys, it is not surprising that Amnesty has had an uphill task in its campaigns over the detainment, ill-treatment, torture and execution of political prisoners.

(Sinfield 2006: 318)

How should development actors negotiate the imbrication of pleasures and dangers in sexuality? This question is important to many aspects of human development – such as dealing with sexual violence, supporting fulfilling relationships, and promoting safer and more satisfying sexual interactions.

Part of the answer must be to tackle exploitation and inequalities in general that blight so many lives as well as construct our sexualities. The new development dogmas of participation, empowerment, and accountability can help here. By participation and empowerment I mean considered and democratic processes, struggles and movements to enable people (particularly people with less power) to voice and act upon their desires and priorities. By accountability I mean putting in place structures to ensure that institutions listen to the desires voiced. Tackling exploitation and inequalities in general, whether material, emotional, global or local, can open new possibilities for people to imagine, feel, and act upon their desires. I expect in a fantasy world free from exploitation, much sex would still be powerful and include power games and gender or other role-play. However, where these took place it would be due to greater freedom to develop and act out individual desires and fetishes, rather than due to a lack of consent or limited options.

Another part of the answer is to shift beyond the negative approaches of sexuality that treat women as victims, men as perpetrators and ignore transgender. Hand in hand with recognizing that sexuality is imbricated with violence, risk, and danger, we can celebrate the pleasures of sexuality to positive effect. The positive effects can include empowerment and affirmation, and greater safety in sex.

Promoting sexual pleasure to empower and affirm

I have argued so far that negative approaches to sexuality risk being disempowering, reinforcing gender stereotypes, crushing space for discussion of women's pleasure, and converging with right-wing discourses around sexual morality. There is evidence that positive approaches to sexuality which include spaces for talking about pleasure can engender confidence and an ability to make positive decisions, while scare tactics and stigma leave people feeling disempowered and less able to assert themselves (Philpott, Knerr, and Maher 2006).

A study of American adolescent girls (Tolman 2002) found that some were paralyzed with fear of the dangers of having sex – to their reputation, and in terms of risks of pregnancy and disease. One such girl explained that she did end up having sex with her boyfriend because he wanted it, although she felt no desire. When she discussed it with him afterwards, he insisted that she had wanted sex. She was confused, and agreed that maybe she had, maybe he knew her better than she herself did. In contrast, girls with a more positive view of sexuality were more assertive. One girl who had enjoyed sex encountered a boy from her school who tried to pressure her to sleep with him. She forcefully resisted and succeeded in deterring him. She was quite clear that she didn't want sex, because she knew what it felt like to want sex. If you are not allowed to imagine or discover what it feels like to want sex, how do you know if you don't want it? Does consent have any meaning if you are only allowed to say no? If you are only allowed to say no, you have to say no, even when you mean yes. This is going to be confusing for adolescents of any gender.

McFadden (2003) argues that many African women are fearful of considering the possibilities for sexual pleasure because of patriarchal concepts of women's sexuality as "bad" or "filthy." She sees sexual pleasure as a life-giving force which can fuel liberation on both a personal and political level, and calls for African women to reclaim their sexual energy and power, both for their own pleasure and in order to challenge the patriarchal practices which oppress them. Pereira (2003) challenges McFadden's essentialist and homogenizing understanding of sexuality, and calls for research into the understandings of sexual power and pleasure by African women and men in all their diversity. However, she too sees the potential of sexual pleasure as empowering, or at least that this idea is worth considering. She suggests further exploration into how sexual power can be used as a political resource, and on the relationship between change around sexuality and change in the economy, society, and politics.

Vasu Reddy sees the relationship between liberation around sexuality, empowerment, and affirmation as mutually reinforcing. He describes how the Durban lesbian and gay community center supported and empowered gays and lesbians and declares:

> An effect of this empowerment, I believe, is ... our celebration of sexuality and sexual cultures that associate sexual pleasure with affirmation of our identities ... Sadly, for the majority of our society, African homosexuals constitute "improper" bodies and homosexuality a "subversive" pleasure ... Such thinking confirms that, for us, sexual pleasure cannot be detached from the urgent need (and responsibility) to mobilise, educate and continue with our liberatory project.
>
> (Reddy 2005: 1, 6)

Practical initiatives are already under way to empower people through promoting possibilities for sexual pleasure. For example, since 1993 Women for Women's Human Rights (WWHR) has run training courses on human rights for women in community centers in 35 cities in the least developed and most conservative areas in Turkey. This four-month training program aims to empower women in a broad sense. It includes three modules on sexuality that talk about "sexual pleasure as a women's human right." These modules come in the ninth and tenth week *after* the women have already built up mutual trust, and had space to discuss sexual and other violence. According to WWHR's director, Pinar Ilkkaracan, "So far we've trained 4000 women and these modules are among those that women value most. Not one woman has said she didn't like talking about sexuality. On the contrary, most say they want to spend *more* time talking about it!" (cited in Jolly 2006a: 78).

Sexual pleasure is sometimes seen as men's prerogative, the stereotype being that in heterosexual sex, men will selfishly take their pleasures without giving enough attention to what the woman wants. However, the pursuit of pleasure is, in reality, not without obstacles for most men. Gender norms influence how and where men are supposed to take their pleasures; for example, in many cultures, men are not supposed to enjoy having their nipples or anuses touched. Taking pleasure in tenderness and intimacy may also be discouraged by ideas around what it takes to be a proper man. The Association of Men Against Violence formed in 2000 in Nicaragua not only works with men to tackle violence perpetrated by themselves or others, but also, through workshops, encourages men to discover the pleasures of tenderness, intimacy, and equality in both sexual and non-sexual relations.

Promoting the pleasures of safer sex

[T]here are increasing indications – from developing as well as developed countries – that public health outcomes may benefit from a greater acceptance of positive sexual experiences ... greater comfort with one's own body will enable greater ability to communicate wishes to others, and to be less "pressured" into unwanted sexual relationships.

(Ingham 2005: 1)

Sexual pleasure can be affirming and empowering. It can also help motivate safer sex.

A study involving participant observations with over 100 men who buy sex in Mombasa, Kenya, conducted in bars, shebeens (illegal drinking establishments), and night clubs where transactions over sex are made found that:

[t]he most important conclusion ... is that men who pay for sex do so because it is pleasurable and many men do not find the male condom pleasurable. Therefore messages targeted at men who have sex with sex workers may not be 100% successful if they only emphasize the benefits of condom use as disease control.

(Thomsen, *et al.* 2004: 231)

In a focus group discussion with sex workers taking part in a UK Department for International Development (DFID)-funded HIV/AIDS project in China, several participants said that while some clients "treated them like meat" which was insulting, they enjoyed sex with the clients who were cute, clean, polite, or "high quality." It was more likely to be enjoyable if they were using condoms, as they were more relaxed and not afraid of getting a disease. Some program strategies linked safer sex with pleasure, exploring how pleasure can motivate people into different kinds of sex, sometimes unsafe, and how safer sex can be promoted as pleasure-enhancing (Jolly and Ying 2003).

Ingham (2005) provides evidence that a more relaxed attitude to masturbation could help promote safer sex. He considers anxiety around semen loss, masturbation, and wet dreams in India as a factor encouraging some young men to seek out sex workers or have sex with other men in order to allow semen release. Ingham also compares the general greater ease around masturbation, bodies, and sex among young women in the Netherlands as compared to the UK, and suggests a link to the lower teenage pregnancy rates in the former.

Pleasure is clearly one motivation for sex, and may, depending on the situation, lead to or be enhanced by either safer and less safe sex. Several initiatives are already attempting to promote the pleasures of safer sex. The Pleasure Project has mapped 27 initiatives around the world which use pleasure as a primary motivation for promoting sexual health. These include programs which eroticize male and female condoms; sex-positive books for teenagers, work with churches to improve sex among married couples, erotica designed for HIV-positive people, and pleasure and harm-reduction counseling for sex workers.

Final reflections: pleasure for pleasure's sake

> People have a right to pleasure, desire, and sexuality, as well as a right not to experience these if they don't want to. How can we tell if these rights are being realized? We don't need to measure sexual pleasure, which would be quite difficult! Instead we can measure rights, and there has already been a lot of work done on how to do this.
>
> (Armas in Jolly 2006b: 1)

The development industry has emphasized the dangers of sex and sexuality. This negative approach to sex has been filtered through a view of gender which stereotypes men as predators, women as victims, and fails to recognize the existence of transgender people. It is time to go beyond this negative and gender-stereotyped view of sexuality, to recognize the imbrication of pleasure and danger in the ways people experience sexuality, and move to more positive framings of sexuality which promote the possibilities of pleasure as well as tackle the dangers.

The promotion of sexual pleasure can contribute to empowerment, particularly but not only for women and marginalized groups. The pleasures of safer sex can be promoted to tackle HIV/AIDS and improve health. These are important ends. However, it would be sad to reduce sexual pleasure to being a means to reach development goals. A variation on "lie back and think of England" becomes "take your pleasure to help meet the Millennium Development Goals."[10]

Sexual pleasure can be a wonderful thing in itself. Sonia Corrêa (2002) calls for sexual rights to be considered as an end in themselves, affirmed in relation to eroticism, recreation, and pleasure, under a framework of development as freedom, as suggested by Nobel prize-winning economist Amartya Sen (1999). Not everyone wants sexual pleasure; some people are not interested, asexual, or have decided for whatever reason that they will not pursue such pleasures. It would be presumptuous and harmful to assume everyone should be seeking such pleasures. However, for those who do wish to pursue these, an environment which enables this pursuit should be fostered by challenging the exploitation and inequalities which construct and channel our desires and actions, and by promoting rights to seek and explore those pleasures and delights which take our fancy.

Notes

1 Here I use the term "development industry" to mean all those involved in giving or spending international development funding. This includes United Nations Agencies, donor governments, recipient governments, international foundations, consultants, non-governmental organisations, activists, and development studies institutions – including the Institute of Development Studies where I work.

2 An old English saying and piece of advice for women reluctant to endure their "marital duties."

3 For example, Tamale states: "Between the age of nine and twelve … a Muganda girl would be guided by her *Ssenga* to prepare her genitals for future sex. This was done through a procedure that involved elongating the labia minora. Known as *okukyalira ensiko* (visiting the bush), this rite was traditionally performed in a clearing among the bushes where the herbs … used for the procedure were found. Pubescent girls would 'visit the bush' for a few hours every day over a period of about two weeks" (Tamale 2005: 12). Most of the women interviewed by Tamale "spoke positively of this practice," and both men and women considered the elongated labia minora to bring pleasure to both the woman and the man, to look more attractive, and to be a stamp of the Baganda identity.

4 Gayatri Spivak describes the collective imperialist fantasy that "white men are saving brown women from brown men," which white women have gone along with (Spivak 1988: 296–7).

5 Although I recognize some individuals from these groups may reject the term transgender – for example, some hijras identify as women, some as a third sex, some transsexuals identify as the sex to which they are transitioning or have transitioned. However, given the limitations of the current language available, transgender still seems the best term to use for now.

6 "Travesti" is a Latin American transgender identity – men who generally identify as men, but see themselves as feminine, are attracted to men, and mostly work in sex work.

7 A note on pronouns: I tend to say "we" because I consider myself, and I expect some of my readers, to be part of this large and messy development enterprise. I am not an external critic, keeping my hands clean while critiquing what's going on. I am implicated, part of the problem as well as the solution.

8 This is based on participant observation in the London S/M scene.

9 I do mean fantasies of rape, I do not mean women actually want to be raped.

10 The Millennium Development Goals are currently among the highest profile goals for most governments' actions on international development.

2 Transgendering development

Reframing hijras and development

Jyoti Puri

I got my name Pia because I danced the song with the words "Pia … pia" at weddings. My name is also Krishna … I am 18 years old … People in the jhuggi (hutments) who know me call me Krishna, others call me Hijra, Hijra. I like the name Pia but I don't hide my name Krishna.

Once, a policeman in Sadar Bazaar beat me, he caught hold of my hair and twisting it, he hit me mercilessly, abused me verbally. I became goddess Kali, and I wasn't going to let him go. So, I hit him, bit him on the leg and hand, I went crazy. Four–five policemen separated me from him and warned me to go away. But, that would mean I was afraid, so I didn't go away. I told them that this would get decided in court. So, they sent the policeman away with the excuse that he needed to change his shirt. They told me to let it go and I forgave him.

(Yamuna Pushta, Delhi, June 2005)

Bobby looks directly into the camera. Her head and shoulders are tilted sideways, her face resting on a hand as her dark hair falls to one side. Her eyes are lightly lined; a bindi (dot applied on the forehead) and pinkish lipstick adorn her face.

She wears a black bra. A white garment covering her lower body merges with a brightly colored bed cover of blues, yellow, and mauve and cushions of purple, black and white arranged against a patterned bed frame. Just beyond the bed is a wall shelf, covered with gilded cloth, and filled with knick-knacks. A blue-green textured wall frames Bobby and fades out of the photograph.

(Max Mueller Bhavan, New Delhi, May 2005)

The accompanying text reads:

I am expressing my in-depth feelings. In this picture I feel like a woman. I live life like a normal woman which is what I have desired. But unlike most women I do not have any restrictions imposed on me.

This is the opening image of a series of nearly 40 images exhibited at the Max Mueller Bhavan art gallery.[1] Entitled *Kaaya: Beyond Gender*, the series is entirely composed of self-portrait photographs of kinnars (also known as hijras).[2] That the photographs on display are taken by kinnars and the attached text is in their own words make this exhibit unusual. Opening day is well-attended, followed by positive reviews. A book compilation of the photographs, also entitled *Kaaya: Beyond Gender* (2005), including a few that were not displayed at the exhibit, is available simultaneously. It is held to be the first such funded and publicly displayed exhibit.

A little background to begin with. Hijras are interchangeably considered "Third Gender" (M. Kay Martin and Barbara Voorhies' term[3]), "Third Sex," or in the language of their most widely known ethnographer, Serena Nanda (1990), "Neither men nor women." A generic description of hijras might read something like this: they are socio-biological males who present women-like within a shifting constellation of meanings; they may undergo castration and penectomy dedicated to their goddess, which gives them said power to endow fertility on newly-weds and bless newborns; the minority that is born intersexed is considered to be especially invested with these powers and is treasured for its uniqueness. Many pay allegiance to or live in a guru's house even as the arrangements can be flexible and loyalties can change. While all hijras belong to a kinship organized around seven houses in India, regional variations persist. Regional languages and cultural differences among hijra are not unimportant; in the Delhi area, hijras draw part of their income from attending ritual observations of weddings and births, but there is no such parallel among those living in and around Chennai, where they rely solely on soliciting money and sex.

Hijras are also varyingly seen as eunuchs, transsexuals, effeminate men, and, increasingly, as transgenders. The frequently derogatory use of the term hijra and its synonyms (ali, for example) has contributed to the circulation of regional terms such as aravani and kinnar; especially around the Chennai area, aravani is the preferred term and kinnar is fast gaining popularity in Northern India as a form of self-identity.[4] In keeping with these changes, I use the term kinnar for the Delhi area and the terms hijras and transgender more generally and interchangeably. These mobile identities also coincide with gaining momentum for hijras' rights as persons and citizens, right to protection against violence and discrimination, right to equality under law, right to vote and stand for election, right to livelihood, including sex work, right to legally and medically change gender status, right to fair portrayals in the media, and right to a life with dignity, among others. Perhaps the list will give indication of what is still socially and legally denied to kinnars and hijras in other parts of the country.

Pia/Krishna recounts routine police violence borne by kinnars as well as the lack of access to justice. In her account, a policeman's severe public beating proceeds and ends with impunity though not without provoking retaliation from her. Fellow police intervene but do not/cannot prevent the physical and verbal violence. Pia/Krishna is not allowed to report the violence to the police station head but she does what she can under the circumstances – fights back, lets herself lose control, threatens to report the violence. With little recourse, she chooses to be magnanimous.

I start with this account and background on hijras not to sketch a portrait of abject life, for a life is hardly just that. My purpose here is to foreground the question: why are Pia/Krishna and other kinnars ignored under the framework of development?

Police violence, bare survival, and lack of rights and protections as tenants and as labor ought to have made hijras among the first to receive development aid. Pia/Krishna is one of several kinnars with whom I spoke in 2005 in the Yamuna Pushta area, the largest slum of Delhi. They detail police violence but also the whims of landlords who throw them out upon learning they are not women but kinnars, the difficulties of earning livelihoods due to the precariousness and dangers of sex work and soliciting, and the lack of civil protections. A report, *Human Rights Violations against the Transgender Community* (2003), by the longstanding and respected People's Union for Civil Liberties, Karnataka (PUCL-K) documents the vulnerability of hijras in the family, the law, the medical establishment, and the media alongside the day-to-day harassment, abuse, and sexual violence at the hands of the police and ordinary people.[5] As an institutionalized but ostracized community, hijras would have been eminently suitable candidates for development's commitments to improving quality of life, poverty reduction, and empowerment. Rather, what is evident is near total neglect until recently.

If this is interpreted as a plea to include hijras into the project of local, national, and international development, it would be a misreading at best. Noting the systematic and systemic exclusion of hijras sets the stage for when and how they do become visible within development. The *Kaaya* photo project is the illustrative case. The project came into being through the collaboration of Deutsche Gesellschaft für Technische Zusammenarbeit (GTZ), a private company owned by the German Federal Government that works toward sustainable development through international and technical cooperation; Sahara, a Delhi-based NGO working primarily with persons living with HIV/AIDS; and Parthiv Shah, Director of the Centre for Media and Alternative Communication (CMAC), who was the supervising photographer. Given the immediate and far-reaching social, economic, and political ramifications of HIV/AIDS, the collaboration between GTZ (development) and Sahara (HIV/AIDS) is hardly unusual. The driving purpose of the project and its acclaim was the opportunity to bring visibility to kinnars in the Delhi area in a distinctive way. Rather than add to the corpus of representations of hijras, the idea was to allow kinnars to self-represent.

The basics of my argument in this chapter are as follows. One, the attempt to bring kinnars/hijras into visibility reveals their neglect within development discourse. Two, the issue, however, is not about a transition into visibility or even to more truthful visibility under the aegis of development. In fact, development has been rightly problematized precisely as a discourse that functions through an "economy of visibility" (Escobar's phrase). The underpinnings of this developmental apparatus have been under scrutiny for a while (Sen and Grown 1987; Ferguson 1994; Kabeer 1994; Escobar 1995; Marchand and Parpart 1995) and should make readers question liberal attempts at giving attention. What remains to be considered is how certain subjects secure the development discourse, not because they are invisible but because they haunt it. Hijras constitute the discourse of development as its "bare life" (after, Giorgio Agamben 1998). Three, as the outliers of development's discourses, kinnars lay bare its heteronormative dictates and the attempts to frame them as development's objects.

This essay can be read as a plea to identify and undo the heteronormative and class-based logic of development, which is secured through hijras in this case. This is an appeal to rethink development from the vantage points of those who help constitute it precisely because they are actively neglected. I do not mean to imply development as a homogeneous discourse but to grapple with the heteronormative underpinnings that give "development" a semblance of coherence.[6] My purpose is to place front and center matters of non-normative gender and sexuality in reflections on development queried by its emerging objects.

Development's mediations

The *Kaaya* photo project was funded by GTZ. Highlighting the language of sustainability, GTZ's mission is directed toward international cooperation, "viable, forward-looking solutions for political, economic, ecological and social development in a globalised world."[7] The *Kaaya* photo project fits this mission by understanding people's lives as a starting point. In his opening essay to the book *Kaaya*, Jost Wagner, the GTZ representative, frames the project as a prelude to "... a direct window into the community. Through photos, the viewer feels more connected to the people, gaining an understanding of their lives and feelings and circumstances (Wagner 2005: 5)." Photographs are especially well suited to document, furnish evidence, invite sympathy, and, no less, as critics have cautioned, bring people into view as objects of knowledge (Sontag 1977; Berger 1981; Jay 1996; Rogoff 1996; Mirzoeff 1998). Coupled with photography's codes – relationship between photographer-subject-viewer, the framing and editing of images, mood, tonality, what is included and what is excluded from the image, among others – Wagner's project to create awareness through documentation is already charged with the uncomfortable politics of gazing.

Sahara played a key role in this project. Sahara has been working with people coping with substance abuse since its founding in 1978. Staffed almost entirely by former substance users, Sahara has a fairly extensive list of services aimed at persons living with HIV/AIDS and their families, including a healthcare center for kinnars and kothis,[8] which is located in Yamuna Pushta and is run by two Sahara staff members, Ajay and Malti. Ajay and Malti have painstakingly cultivated these relationships over several years and earned a degree of trust from kinnars in the process.[9] According to Shah, an established photographer, Sahara staff approached him to supplement a survey on kinnars with photographs to which he counter-proposed a self-photo project of kinnars.[10] Self-representation, according to Shah, is especially effective in the case of kinnars, who have always been represented by others; he was convinced that photographs would help alleviate the stigmas that force kinnars "... outside the normative – the parameters for which are determined by mainstream society" (Shah 2005: 13).

If photography is well-suited to bring attention to subjects, then self-photography is its most legitimate mode. Self-photography aims to present the self to the viewer with minimal mediation, while giving the subject-photographer say over what, how, and to whom the self is made visible. The affinities between seeing and knowing make us viewers believe that self-photographs have the ability to depict the photographer's viewpoint, for us to know their perspective, even hear their "voice" through representation. What makes this perspective especially compelling is that it cuts against criticisms of how photography reproduces unequal relations of seeing and knowing between the viewer/photographer and the object of the gaze. This is precisely the kind of criticism that Shah seeks to offset by letting kinnars photograph themselves. Self-photography promises authenticity by reducing the triad of photographer, subject, and viewer into a dual relationship between the viewer and a composite self-photographer-subject.

Nowhere is the commonplace of self-representation, truthful visibility, and "giving voice" more at play than the *Kaaya* photo project. The project is part of a broader trend cutting across the domains of development and photography driven by the logic of authentic representations and giving voice to the marginalized. The move to "give voice," to hear the point of view of others, especially the marginalized, has come to occupy center stage in the development discourse (Marchand and Parpart 1995; Parpart, Rai, and Staudt 2003). It is curiously linked to the rhetoric of empowerment. So powerful and widespread is the language of empowerment that Jane L. Parpart, Shirin M. Rai, and Kathleen Staudt (2003) rightly ask how empowerment can be meaningful if it is a catchword among ideologically disparate groups. Further, Parpart (2003: 177) expresses doubts that giving people voice leads to empowerment, and calls, instead, for understanding the play between power, voice/silence, and gender, along with relevant material and structural forces. Yet, attempts to give voice to socially marginalized groups by eliciting their perspectives through self-representation persist. Nowhere is this more troublingly illustrated than in the film *Born into Brothels* (2005), and in its subsequent acclaim, especially in the US.[11]

The *Kaaya* project, unfortunately, is similarly troubled: the process through which the photographs come into being; and the intended products. How this project took shape and the role of Parthiv Shah and the Sahara team dismisses harborings of authentic unmediated representation. According to the published account of the process (*Kaaya* 2005), *GTZ* supplied the cameras and the kinnars worked in pairs. The 11 names of kinnars who are part of the final photo project are mentioned as: Saiba, Sapna, Vidhan, Mandakini, Munni, Bijli, Chanda, Neha, Chanchal, Bobby, and Asha. The narrative suggests that they exposed ten rolls of film in about two weeks, which yielded the final 42 photographs. The 11 photographers were then asked to select five photographs each and create text in Hindi for each of the final images, which were translated loosely into English to preserve the original texture of their words.

In fact, the process was neither so transparent nor so simple and the published and unpublished accounts vary.[12] Shah suggests that several meetings were necessary to convince kinnars of the usefulness of the project and how to go about it. Shah took books on photography to the first meeting and the Sahara staff, especially Ajay and Malti, later coached them on the use of the camera and visualizing the images that they might capture.[13] Kinnars' participation across the series of meetings varied greatly. From the 25 to 30 kinnars present at the first meeting, most did not show up again, and others attended later meetings. According to Shah, many photographs were unusable because of exposure problems or because they had taken photographs "just for the heck of it." The resistance and refusal presented by kinnars, and the necessary coaching by the Sahara staff, point counter to the possibilities of spontaneous self-representation.

While the kinnars/photographers were asked to select five photographs each, Shah and his team made the final cut of the 42 photographs, published in the book version. Contrary to how the process of selecting the photographs was described in the book, the final selection does not appear evenly distributed across the ten kinnar/photographers; Bobby accounts for the most with ten photographs, Vidhan and Chanchal with seven each, and Neha and Asha have the least, with only one photograph each. To his credit, Shah kept the editing and cropping of the photographs to a minimum. As he explains it, some of the film was developed hastily by Sahara staff at local photography outlets, and therefore needed masking of scratches, for example. Still, the process of deciding which photographs are usable, what gets dismissed as "just for the heck of it," and how Bobby's photograph is chosen to headline the exhibit and book speaks to the heavily mediated nature of such projects.

My point is not to gesture toward unmediated representations; on the contrary. The nuances between the published and unpublished accounts of the process of producing the photographs alert us to their power-laden socio-cultural, technical, and discursive contexts. In a nutshell, the photographs are the product of: the socio-political context under which kinnars/hijras are known and shunned; photographs as tools of understanding the unknown; the camera as a democratic tool; the Sahara research survey of kinnars; the role of Shah and the Sahara staff; photographic conventions; the presence of an audience.

That the audience for the photo project was pre-constituted and external to kinnars is a matter of particular significance. The photographic exhibit and the book compilation were intended primarily for circulation among those who likely revile kinnars and know least about them, namely the middle and upper classes in urban India. These are the relatively privileged urban elite, local and transnational, myself included, who are most likely to hear about and visit the Max Mueller Bhavan gallery in New Delhi. The established codes and conditions of photography shape how and which aspects of the composite self are positioned in relation to this audience. Thus, the images taken and selected for the *Kaaya* project may not be any truer or revealing than the images of kinnars that already exist – for example, Dayanita Singh's *Myself, Mona Ahmed* (2001) or Mary E. Mark's *Falkland Road* (1981) – or pictures that Shah might have taken. Despite their differences, the numerous representations of hijras share an intended audience. Insofar as intended audiences remain stable, self-images may mimic (after, Homi Bhabha) the historical conventions of photographs and portraiture, and mirror the social inequalities that make it at all necessary to present the self to a privileged audience.

Thoroughly confounding self-representation in the *Kaaya* project is the notion of the self. Who counts as the self in the self-images created by kinnars is not easy to determine. It is difficult to decipher whether the photographer and subject/self in the photographs are the same and these are self-images in the strict sense. The cameras distributed by GTZ were of the "aim-and-shoot" variety, which are hard to turn upon oneself. This, however, does not preclude the possibility that some of the photographs are, in fact, self-images, narrowly defined. Kinnars were asked to work in pairs because there weren't enough cameras to go around, according to Shah.[14] Which photographs are self-images, which are the result of paired kinnars taking photographs of each other, to what extent are they directed by the subject or reflect the view of the photographer/kinnar behind the camera, and which have been taken by a third person are among the questions that Shah found impossible to sort by the end of the process.[15]

I am loath to glibly dismiss attempts to provide a different point of view through the eyes of the kinnars who participated in the project. Further, my argument rests on the proposition that the photographs exceed the limitations out of which they were produced, a point that is not developed in this chapter due to constraints of space. But, the limitations cannot be ignored, especially if one were to understand how the photographs push against the mold from which they are wrought. The limitations cluster around how the photographs were produced and the kinds of photographs thus produced. Of concern is that the process shows little transparency or reflexivity about self-representation, about making the self visible to those who are ignorant or disapproving. The project may have been voluntary but the implicit instruction to take photos of the self for an external audience was the received mandate!

Development's imperceptibilities

Seeing development as a discourse through which subjects, assumptions, strategies, and central concepts are rendered as objects of knowledge has been useful (Escobar 1995; Ferguson 1994, 2006). Critical scholarship has moved us away from crude materialist assumptions of "good" versus "bad" development toward its omissions, failures, and fractures that are not missteps but inherent to its functioning; writers bringing to bear a poststructuralist lens to development studies (Escobar 1995; Ferguson 1994, 2006; Sylvester 2006) and feminist scholars (Kabeer 1994; Marchand and Parpart 1995; Parpart, Rai, and Staudt 2003) have been at the forefront. Development can no longer be seen as an unquestioned value. Thrown into doubt are the ways in which the apparatus works through a politics of visibility, underpinned by universalist though Eurocentric notions of quality of life, modernity, and progress. For example, using the concept, "economy of visibility," Escobar notes the successive shifts between "peasants," "women," and "the environment" as the objects of development for each of the decades between the 1960s to 1980s; not only were these categories the means through which people became targets of control but also the mechanisms through which the development discourse sought to transform the conditions of normality.

One question that might be derived from this critique of development is: why have hijras not been visible as one of its categories? Clearly, this visibility may not be desirable, given the criticism, but the question points toward how hijras are gradually becoming intelligible objects of development. It is not that hijras have been neglected within development discourse until recently because they are socially invisible; indeed, they are hard to miss in public places of metropolitans and in institutional and popular discourses. On earmarked days of the week, often Tuesdays and/or Fridays, hijras are noticeable around railway stations, traffic crossings, and markets, among others, where they solicit money. Their distinctive staccato clap and typically bright saris draw attention from non-hijras persons. In Delhi, their presence is vivid, although on the decline at ritual ceremonies, such as the birth of a son, or a wedding celebration among the middle classes. Even as they are increasingly shunned by them, middle-class men are known to cruise public parks seeking their sexual services.

This hypervisibility is paralleled in anthropological discourses on hijras, as well. Hijras are widely characterized as symbols of "Third Gender" and, especially within popular discourses, hearkened as ancestors from a non-Western culture that can help construct genealogies of (Western) transgender identities. Despite well-placed criticisms (Cohen 1995; Towle and Morgan 2002; Reddy 2005), this narrative has not been easy to dislodge and hijras remain firmly entrenched as icons of sexual difference.[16] The discourse of sexual difference does not stand alone but is charged with notions of gendered difference – where there is a preoccupation with socio-biological maleness of hijras (Patel 1997), national cultural difference – where hijras come to represent India (even though they are present in Bangladesh and Pakistan), and historical difference – where hijras stabilize a trans/national present-day politics of gender and sexuality by representing a bygone past. Therefore, it would be simply erroneous to say that the *Kaaya* project's contributions lie in moving kinnars/hijras from invisibility to visibility under the aegis of development.

A different set of questions might be posed regarding the *Kaaya* project: how is it that hijras remain imperceptible within discourses and policies aimed at the improvement of quality of life and alleviation of poverty? What places those who are a part of society outside of developmentalist interventions? Giorgio Agamben's thinking on bare life in *Homo Saccer* sheds light elliptically on these questions. Defining bare life as the living that is common to all living beings, Agamben (1998: 4) argues that it is the vexed basis for political community. Founded as a means to protect life anthropomorphized as humanity, political community simultaneously excludes the basic regard for life by yoking rights to citizenship. He notes that even though bare life is "inside" the political, it is shorn of political and social rights and, indeed, humanity. Drawing on the work of Carl Schmidt, Agamben emphasizes the exception to suggest how figures (for example, those who are targets of state violence even as they constitute state sovereignty) and idioms (the concentration camp) of bare life are excluded from the political.

Agamben's approach opens up the possibility of rethinking the simultaneous inclusions and exclusions of bare life at its most iconic – hijras – but not without revisions to his arguments. Agamben's exceptional figure is presented without attention to the constitutive influences of sexuality and gender. Insofar as bare life is understood as that which we all share and to which we are all equally entitled, gender and sexuality can be seen as the hierarchical effects of political community. Sexuality, gender, and, for that matter, class are deeply relevant within the context of political community as they serve to sift bare life from citizenship, and humanity from political community. Some lives are seen outside the pale of citizenship and a politicized understanding of humanity precisely because of transgressions, in the case of hijras, of sexuality, gender, and class. Like the figure of the refugee, then, hijras reveal the disjuncture of humanity and citizenship. But, and this is the crucial point, they also reveal the anxieties of political community by standing in for the most egregious violations of gender and sexual norms, of the shamelessness of those who barely survive. In fact, hijras show the heteronormative insecurities of citizenship to which we resolutely cling; they continually trigger anxieties of the precariousness of political communities and their promises of citizenship. They are the exceptions that though hypervisible remain imperceptible to political community, and are actively neglected by the discourse of development that serves it.

Non-normative sexualities have been noticeably absent in development discourse until recently in stark contrast to the preoccupations with population and reproductive health, for example. Putative subjects of development are assumed as normatively gendered and sexual. Is it any wonder, then, that HIV/AIDS concerns within development discourses and policies become the turning point of interest in hijras? In the past decade, hijras have been increasingly the target of HIV/AIDS intervention programs in India. This has meant heightened surveillance and scrutiny of hijras, especially by non-governmental organizations with ties to the state as well as international donors and agencies. Along with non-transgendered women sex workers and men truck drivers, hijras are becoming the most maligned risk groups in the HIV/AIDS discourse in India. The consistent problem remains that hijras are positioned as little more than carriers of sexual contagion. In some cases, though, self-identified hijras have sought to counter such pejoratives by leading several HIV/AIDS-focused NGOs and reaching out to hijras and other gender and sexuality nonconforming persons; for example, the South Indian Positive Network (SIP+) in Chennai and Dai Welfare Society in Mumbai.

The move to bring hijras into visibility says less about the hijras than it does about development's neglect of them. The heteronormative logic of development continues to place them inside and outside this discourse. Hijras secure its margins and haunt this discourse, which also explains why they are ignored under its purview. The next section shows the limitations of the attempt to make hijras visible within development discourse and suggests that the photographs reveal its heteronormative framework. Read from a critical angle, these photographs are layered and provocative – simultaneously revealing and defying the heteronormative logic of development.

Imagining (our)selves

According to Shah (2005), the supervising photographer of the *Kaaya* project, a series of photographs is valuable since a single photograph or an image by itself is mostly out of context. What stands out from the series of 42 images is the mundane settings and the mundane content. If the audience at Max Mueller Bhavan was expecting startling revelations about the lives of the kinnar/photographers, there surely must have been disappointment. The photographs are taken in the unremarkable settings of kitchens, in the ordinary home, in bathing areas, by the car parked outside the home, on the streets of the neighborhood. The content is also commonplace. Photographs of offering prayers, cooking, bathing, and heading to work are alongside the occasional occurrence of death and social gatherings among friends. The images reinforce the banality of life without being banal.

The series of photographs presents an intimate view of the kinnar/photographers. More than three-quarters of the photographs (32) are taken in interior spaces: inside rooms, kitchens, bathrooms, and nondescript common rooms and hallways. Even when taken in exterior spaces, the photographs tend to be within neighborhoods and are tightly framed. One photograph centers Bobby at the threshold of a kitchen, wearing a black sleeveless kameez (long top) and a black bottom. Pots and pans and cooking utensils occupy part of the image, and a bright red bureau with a framed photograph of her, flowers, and a few odds and ends reflecting in a narrow mirror fill the other half. Bobby's eyes are closed; her right hand is raised, as if she were photographed in an unplanned moment. The intimate portrayals work together with the commonplace settings and content to make them all the more compelling to the putative audience; the series seems to present things "as they are."

How the photographs can be understood has everything to do with the relationship between the kinnar/photographers and the audience, a point which critical writing on photography has reiterated. Not only were kinnars asked to take photographs of themselves for an external audience, as noted in the section above; they were also asked to generate text that would explain selected photographs to the audience. W. J. T. Mitchell's term "image-text" is useful, here, for the text, along with the image, orients the viewer to the kinnar/photographer.[17] The narrative attached to Bobby's photograph is brief and aimed at the audience, "Since I left home, I have been managing my house myself. Whatever happens, I am very happy."

Self-kinnar-photographer

The images collectively and in conjunction with the audience produce an ordinary and, especially, a normalized self. For subjects who are socially hypervisible for all the ways in which they transgress norms of the sexed body, gender, and heterosexuality, the selves depicted in the photographs are remarkably heteronormative. The relations between the sexed body, gender, and sexuality are the building blocks of what we have come to understand and critique as heteronormativity.[18] Judith Butler's (1990) work in *Gender Trouble* clarifies how the heterosexual mandate is circuitously predicated on sex and gender: that sex is pre-discursive, dual (male and female), gender is the cultural overlay on biology (manhood and womanhood), and the two sex/genders are necessary for the heterosexual reproduction of the species.

If all sexed bodies are shaped by the cultural premise of difference – males are different from females who are different from males – the photographs cannot but claim difference in order to normalize sex. The photographs present feminine bodies not so much as female, but as *different from male*. In an image taken in a bathroom, while Vidhan and another are bathing, the photograph provides evidence of sexual difference within the well-established and gendered codes of visual culture. Lathered and seated sideways on the bathroom floor, Vidhan turns to look up at the camera. Her wet hair clings to her face, the left arm extends to the other one shielding breasts from view, while the rest is tucked under the folds of her body and her legs. Like many, many such images, the feminine body is simultaneously open and shielded form the viewer's gaze.[19] What's crucial is that the non-male body is marked not through evidence of female breasts or absence of male genitals. Rather, it is the photographic convention through which the image is produced and the *presence* of woman-like hair. Sexual difference and femininity work to depict a normal self.

Another photograph in the series reflects the significance of heterosexuality in representations of the self. It bears Bijli's name, and is taken in the exact manner of photographs of middle-class newly-weds in India. A mid-shot focuses on a couple, seated close together, their shoulders touching. Taken a bit right of center, Bijli appears to lean slightly forward in the photograph, head draped in a red duppatta, adorned with necklace, bindi, lipstick, and the red mark of a married woman in her hair. She smiles at the camera. Looking diffidently but pleasantly at the camera, the boyfriend is wearing a beige suit and a buttoned-up white shirt. The photograph captures a special moment for Bijli. She says to the audience, "This is the most beautiful photograph because my boyfriend is in it and I am dressed like a woman. I love my boyfriend very much and like to stay as his wife forever. This photograph reveals the real me; it shows how I really want to live my life." Desire, not just sexual, but sexed and gendered, is everywhere in these photographs.

Work and leisure also figure prominently. Asha says, "We are going to work at this time along with our leader 'Guru'. We prefer to go to work than sitting at home." The attached photograph shows two kinnars dressed in salwaar-kameez in a blue Maruti car. One is seated on the passenger's side in the front and another directly behind her. They look smilingly into the camera from the open windows. Another photograph shows a kinnar getting into a car while another waits outside, caught looking down at her feet. The text reaffirms the importance of work, "Sometimes we hire cars and to work in groups. We like to be productive and self-dependent." Even though the nature of work is not explained in these images, the importance of labor, of being productive and independent, is emphasized.

On the page across from Asha's image-text related to work is a photograph associated with Bobby that shows a group of kinnars in the midst of leisure time. Many photographs of leisure and play are included in the series and serve to complement the other side of the laboring, diligent self. Six kinnars are seated on a rug on the floor, perhaps taking a break from the singing and dancing that Bobby describes in the text. She says how much she enjoys herself at the parties when someone plays the drums and others sing and some dance. Sure enough, a dholak (drum) is visible, and a few of them appear to be in lively conversation, while two of them look at the camera.

It would be difficult to depict a normal, ordinary self without giving some clues about patterns of consumption. The abject poverty thought to be true of at least some, if not many, kinnars and hijras is nowhere to be found in the photographs. Cars used for work is one way in which the presence of consumables is established. Scenes of leisure present further evidence. In a set of photographs on adjacent pages, Bobby and her kin are seated on and around a bed playing ludo. Objects of everyday utility – a bed, a stack of shiny stainless steel glasses, an altar, audio tapes, and a music system – are visible, as is a poster of a white infant in one of the photographs. Beds, televisions, decorative objects, cups and saucers, steel glasses, cushions, covers, pots and pans fill the frames of indoor photographs. The traces of grittiness as a result of peeling paint, electrical wiring, and floors worn with use are complemented with an array of household objects in ways that are not unlike lower middle-class homes in Delhi. Indeed, a colleague who read an earlier version of this chapter and the descriptions of the photographs, exclaimed, "I thought hijras were supposed to be very poor." The photographs deliberately don't confirm such perceptions.

Much like the way in which photographic techniques are used to depict images of a heteronormative self, they can also be used to suggest plenitude. One of Saiba's photographs is worth noting here. In it, five people are seated, including her brother-in-law, her friend, her boyfriend, and herself. She expresses pleasure at how they live together as a family and draws the audience's attention to the stack of utility and decorative items on the left of the frame, by noting that the photograph shows part of her room and how things are properly arranged. What confounds this description is that another kinnar, Munni, has a photograph that has been taken with her boyfriend in the same room, although it becomes clear only through careful attention; the background wall shelves with the stacked shiny steel glasses, the inverted teacups, and neatly arranged knick-knacks are the same as the color on the wall, though shadowed by a different light.

The photographs of the ordinary, normal lives and selves of kinnars are about desire. It is possible that the photographs help the kinnar/photographers represent their desires for a life with dignity – some desires that are lived and others that are imagined. Seen this way, they are instructive about what it means or would mean to live a life of dignity, to enjoy the sanctity of social personhood. These photographs may be about how the photographers would like to be perceived – as normal persons. They present themselves as normally sexed, normally gendered, with normal desires, and leading normal lives. The need to work, to be self-reliant, is balanced with leisure time spent in the company of kin and friends. Domestic work straddles the divide between work and play as a number of the image-texts speak to its pleasures.

Yet, the cautions about the process through which these photographs were produced ought to be taken into account; the process alerts us not to treat the series as authentic self-representations, to be wary of the unequal relations through which the photographs came to be. That the audience was pre-constituted and external suggests that the photographs were about how the kinnar/photographers might conceive the audience and *its* desires. Aimed at a non-kinnar, middle to upper-class urban audience, the kinnar/photographers have to contend with what will make them perceptible to outsiders. Kinnar/photographers are most aware of their hyper-visibility, and the ignorant, pejorative attitudes and beliefs of this audience toward them. Therefore, how they may want to be perceived by this audience is not unrelated to what they think will make them perceptible. Depictions of normal lives and ordinary selves of kinnars are presented to the audience. In that, they mirror lives and selves similar to those of the audience. The photographs indicate that what would catch the attention of the audience is a mirror image of itself.

The lives and selves projected in the photographs are recognizable in one more register, namely development discourse. It turns out that the putative subject of development, or rather development's success, is remarkably similar to the subject presented in the photographs – persons who are normatively gendered, normatively sexual, lead a life balanced between work and play, who may not be wealthy but can afford the necessities of life and at least a little beyond. GTZ's project was informed by its mission to bring awareness among the public at large as a first step in improving the lives of abject groups. But the outcome of the photographs is not a self in desperate need. The series is no plea for intervention by NGOs or, for that matter, other parts of state and civil society. The photographs are a mirror of ordinary lives per hegemonic perceptions, even as the photographs cannot help but make these lives a little less ordinary.

Endings

The *Kaaya* photo project and the photographs taken by the kinnar/photographers provide a rich archive of the conjunction between development, photography, and non-normative personhood. The attempt to bring hijras into visibility for a middle-class urban audience as a precursor to becoming full subjects of development drives the project. Visibility captures the reasoning that little is known (to the privileged) about kinnars/hijras, that seeing their photographs will help the audience know more about them, that the self-images will allow kinnars to "tell their story," which cannot but be compelling to this audience, and will eventually lead to improvement in their lives. The long-standing codes of visual culture lend credibility to beliefs that seeing is knowing, knowing leads to better understanding, and that giving voice to the marginal is beneficial to the audience and empowering to subjects. Not surprisingly, then, photography and film are playing an increasing role in development projects.

The causal relationship between development, visibility, and empowerment is deeply flawed. Kinnars have not been invisible but, rather, actively neglected within the framework of development. Indeed, this impulse to bring them into the spotlight focuses on their active neglect, the ways in which they both haunt the development discourse and are excluded by it. The bare life that must be actively neglected for it simply cannot be ignored. The various introductory accounts included in the *Kaaya* book rehearse the relationships among the denial of humanity, the rights of citizenship, and empowerment. What they assiduously omit are explanations for why hijras remain imperceptible to development and the political community, the extent to which their neglect reveals the power of heteronormativity, and why photography is ill-suited to bringing empowerment.

In the photographs, kinnar/photographers present themselves as subjects of development. Notwithstanding the selection process, the photographs present the likeness of normatively gendered, sexed subjects, with all the desires of respectable womanhood. These are laboring, leisure-seeking, consuming subjects. Nothing out of the ordinary. What is as important as, if not more important than, the mirroring of the putative subject of development is that this is no plea for development's aid; it is no plea for assistance or empowerment. Rather, the photographs are images of what may be recognizable to the projected audience, what may be *perceptible* to it. Nothing could be more powerful or telling than to project back likeness through the eminently suitable tool of photography.

The photographs represent desire – the audience's desire for authentic self-representations of kinnars/hijras. GTZ, Sahara, Parthiv Shah, the many people who see the exhibit at Max Mueller Bhavan, including me, and those who have copies of the book compilation are all implicated as the non-kinnar audience. Even though this audience is not homogeneous and is unlikely to share a heterosexist, class-based, normatively gendered view of the kinnar photo project, the audience is nonetheless privileged and external to kinnars. Perhaps the kinnar/photographers are aware that the audience's abiding pejorative view of kinnars can only be offset through images of normally gendered, sexual, productive, and consuming selves. The kinnar/photographers' desires may be present in these images but they are selectively refracted from the point of view of the audience. What is omitted in the images is as telling as what is shown – no hints of police violence and violence at the hands of gurus, for example. In the final analysis, the kinnar photographs give the audience what it expects to see – itself – and in so doing the photographs exceed the limitations of the project.

Notes

1 My deep gratitude to Vaughn Sills, a remarkable photographer in her own right, for our early conversation and her insights regarding self-photography and reading photographs.
2 In Hindi, *Kaaya* means body.
3 Cited in Towle and Morgan (2002).
4 Concerns about the extent to which the term kinnar heralds the Hinduization or, really, the Sanskritization of what is surely a dynamic and ethnically hybrid form of person-hood are relevant, but not taken up in this essay. The term Sanskritization was coined by the sociologist M. N. Srinivas (1952) in which those placed lower in the caste hierarchy seek upward mobility by emulating the "upper" castes. See, M. N. Srinivas (1965).
5 See also, Puri (forthcoming) on the issue of violence against Kinnars and others.
6 As Amy Lind lays out usefully in her introduction to this volume.
7 GTZ's website is available: http://www.gtz.de/en/unternehmen/689.htm (accessed June 27, 2006).
8 Kothi is a form of self-identity among feminine-identified men typically from the working classes who have sex with normatively gendered or hypermasculine men. Sexual partnering with men and women (some are married) varies according to circumstance and while some choose to cross-dress occasionally or mostly, others do not.

9 Based on personal communications with Ajay and Malti (June 2005).
10 Personal communication with Shah, January 2006.
11 For a useful critique of the film, see Svati Shah (2005).
12 By published accounts, I refer to the descriptions of the *Kayaa* project presented in the book by Jost Wagner and Parthiv Shah. As suggested above, I spoke separately with Parthiv Shah and Ajay Kwatra about the details of how the project came into being; I refer to these as unpublished accounts. None of the kinnar/photographers who participated in the project could be contacted for their perspectives.
13 Personal communication with Ajay Kwatra, June 2005.
14 Personal communication with Shah, January 2006.
15 Ibid.
16 By sexual difference, I mean the following: an understanding that sexual dimorphism is normal so that hijras become the embodiment of difference; that gender analyses are based on the notion of two sexes so that "third gender" is seen as a variation on sexual dimorphism.
17 Cited in Marianne Hirsch (1997).
18 Michael Warner's definition still remains the most precise and useful starting point to capturing heteronormativity: the understanding of heterosexuality as an elemental form of human association, the model of inter-gender relations, the indivisible basis for community, and the means of reproduction without which society would not exist (1993: 21).
19 See John Berger's (1981) *Ways of Seeing* for a useful analysis of how visual codes are profoundly gendered in how they present women.

3 Querying feminist economics' straight path to development

Household models reconsidered

Suzanne Bergeron

Among the many obstacles to be overcome in the project of integrating diverse sexualities into development is the way that economic growth and international aid initiatives work to normalize gender and sexual identities. Standard accounts of economic development generally ignore the entrenched nature of heteronormativity in their thinking, in which reproductive sexuality is seen as the only functional form of sex (Kleitz 2000). Because of this, the diversity of affective relations that do not fit the functional model is rendered imperceptible in nearly all discussions of poverty alleviation, growth targets, and economic policy reforms. While the prioritization of HIV/AIDS by international financial institutions, such as the World Bank, has created some space for adding sexuality to the equation, this has been limited by a general confinement of these conversations to health concerns only (Gosine 2005a). As a result, there continues to be little explicit attention paid to diverse sexualities in either mainstream economic development thought or in alternative frameworks which draw inspiration from feminist, anti-poverty, and ecological movements. Thus, in order to challenge the heteronormative aspects of economic development theory and practice, it is important to explore how and why such narrow accounts persist in order to adequately re-frame economic development to move beyond these limits.

There is also a need to recognize and challenge the ways that development policies are implicated in the production and transformation of normative heterosexualities themselves, particularly in regard to how teleological visions of sexuality have dominated development discourse (Pigg and Adams 2005). Such visions have informed many attempts to transform multiple and diverse sexual practices into a mythical norm of the stabilized, westernized, and "modern" heterosexual family, while reconstructing forms of resistance to these efforts as elements of pathology that need to be contained (Ferguson 1999). Development policies implicitly rely upon, and push, particular sorts of affective arrangements. For example, neoliberal structural adjustment policies are based on the assumption that women in gender-normative, heterosexual-couple households will pick up the care work formerly supported by the state (Elson 1996; Peterson 2003).

This heteronormative thrust of development discourse is the result of a complex confluence of forces. In this chapter, I examine one strand of this in the economic theories that inform development policy. Here, I focus specifically on meanings about affective life that are produced in economic models of the household. Utilizing Judith Butler's concept of "a heterosexual matrix" (Butler 1990: 37) through which constructions of gender difference rely on a heterosexual norm, I unpack and examine how particular ideas about intimacy are naturalized in order to highlight the ways that the normative heterosexuality presumed within economic household models is artificial and unstable.

My focus on household models is in part due to their lingering importance in development thinking. These models have had a significant impact on what it means for an economy to grow and modernize, so examining them allows us to get to the conceptual heart of many development initiatives. Further, household models have considerable contemporary currency, particularly through their role in forming the conceptual basis of gender and development policy. Recently developed household bargaining models that incorporate game theory to make sense of gender conflict have given legitimacy to feminist economics in development circles, and are used to support arguments for pursuing gender justice as a way to fight poverty and foster economic growth in a host of texts such as World Bank reports, country poverty-reduction strategy papers, websites of bilateral donors, and working papers produced by organizations such as the United States Agency for International Development, the International Labour Organization, and the International Food Policy Institute.

Despite their attention to certain aspects of gender power dynamics, however, these newer models and the policies that they inform still generally exclude those outside the boundaries of conventional gender roles and heterosexuality. Even the most sophisticated household bargaining accounts of women's empowerment in the global South that take diversities of culture, race, class, age, and nation seriously (e.g. Agarwal 1994; Kabeer 1994) register a silence on sexuality. While a handful of feminist economists have made an important empirical contribution to economics in general by adding same-sex identities to the mix (Badgett and Hyman 1998), they have not examined the sexual assumptions that lie behind these newer economic models of the household. Further, they have not asked the broader question of why even scholarly works by progressive feminist economists often privilege, and sometimes promote, normative sexualities.

Noting these gaps and omissions, this paper aims to challenge the naturalizing of heterosexual roles, institutions, and practices in this literature. My strategy is to delineate the methodological and conceptual slippages and assumptions that pervade feminist economic accounts of the household. The aim is not to diminish the contributions of feminist economists, but rather to highlight alternative frameworks of analysis. To the extent that feminist economics participates in a broader discourse of producing heteronormative ideologies and conventions, making them seem natural and universal, it may be underwriting rather than subverting the gender order that it is attempting to challenge. By demonstrating that attention to sexuality should play a role in the future of feminist development economics research through a critique of implicit assumptions that normalize family, heterosexual reproduction, and marriage, I hope to contribute to a richer and more inclusive portrait of gender, sexuality, and development.

In the first section of this chapter, I briefly trace the evolution of household models. I begin with the unitary model that was in use in the immediate postwar period, then discuss the impact of Gary Becker's "new home economics" on development thinking, and, after that, introduce contemporary feminist bargaining models that are currently in vogue in gender and development circles. In the section that follows, I examine the unspoken assumptions about sexuality that are deployed in feminist economic constructions of the household. Here I also draw attention to the slippages and elisions that feminist economists engage in to support their construction of normative sexuality in these models. In the concluding section, I outline some of the implications of these heteronormative framings for development economic policy-making. Here I also make a case for more critical interpretive work that can reframe the view of the household so as not to reproduce the marginalization of household and family configurations that are not constituted around heterosexual partnership.

From the unitary model of the household to feminist bargaining approaches

Many feminist criticisms of development economics have focused on how mainstream narratives have tended to invisibilize women's reproductive labor, rationalize inequality within families, and elide the existence of power dynamics within the household (Waring 1988; Benería and Feldman 1992). One major target of this feminist critique has been the economic model of the household that framed development policy in the early postwar period. This model assumed away differences among members by positing that decisions about investment, labor supply, and consumption were made collectively by a household unit with a shared, single set of preferences. Further, this model created no space for examining non-nuclear family arrangements because it defined the household a priori as a unit made up of a husband, wife, and children (e.g. Samuelson 1956). Finally, the unitary model did not include recognition of non-market economic activity as economically productive. Instead, it viewed what goes on in the household as unproductive, thus contributing to a relative inattention paid to the enormous amount of subsistence and reproductive activities undertaken by women and men in developing economies (Wood 2003).

This picture of the domestic sphere as unproductive and characterized by a harmony of interests was further codified in economic development as it began to adopt ideas from Gary Becker's new home economics in the late 1960s. Becker's version of the unitary model assumes a gendered productive/unproductive dichotomy in which men labor outside of the home, while women engage in what Becker refers to as the "leisure" activities of care in the household (Becker 1991). While offering a different view of the decision-making process in the household that replaces collective, harmonious choice with an "altruistic husband" who makes decisions about consumption, production, and investment for the well-being of the wife and children, the new household economics, like the model that preceded it, also elides gender conflict. Unlike earlier economic household models, however,

Becker explicitly addresses gender difference in task assignment. Men should be breadwinners, and women carers, he argues, based largely on their biological differences. Here, Becker portrays the husband/wife, breadwinner/carer version of heterosexuality within the household as natural, normal, and obvious (Hewitson 2003). He also privileges it within neoclassical economics' own moral term: efficiency. For instance, Becker writes that "normal" women "depend on men for the provision of food, shelter and protection," and "normal men depend on women for the bearing and rearing of children and the maintenance of the home and men themselves" (Becker 1991: 43, cited in Hewitson 2003). Becker contrasts these normal individuals with less efficient "deviants," such as women who are drawn to the labor market instead of reproduction, and homosexuals, whose affective choices are inefficient because they cannot capture the inherent comparative advantages of men and women (Becker 1991: 30–41).

This variant of the unitary model, with its emphasis on the efficiency of a strict gender division of labor in the heterosexual household, gained significant traction in development economics by the early 1970s for a number of reasons. It helped to shore up ideas about family life and gender roles that were already in wide circulation by tying them to economics' own moral term: efficiency. It contributed to development's managerial imperative by positing a universal form of household organization and making invisible the variety of household forms and practices that might exist, therefore rendering household production and decision-making as something manageable, predictable, and susceptible to development planning (Bergeron 2004). By assuming that all resources and incomes are pooled and allocated altruistically by the father/husband, the model also dovetailed with dominant thinking on gender that masked inequalities and conflicts in the distribution of household resources and tasks. In this, the unitary model contributed to what a later generation of feminist scholarship would show to be the empirically flawed assumption that women's role in development was limited to reproduction in the private sphere of the household (Moser 1993; Kabeer 1994).

While the male breadwinner/female carer model of the household was simply assumed by some economists and policy-makers, others viewed the affective norm contained within it as not existing, but rather potentially emerging, if only the right policies were put into place. For instance, an economic theory account of households in rural Cameroon notes disapprovingly that sometimes "husbands and wives do not act as unit" to highlight the "inefficiencies in these households" and call for policies to restore household harmony and economic efficiency (Jones 1983). Similarly, according to Ferguson's ethnographic study of modernization efforts in Zambia, development policy-makers in that country aimed to reduce the "economic inefficiencies" associated with antagonistic male/female relationships, illicit cohabitation, and people living in extended families in order to create more modern and efficient households that reflected the dominant economic model (Ferguson 1999).

But the idea that the modern, efficient household is made up of a female carer and a male breadwinner who is the altruistic decision-maker was already becoming archaic in some economic circles at the time that these issues were being discussed in Cameroon, Zambia, and elsewhere in the 1980s. In its place, a new model of the household was emerging. This model, drawing upon game theory and other theoretical innovations, supported the claim – long made by feminists but resisted by mainstream economic thinkers and development policy-makers – that the unitary household is a fiction.

Rather than presenting a picture of household unity and harmony, the new model imagines each individual within the household as an independent agent using her/ his resources to bargain with the other members over shares of work and income (McElroy and Horney 1981; Haddad, Hoddinott, and Alderman 1997). This approach, unlike Becker's, is able to take power and difference within the household into account, because it views decisions regarding resource distribution not as determined by a benevolent patriarch, but rather as the outcome of bargaining between household members.

The innovations offered in these game-theoretic models were quickly adapted by feminist economists such as Folbre (1994), Agarwal (1997), and Katz (1997) to explain changing asymmetric power relations in household allocation of resources and labor by gender, and to take seriously the role of social gender norms in determining the bargaining power of men and women. In these feminist approaches, women are identified with caring and men are painted as more egoistic. But unlike the unitary model, the gendered division of reproductive labor and care is here viewed as something subject to negotiation and change through increased bargaining power when women gain access to independent wage income, assets, or social capital. Feminist-inspired research has also successfully used bargaining models to support the argument that gender inequality in households is inefficient. When households do not pool their resources for production, inefficiencies result that decrease individual household income and well-being, as well as economic growth in the macroeconomy. For example, in an oft-cited study of gender inequality and agricultural output based on a bargaining model approach, it has been shown that when male household members have control of resources they over-allocate fertilizer and labor to their own fields, while these inputs are under-allocated to their wives' plots, thus resulting in lost agricultural output overall (Udry 1996). A further argument made in the literature with regard to the inefficiency of gender inequality relates to women's roles as carers in households. Because women are more attentive to family well-being due to their roles as mothers, it is argued, giving women access to wage income and credit, and thus more control over household expenditure, results in better nutrition and health for the household as a whole, and particularly for children (Blackden and Bhanu 1999).

This intrahousehold bargaining model approach, and the policy prescriptions that it underwrites, has by now become quite influential in feminist economics, and is considered by many to be the "*sine qua non*" of the field (Seiz 2000). This approach has gained ascendancy in gender and development policy circles as well. For example, the World Bank's flagship document on gender, *Engendering Development through Gender Equality in Rights, Resources and Voice* (World Bank 2001a), uses insights from this model to argue for the importance of promoting gender equity to increase efficiency and promote growth. There is an entire chapter devoted to a discussion of household bargaining models, and the report's other chapters rely on the language of these models to explain gender differences and inequalities and support the argument that poverty can be reduced by channeling resources to women in households. The language of bargaining approaches is also used to advocate for gender equity in other international development institutions such as USAID (2000), International Labour Organization (2000), and the International Food Policy Institute (Quisumbing and McClafferty 2006).

Sexuality assumptions in household bargaining models

The adoption of intrahousehold bargaining models has effected a significant shift in the way that development economics imagines the household and gender relations within it. It has made women's reproductive labor and conflicts around domestic work more visible. It also challenges the implications of previous household models with regard to limiting women to the reproductive sphere. In fact, these new models often serve as a conceptual basis for arguments regarding both the empowering and efficiency-enhancing effects of integrating women into paid labor in order to increase their bargaining power and thus reduce inequality at home. However, like the earlier unitary model, these bargaining approaches still present heterosexual partnering as the sole form of family life, and care as something that is always already produced and bargained over within the private sphere of the heteronormative household. Bargaining models, at least as they are currently constructed and deployed by feminist economists, help to normalize dominant notions of heterosexuality in a variety of ways. First, they do so by unwittingly presenting the normative household as the only family form. For example, articles on the topic by Katz (1997) and Agarwal (1997) engage in an unproblematized slippage that pervades much of the feminist household bargaining literature by interchangeably using the terms "household," "family," "married couple" and "husband and wife." For example, Katz writes: "People in a *household* bargain based on the well-being they would expect to have if they broke up the *marriage*" (Katz 1997: 31). While it is not a methodological error in itself to focus on heterosexual partner households, without context this focus lends itself to normalized and naturalized conceptualizations of sexuality, domesticity, and social reproduction that renders other alternatives invisible.

Another example of a slippage that pushes alternative household arrangements to the margins is found in Folbre's *Who Pays for the Kids: Gender and the Structures of Constraint*. While the author includes data from Latin America and the Caribbean on the percentage of female-headed households, ranging from about 15 percent in Argentina to 45 percent in most of the Caribbean countries, she nonetheless concludes her discussion of women's well-being in this region by framing her analysis around "the primary wage earner (typically male) versus the person specializing in family labor (typically female)" (Folbre 1994: 257). In making this assumption about gender roles in households, Folbre reinscribes a heterosexual model onto data that doesn't support such a narrow view of family life. And she also essentially makes many of the needs, constraints, and tensions of the very large percentage of female-headed households in her study invisible.

But even when they acknowledge and explicitly analyze female-headed households, feminists using household bargaining models often impose a troubling variant of heteronormativity onto these arrangements. For example, McCrate (1987) and England and Kilbourne (1990) use bargaining models to explain the existence of female-headed households only in the context of failed heterosexual coupling, in which women choose to be single as a way to voice their unhappiness over doing an unequal share of domestic labor. In a study of women in Colombian floriculture that utilizes these models which was published in the journal *Feminist Economics*, Friedemann-Sánchez comes to much the same conclusion. She states that women in the flower industry who choose to remain single have only do so because of a flawed heterosexuality of excessive machismo in which "being partnered means living under unequal conditions with regard to men" (Friedemann-Sánchez 2006: 173). Thus when women-headed households are taken into account, it is generally through a set of assumptions that can only see them "broken" or "headless" because the male is perceived to be missing (Paulson 2006; see also her chapter in this volume). And when female headship is framed as "broken" or a "disorganization of the family" it implies that such disorganization can be contained through pro-family interventions and policies aimed at fixing and making the heterosexual household intact again (Chant 1999).

An additional element of bargaining approaches that contributes to their heteronormative vision is their reification of stereotypical gendered notions of domesticated female altruism and undomesticated male egoism in their assumption that women are more caring. Women's nurturing and altruistic tendencies are increasingly the reasons given by feminists using household bargaining models, and by extension the gender and development experts who cite their research, for targeting women as agents of development. An oft-repeated argument to emerge from bargaining frameworks is that giving women credit and/or access to wage labor increases their bargaining power in the household which in turn results in better care for the family. Arguments for equality that rely on a narrative that those predisposed to care (women) will use resources more efficiently than those who are not (men), however, reflect a slippage in which arguments for gender equality are linked to maintaining heteronormative gender roles – hardly a goal one would think might be espoused by a feminist approach. One reason for this slippage is that the vision of the household used by feminist development economists unwittingly relies upon an inherent gender role binary that maps heteronormative affective relations, child-raising, and domestic life together, and gives no attention to the heterosexual matrix through which these constructions of gender difference themselves rely upon sexual norms. As Hewitson (2003) argues, this move reinforces rather than challenges hegemonic representations of binarized gender.

Such representations of gender relations within the household further conceal the ways in which decisions about labor and resource allocation might be made differently by people who do not conform to this gender or sexual norm. As Cameron (2000: 61) suggests, these models can't think beyond two types – the traditional exploitative heterosexual household, and the modern, progressive heterosexual household where power and decision-making are somewhat more equally shared – and can only see feminist equity in terms of moving households from the traditional type to its opposite. But in the global South there is diversity of domestic arrangements even in heterosexual households that does not always conform to the gender norms offered in the simplified accounts of feminist household models (Cleaver 2002; Wood 2003), not to mention a diversity of other arrangements based on same-sex relationships, single-headed households, and so forth.

Policy implications of heteronormative household models

Put together, these unexamined ideas about sexuality in household bargaining models have significant implications for gender equity policy in a development context. First and most obviously, they contribute to the continued marginalization of non-normative sexual and household arrangements from analysis and policy-making. As Lind and Share (2003: 62) discuss, when the concepts of household and heterosexuality merge, it restricts the space for kinship and care to broaden its meaning to include transgendered, same-sex desire, and homosocial relations among others. Examinations of care work and reproductive labor from a non-heteronormative perspective, for instance, might recognize its production in friendship and other extra-familial networks (Roseneil 2004). Further, the unmarked status of sexuality in these models does not allow for an examination of how processes of development in general, and integrating women into paid labor specifically, might change sexual arrangements beyond making heterosexual households more equal.

In their assumption of household homogeneity, feminist bargaining models also shore up policy arguments that paid work liberates women. The language of household bargaining models is used to support policies such as export promotion strategies as both good for economic growth *and* good for women, because jobs in these industries gives women bargaining power in the home (Barker 2005). But such arguments only hold if one presumes that all households were inequitable heterosexual patriarchies before these jobs arrived. Further, economic development researchers and policy-makers have used the language of bargaining power and labor market integration to discount the idea that women who do engage in paid labor face a double burden of work, because paid work allows these women to bargain with their previously uncooperative male partners to share in household tasks (e.g. Newman 2002: 394). As Bedford's analysis of the heteronormativity of Ecuador gender policy demonstrates, this argument has gained significant traction at institutions such as the World Bank, and is now embedded in policy prescriptions (Bedford 2007; see also her chapter in this volume). This is troubling because even if this modernization tale of capitalism as liberating *were* true for the heteronormative households under study, the argument that "men will pick up the slack" fails to explain the empowerment or care burdens of those in other domestic arrangements, such as women in female-headed households, who are drawn into the paid labor market. But the concerns of these others are pushed to the margins in these modernization and empowerment narratives that rest so heavily on investments in sexual norms.

For example, the way that the "care crisis" is currently framed in the development policies that use feminist economic household models as a conceptual base is in the context of the heterosexual household in which women, socialized to be carers, do a disproportionate amount of the work. The solution proposed, then, is to create the conditions by which their male partners will share domestic tasks. As discussed above, the path to achieving this equitable result suggested by economists and policy-makers is to integrate women into paid labor in order to increase their bargaining power at home. But, sometimes, additional policies are proposed to push this effort along. For example, World Bank-funded programs in Mexico, Argentina, and Ecuador currently give priority to projects aimed at reorganizing behaviors within the family through workshops and other efforts aimed at creating equitable partnerships for men and women at home (World Bank 2001b; Molyneux 2006; Bedford 2007). "Taking care seriously," as Molyneux (2006) points out in her analysis of Mexican household policy, should include giving priority to public funding for childcare and elder care, or promoting work/life balance through paid maternity leave or flexi-time. But given the discourse around households and gender equity constructed through household models, it has come to mean a focus on promoting changes primarily in the private realm of the family. Similarly, recent anti-poverty policies in Argentina draw upon the language of household models and seek to strengthen and reorganize the family through a number of avenues, including policies to promote the inclusion of men in household chores and childcare (World Bank 2001b). And, as Kate Bedford's analysis of gender-equity policies in Ecuador demonstrates, similar efforts are in place there to reinforce normative family attachments by producing, through workshops and other mechanisms, an ideal of "sharing couples" and "domesticated men" (Bedford 2007).

Among the number of conceptual attachments at work in these discourses on households and care work is a hegemonic form of heterosexuality associated with so-called modern, developed societies as the ideal toward which people in the global South should aspire. World Bank studies and policy reports that draw upon household bargaining models often counterpose representations of backward patriarchy in the South with romanticized versions of household gender equity in the North. As Hart (1997: 16) has argued, household bargaining models have conceptually underwritten colonial, pathologizing accounts of households in the global South as being made up of "good, nurturing (working) mothers" on the one hand and "profligate fathers" who are portrayed as traditionally patriarchal and uncaring. Economic development policy, then, aims to transform these households into modern, sharing ones that resemble the supposed North Atlantic ideal. In this manner, the conceptual framework of household bargaining models, when translated into policy, not only contributes to the lack of visibility of non-normative sexual and household arrangements. It is also implicated in the production and transformation of normative heterosexualities themselves by regulating people across a whole spectrum of sexual and familial arrangements who do not conform to the hegemonic ideal (Cohen 2004: 27–8).

Without question, this heteronormative framing of development discourse is not determined solely by feminist household bargaining models. But the work that feminist economic accounts of the household have done, through a series of slippages and elisions, to create a vision of a heteronormative household made up of domesticated women and undomesticated men has been utilized by institutions such as the World Bank to shore up arguments in favor of privatizing care burdens through the restructuring of heterosexual family life, while simultaneously rendering non-normative households invisible. The use of household models in development policy discourse has led to naturalized accounts of women as carers, and has helped to underwrite exaggerated, colonial accounts of male profligacy in the global South. Finally, these conceptualizations of gender and sexual relations in households have allowed development policy-makers to rewrite the script of capitalism and wage labor as the sole salvation of women – the very script that many feminist economists have spent their careers challenging. Attention to assumptions about sexuality by feminists working in economic development would challenge these framings instead of unwittingly reproducing them. A feminist theory of household production and distribution which acknowledges that existing economic representations of households have been powerfully shaped by normative ideas about sexuality could better challenge the dominant discourse of gender and development policy, instead of fitting comfortably in a set of development knowledges and practices which fail to imagine gender identities and emancipatory aims outside of the heterosexual matrix.

Part II

Negotiating heteronormativity in development institutions

4   The World Bank's GLOBE

Queers in/queering development

Andil Gosine

In fall 1992, draft versions of a proposed anti-harassment policy were being circulated at headquarters of the International Bank for Reconstruction and Development – the World Bank – at 1818 H Street in Washington DC. One section caught the attention of Hans Binswanger, then a senior agricultural economist at the Bank. "I was surprised to see it offered protection from harassment on the grounds of sexual orientation," he recalls (2006). The reference to sexuality survived subsequent revisions, and was included in the Bank's "Policy on Eradicating Harassment."[1]

Binswanger anticipated an "en masse coming out" by gay and lesbian staff at the Bank would soon follow. "I thought that with the policy there was no more reason for people to hide their sexualities," he remembers, "but this didn't happen. Almost nobody came out; most stayed in the closet" (2006). Determined to seize upon the opportunity afforded by the policy, he decided to take steps toward the formation of a staff association. A gay couple employed at the Bank offered their home for a first meeting, and after overcoming efforts by some of their (presumably heterosexual) colleagues to stop the gathering,[2] 60 men and women came together at a private residence in January 1993 and founded GLOBE, the Gay, Lesbian or Bisexual Employees staff association of the World Bank Group.

By 2005, GLOBE had 165 paid members, up from 146 in 2003 and 122 in 2001. The group continues its work "to advance the fundamental principle of non-discrimination on the basis of sexual orientation" by:

> holding regular business meetings, social gatherings and film showings; encouraging Bank management to adopt administrative policies that treat gays, lesbians, bisexuals and transgenders equitably (e.g. domestic partners benefits); liaising with counterpart organizations in related agencies; and promoting debate and action on issues relating to sexual minorities in developing countries.
>
> (http://globe.worldbank.org, accessed June 14, 2004)

Membership in GLOBE is limited to "all active or former World Bank Group staff" and their partners, although colleagues at the International Monetary Fund and from other similar institutions, and all of their partners and friends, have also usually been invited to participate in the group's activities. It also collaborates with local gay and lesbian organizations in Washington, most often with Gays and Lesbians in Foreign Affairs Agencies (GLIFFA), and has sponsored film screenings at the local gay and lesbian film festival, Reel Affirmations. Thirteen years into GLOBE's existence, and with many of its original objectives now apparently achieved, it seems appropriate to now ask: What do we make of queer organizing at the World Bank? How has the existence of a gay/lesbian/bisexual staff association influenced the institution's work culture and its articulation of international development?

Through review of the organization's history and activities, this chapter seeks to identify and begin to evaluate some of the ways in which GLOBE has interpreted, negotiated and sometimes challenged the heteronormative terms mandated by the World Bank's constitution and implementation of its development programs, and in its institutional practices.[3] The first section, "queers in development," describes and evaluates some of GLOBE's efforts to achieve better working conditions for gays and lesbians, including through its challenges to the institutionalization of heterosexist claims in its human resources (HR) policies. The second section, "queering development," underlines the specific institutional location of GLOBE, a group operating within and contributing to the knowledge and policy production processes of perhaps the most powerful institutional actor in international development, and considers how GLOBE has and/or could potentially interrupt the production and promotion of heteronormativity in development policies and practices. This discussion has broader relevance; it reveals some of the implications of queer organizing in development institutions, and provides insight into the ways in which sexuality issues are being framed in development theories and practices.

I draw on many sources in this study, including feminist and queer scholarship, World Bank publications, documents provided by GLOBE, and from interviews conducted with World Bank staff. In 2005 and 2006, I interviewed seven men and two women employed at the Bank, four of whom are identified in the essay: current President of GLOBE, Daniel Crisafulli, past President Jeffrey Waite, Diversity Advisor for the World Bank Group, Julie Oyegun, and the already mentioned Hans Binswanger, who retired from his position as a Senior Advisor in 2005. Aliases are provided for the remaining five interviewees, of whom three were employed as permanent staff at the Bank and two were full-time consultants when the interviews were held.

Queers in international development

That the World Bank has a gay/lesbian/bisexual staff association surprises many people, as imaginations of the preconceptions historically associated with economic liberalization, environmentally and socially destructive policies, and burdening Third World countries with debt are unlikely to feature queer organizing in the mix. Yet the introduction of GLOBE was hardly a unique event. The 1990s brought about a series of organizing efforts in North America and Europe that sought to improve working conditions for gay men and lesbians at private and public corporations. In Canada and Western European countries, advocacy efforts resulted in legislated workplace protections and reforms to insurance, partnership, and marriage regulations. But as similar legislative protections were not available in much of the United States, changes at the workplace depended on lobbying from employee groups and a supportive management (cf. Raeburn 2004).[4] Advocates shared similar ambitions: opportunities for queer-identified men and women to meet, and better working conditions, including protections against discrimination based on "sexual orientation." Results have been quickly achieved. In 1990, no *Fortune 500*-listed company offered domestic partner benefits to employees in same-sex relationships, but, by 2004, more than one-third of them did (Davison and Rouse: 2004: 22).

When Binswanger moved to organize GLOBE, he believed it could work on two main goals: "getting gays at the Bank together to socialize," and "achieving equal rights." GLOBE's current by-laws emphasize the latter in their statement of objectives:

1   To advance, in the World Bank Group, consisting of the International Bank for Reconstruction and Development, the International Development Association, the International Finance Corporation, the Multilateral Investment Guarantee Agency and the International Center for the Settlement of Investment Disputes, the fundamental principle of non-discrimination on the basis of sexual orientation or gender identification.

2   To establish an organization which promotes better integration of Gay, Lesbian, Bisexual and Transgender employees into the World Bank community; assists in the affirmation of their identity; and encourages and stimulates interest in, and understanding and acceptance, of Gay, Lesbian, Bisexual, and Transgender people.

3   To enhance awareness in the World Bank Group that sexual orientation and gender identification are an integral element of an individual's character; it is not the sole component of personal and professional conduct.

4   To encourage respect for legitimate standards in World Bank Group operations on the premise that discrimination against a group or individual on the basis of perceived sexual orientation or gender identification is unacceptable.[5]

This agenda may be read as a not atypical liberal call for gay and lesbian rights, aimed at the normalization of (some) homosexual practices and the assimilation of (former) sexual dissidents into mainstream institutional and cultural practices, and which are configured around the demands of capitalism. Despite the important limitations of this approach,[6] GLOBE's efforts have brought about some real material gains for queer men and women, and interrupted the production and reproduction of heterosexism within the Bank, including recognition of same-sex domestic partnerships, successful challenges to assumptions of universal heterosexuality, and creation of a "gay friendlier" work environment. As outlined below, these changes have been universally celebrated, but not always equally experienced, by queer men and women at the Bank.

GLOBE's most valued victories have been its achievement of domestic benefits for same-sex partners and healthcare coverage for HIV-positive staff, both won after votes taken by the Bank's Board of Directors in January 1998. Same-sex spouses and partners now hold almost equal privileges as opposite-sex couplings, including: medical coverage, access to Bank premises and resources, travel and relocation allowances, accident insurance, education payments for children, health club membership, immunizations, and other benefits. There are still some exceptions; for example, through a points reward system, opposite-sex spouses are permitted to travel with Bank staff on some work missions, but the same privilege is not afforded to same-sex spouses.[7] Still, these gains surpass those sought by other gay advocacy groups at similar institutions.[8] Other interventions made by GLOBE have included the addition of "sexuality" (alongside race and gender) in the Bank's "360 feedback" forms, the launch of a website in 2002, and the removal of "gay" and "lesbian" as alert words in the Bank's e-mail filter system. In 2002, GLOBE's then out-going president was also appointed to a "Diversity and Inclusion Advisory Group" working on HR policy.

Advocacy on HR issues has been accompanied by a promotional strategy to ensure high visibility of GLOBE inside the Bank. Since 1999, the group has staffed table displays at the Bank's annual Staff Week event, organized special events, film screenings, and lectures (Brazilian gay activist Roberto de Jesus and queer feminist Charlotte Ross have both accepted invitations to present their work). This effort to claim institutional space has served at least two important functions: assert the presence of queer men and women, and to generate a more secure work environment for them.

We're queer, we're here!

The announcement of a staff association for gay and lesbian employees at the World Bank made more visible the reality that not all of the Bank's employees are straight. All of the men and women interviewed characterize the World Bank as a "gay friendly" organization, but they also agree that workers are generally presumed to be heterosexual. Geir, a consultant in the Bank's Africa Region section, recounted a not uncommon experience among gay men and lesbians of "outing" himself to a workmate. A man Geir had been dating had just left Washington and he had an unusually sullen demeanor at work, prompting curiosity from a colleague. "I came to work and she could tell I was looking fairly depressed," Geir (2005) explained. "She kept asking me, 'Okay, who is she? Who is causing this?' I said, 'Uh, actually, *his* name is Fernando.' She smiled." Gavin, an American technology advisor and founding member of GLOBE, argued that the group's existence and high visibility communicate an old message of gay movements: *We're queer, we're here!* He explained:

> ... you need to have a visibility of gay and lesbian people, because too often you meet someone and they say, "I don't know any gay people." And you say, "Actually, you do. You just don't know that you do." It is also important for heterosexual people at the bank of any culture to know that there are gay,

lesbian, transgender, bisexual employees here and that it is important for them to be aware that they do exist and they have to be aware of their own actions, and their thoughts, and their comments … you really do not know who might be sitting next to you.

(2005)

"Sometimes the goal of the staff association," he adds, "is not so much to get a lot of people to come to the table and sign up but … to see that there is a group here." Julie Oyegun, the Diversity Advisor to the President of the World Bank, agrees that GLOBE has made an important impact "in the areas of conscious-raising and awareness-raising".

(2006)

A gay-friendlier World Bank?

Knowing that "there is a (gay) group here" has made many gay men and lesbians feel more secure about their status at the Bank. Prior to GLOBE's formation and the adoption of an anti-harassment policy, many of them believed they were vulnerable to homophobic discrimination at work.[9] Although he was already a senior economist at the Bank when he got GLOBE off the ground, even Binswanger was worried about the repercussions for his activism:

> I also thought through whether it would be difficult to work in the Bank [but] I was a very senior member of my profession and I had a lot of independence. I thought I was taking a calculated risk, and if worse came to worse [sic], I could manage the consequences. I could go to a university.

(2006)

Alex remembers that some gay and lesbian staff didn't want to come to an on-site meeting in the early days of GLOBE, so meetings were also held at private residences and at local gay bars. After the domestic partnership policy was changed, many gays and lesbians hesitated to take advantage of the new benefits plan, on account of their fears about repercussions for "coming out." Gavin recalls:

> Early on my current partner and I … did register for domestic partnerships at the bank when [GLOBE was] pushing for that because it became available but nobody was signing up for that … they had to push to make sure that as many people as possible register for that.[10]

(2006)

Organizers also encountered opposition from some staff when they tried to stage special events.[11]

Race, gender, (class)

GLOBE's leading actors suggest that these anxieties have now subsided. Speaking about his own experience, Binswanger says, "I became famously gay, but there were no consequences for my work at the Bank. I got two big promotions after 1993." He believes:

> GLOBE has been incredibly effective in creating a gay positive environment … I think we can still count on one hand the number of cases brought forward on sexual orientation discrimination, and you might still not need all your fingers![12] Its existence, even for people who never came to meetings, who never came out, they were absolutely ecstatic about it. It made such a big difference emotionally, they felt safer, more valued … especially with those people in more precarious working conditions, like the consultants. It was a very positive thing for them.
>
> (2006)

Most of the people interviewed for this chapter agree. But a more careful review of its membership raises questions about whether all gays and lesbians feel as confident. Right from the start, GLOBE has attracted a homogeneous membership. Recalling its first meeting, Binswanger says:

> When we had the first meeting in January [1993], 60 people showed up. What was striking was that almost all were white men. Women found it more difficult, as did people from developing countries.
>
> (2005)

In 1999, of the 119 paid members of GLOBE, only 21 were women (18 percent). By 2000, membership stood at 132, including 26 women (20 percent), and by 2002, 27 of the 145 members were women (19 percent). These disparities are also reflected in the main communication instrument among GLOBE members, its listserv. In 2005, there were 165 members signed up on the listserv, of whom 106 were on the "cc" list and 59 on the (blind) "bcc" list. Since the list was started, more and more staff have either moved from the blind list to the visible "cc" list or signed up directly to the cc list. However, there were no people from developing countries visible on the cc list and almost no women.[13] This picture stands in contrast with the overall make-up of the World Bank's population of 10,778 workers representing almost every one of the world's countries – 6,428 of these workers are from "Part 2" (i.e. developing) countries – and more than half of whom (5,539) are women. Additionally, no data was available on the professional status of GLOBE members, but there appeared to be little evidence of involvement in lower-waged, "blue-collar" workers in the organization.[14]

Both of the queer Bank workers from developing countries interviewed for this project expressed anxieties about their sexualities being made public. Ravi, an Indian national employed as a policy analyst, said, "I think GLOBE makes a big difference, and I am grateful for what they are doing, [but] I have chosen to stay away" (2005). Explaining why he would not be comfortably "out" at work, he says, "The Bank is still a place which is evolving in terms of its attitudes ... The countries I work on are fairly conservative and traditional, and it affects the comfort level that I have ..." (2005).[15] Iliana, who came to the Bank after working with various development institutions in Latin America, says, she "really appreciates all the work that GLOBE has been doing to make [sexuality] a non-issue, to make sure that the benefits are equal." The group, she says, "is a jewel. If you know you have a problem you know you can go to GLOBE and GLOBE will certainly respond for you." But, she adds:

> There are more gay people working at development institutions than those who have come out of the closet. I think the struggle really ... is to give people the security to come out of the closet. To see that that does not affect growing in the institution, taking important positions, or being this object of horrible things ...
>
> (2005)

As people in the international development field are so well versed in politically correct language and social etiquette, Iliana also suggests, "you can never really know when you are not being given the opportunity because of your sexual orientation" (2005).

Current GLOBE President Daniel Crisafulli conceded, "white males from U.S. and Europe backgrounds are the ones who are most out and active clearly" (2005). Of the low representation of women, he suggested:

> There [ha]ve been different theories put forward ... maybe because women are still in more junior positions within the organization, they feel a bit more vulnerable, perhaps, and therefore more reluctant to come out, if you will, or even to be associated with GLOBE.
>
> (2005)

Asked to explain the low participation of men and women from developing countries, he says, "I think that the majority of the members who are comfortable with the group tend to be from developed, Eastern European, or North American countries" (2005). He believes "it's more of a personal issue ... about own sense of comfort and knowledge about outing yourself to more people than you need to."

Iliana offers a different explanation:

> To me, that says that it seems to be hard for women to come out of the closet at big institutions, you have to compete very hard, you have to be twice as good, and we don't need another handicap ... There is a gender imbalance in terms of opportunities in the Bank. There is a nationality imbalance in the Bank. What are the possibilities to go through the ranks? Just look at the management ...

normally male, white, from a Western country. Those who are in a less privileged position do not need another factor to fight against.

(2005)

Oyegun, who is charged with directing the Bank's work on equity and diversity issues in HR, agrees with this assessment. She asks:

How many layers can people deal with? In this organ it is still true that if you are not white, if you earned your credentials outside the West, you have a lot to deal with.

(2005)

Many queer people of color, she says, do not need to take on "another layer" that may hinder their progress (2005).

What emerges from this discussion about the make-up of GLOBE is revelation of complicity with dominant gendered and racializing narratives in explaining why women and non-white men are under-represented in the group. Two thinly veiled assumptions are repeated in the analysis offered by the interviewees: (1) heterosexual people who are non-white or not from Western countries are predisposed to be homophobic, and (2) women and non-white men, if they are not heterosexual, do not "come out" or participate as members of GLOBE because they face these overwhelming "cultural" pressures to remain closeted, or because they are not strong enough individuals. For example: Binswanger says women did not come to the first meeting because "they found it difficult"; Crisafulli says it's a "personal issue" for non-white men not to identify themselves on the "cc" list or join GLOBE, "whatever the reason, cultural or generational"; Iliana describes non-white men and women less apt to be active, visible members of GLOBE as "less strong" (2005, 2006). In this explanation of marginalization, racializing "cultural" assumptions often offer the opportunity to distract from critical interrogation of the potential production of sexism, racism, or classism within the organization. Consider this episode described by Alex:

I remember a couple of years ago, Hans [Binswanger] and I were working at the table. It just said "GLOBE." Just "GLOBE," unexplained, sounds like some sort of a generic world bank [thing]. I remember I was standing there. And an Indian friend of mine, a colleague of mine, came over, and was standing beside me, chatting for about five minutes. And after ten minutes looked up and said, "So what is this? GLOBE?" I said, "This is for gay and lesbian bank employees," and I could see him go thinking that he has been standing and associating himself with this group. That's kind of amusing.

(2005)

His Indian colleague said or did nothing to indicate he was uncomfortable being associated with a gay organization, but Alex references dominant ideas about culture and difference to anticipate that an Indian *would* be uncomfortable standing at a table for a gay organization. Claims about the homophobic predisposition of non-Western cultures were also often made in some interviewees' descriptions of their interactions with fellow workers; for example, Geir says he hesitated to "out" himself to his colleague because "she was from a Muslim country" (2005). While these and other allusions to the social conservatism of developing states are grounded in empirical evidence (criminalization of sodomy, etc., in much of the developing world), the repeated characterization of developing states as homophobic may also serve to reaffirm orientalist fantasies of non-white, non-Western cultures as barbaric or, at the very least, less civilized.[16] It also fails to recognize that state-mandated sexual repression does not always reflect cultural norms, and betrays the active resistance to homophobia and heterosexism by individuals and organizations across the South.[17]

In its primary function as a staff club, GLOBE has presented important challenges to the production of heteronormativity in the workplace, through its successful pursuit of domestic partnership benefits, commitment to high visibility within the institution and organization of activities that promote queer culture. Yet, as analysis of its membership suggests, these advances have only limited impact in the absence of critical analysis of gender, "race," and class, and may not ultimately be accessible to the Bank's most vulnerable queer workers. Turning attention to an examination of GLOBE's influence in "queering development," a more complex picture emerges.

Queering development

What does it mean to "queer development"? Lind and Share use this term to characterize the ways in which "sexuality and gender can be rethought and reorganized in development practices, theories and politics" (2003: 57). For them, a queer analysis of development thus examines:

> how heterosexuality is institutionalized, naturalized and regulated, both explicitly (by excluding LGBT people from the analysis) and implicitly (by assuming that all people are heterosexual, marriage is a given and all men and women fit more or less into traditional gender roles).
>
> (57)

Applying this definition to examine GLOBE's influence in the formulation and implementation of the World Bank's development programs, two kinds of "queering" interventions and impacts may be identified: ones directed at achieving specified policy and program objectives, and ones aimed at creating or resulting in cultural conditions under which heteronormative claims about sexuality and gender may be reconsidered and reconfigured.

Efforts on the part of GLOBE to actively influence World Bank policy have not been overwhelming. Crisafulli says that as GLOBE is "just another staff club," it has not privileged any political agenda beyond its HR objectives. He explains:

> I have to admit that most of what the group is, is a social network and that's
> what people want out of it for the most part. Happy hours, and parties, and
> women's events – that's really what it's about. It functions a lot like the South
> Asians' group … or … like the Chinese group …

"There is not this groundswell within Bank staff and GLOBE members to run out
there and really champion gay issues in development," he also suggests, because
"most of our members … tend to be pretty discreet. So there aren't a lot of activist types. The bank itself does not typically attract more activist types" (2005).
GLOBE's own research suggests a slightly more complex picture, but appears to
bear out his analysis. Some members seem eager to expand the kind of intervention-
ist role the organization can take, but not the majority. In annual surveys of GLOBE
members conducted since 1999, a significant number of participants have continued to identify work on "HIV/AIDS issues in developing countries" as a priority.
Eighty-nine percent of the 68 respondents to the 2002–3 survey ranked "need for
more involvement with GLB issues in developing countries" as "important (31 percent), very important (26 percent) or extremely important (15 percent)". However,
taking the highest rating alone ("extremely important"), this issue finishes behind
most others listed in the survey: "improved implementation of domestic partner
benefits" (46 percent), "HR issues with regard to sexual orientation" (46 percent),
"improved staff awareness of domestic partner benefits" (34 percent), "greater
management visibility in support of GLB awareness in field offices" (24 percent)
and "greater management visibility in support of GLB issues" (21 percent). In fact,
only two items ranked lower: coordination with other GLB groups on GLB issues
(3 percent) and "increased outreach to the local DC community" (4 percent).

The 2002–3 survey also asked respondents to identify additional activities
GLOBE could undertake. Suggestions included "adding a GLB perspective on
the Millennium Development Goals" and "outreach with GLB groups in developing counties, especially where there is anti-gay discrimination." Yet, as Crisafulli
suggested, many are resistant to organizing efforts to "queer development"; in the
2002–3 survey, one member commented:

> GLOBE has done a good job of advancing our interests as GLB employees of
> the World Bank. In my personal opinion, its mission should remain focused
> on its role as an advocate for GLB employees and job-related issues, including
> fostering a community. It is not the role of the World Bank to advance politi-
> cal or cultural change in our client countries, so I am uncomfortable with the
> idea of GLOBE becoming activist in this area.

Oyegun suggests, however, that the mission of the World Bank inevitably gets
taken up in various ways by staff clubs. "In an organization like the World Bank,"
she says, "you would expect that there would be some link to the Bank's mission,
to reduce poverty, to improve people's lives" (2005). GLOBE, she considers, "has
had a checkered history" which has depended very much on the commitments of
key individuals, especially those who identify linkages between their operational

work and the issues around which staff clubs have formed. After three years at the Bank, Oyegun says that she's "beginning to realize that there are catalysts and champions, even in staff associations, which can radically change the organization" (2005).

Indeed, efforts aimed at achieving specific policy or program issues on gay or lesbian issues have tended to come from GLOBE's universally recognized "champion" of gay rights, Binswanger. As is widely acknowledged by his peers, Binswanger's efforts to integrate gay and lesbian issues in the institution's policies and programs began with his public announcement that he was HIV positive:

> When Hans came out to the Board as an HIV-positive person I think that it was major, major means of changing the attitudes of a number of high-level staff in how they look at it. Because here's the member that they know and respected for a long time who was being open about it … and it brings it all home, saying that it is not such a distant issue for people elsewhere in the world, something that is a problem elsewhere, but it is an issue here.
>
> (2005)

Binswanger in fact has been widely identified in the international development professional community as being personally responsible for transforming the Bank's attitude toward HIV/AIDS. When the World Health Organization set up UNAIDS in 1995, for example, the Bank was "badgered" into joining it. In *The World's Banker*, Mallaby notes:

> The Bank ceded with bad grace; it emphasized that it would "assume no liability" for the new outfit and wished to have "as little involvement as possible." The Bank's AIDS lending coasted along at a modest level in the next years, and [Bank President] Wolfensohn ignored the plague … by 1999, the Bank was funding only three substantial projects in Africa – in Kenya, Uganda and Zimbabwe … Most astonishing of all, no new freestanding AIDS projects were under preparation in the region.
>
> (Mallaby 2004: 319)

Mallaby credits Binswanger and an Ethiopian doctor, Debrework Zewdie, with forcing the Bank to undergo a radical change in the way it viewed HIV/AIDS. Among the many valuable tools each used separately and together in trying to advance support for prioritizing HIV/AIDS interventions, Mallaby lists Binswanger's size and medical status: "He stood at over six feet tall and he had the particular moral authority that comes from being HIV positive" (320). Zewdie's and Binswanger's persistence, Mallaby argues, resulted in the consideration of AIDS at meetings of the Bank's powerful policy-setting Development Committee in April 2000 and, subsequently, creation of a Multi-Country HIV/AIDS Program for Africa, and the setting aside of $500 million in soft International Development Assistance credits (and a promise to set aside another half billion) for AIDS programs.

"When I first started working on HIV/AIDS,"[18] Binswanger recalls:

there were two priorities: the Bank needed to take political leadership on HIV/AIDS issues and fund viral treatments. After this were gay and lesbian issues. These were less pressing [and I worried that they would] distract from the two main priorities.

Believing that the first two objectives had been accomplished, in the last few years leading up to his retirement from the Bank in 2005, Binswanger turned his attention to gay and lesbian issues, and tried to wrest a range of policy and program commitments from the Bank. In memos and presentations to his managers and peers, Binswanger called on the Bank to support UNAIDS in its advocacy for attention to issues relating to men who have sex with men at the international and national level, to use the Bank's influence and resources to provide funding and training for LBGT groups in South countries, and to insist on the integration of MSM and LGBT issues in national HIV/AIDS programs. He also worked closely with the organization, Gays and Lesbians of Zimbabwe (GALZ), towards preparation of communication tools to support queer organizing initiatives. Certainly, Binswanger was not the only one, either inside or outside the bank working on these issues, but his efforts to link the interests of gays and lesbians employed at the Bank to those of sexual minorities in the developing world were unique. Throughout the period of GLOBE's existence, and especially after the domestic partnership benefits were won, Binswanger challenged his gay and lesbian colleagues in the group to become more actively engaged in integrating queer issues into the operational work of the Bank.

Early on, his efforts were rebuffed. At a special meeting of representatives from the World Bank's GLOBE, the more recently formed International Monetary Fund GLOBE and USAID on "HIV/AIDS Outreach to developing countries" held on June 12, 2002, Binswanger led a discussion about ways in which the staff clubs could support HIV/AIDS groups run by or for gay men and MSM in the poorest developing countries, through fundraising and knowledge transfer. But those present agreed that "rather than involve GLOBE as a staff club … it was more appropriate to invite members from GLBT groups within development organizations to participate as individuals on a voluntary – and volunteer – basis" (2002). Crisafulli says operational activities are not within GLOBE's mandate:

> [T]here is work that is being done on the operations side, with ties to GLOBE, but it's not done through GLOBE, if you will. GLOBE is more of a staff organization, for the staff themselves. The group of individuals who are pursuing these issues in the bank are doing that in sort of a parallel to GLOBE.
>
> (2005)

Asked about the reluctance on the part of many of his GLOBE colleagues to take up queer issues in the Bank's operational work, Binswanger says:

> There are so many competing priorities, it's hard if you're not determined. I have sympathy for anyone who does not want to get involved. To me, moving

MSM into Operations was the most emotional and most difficult thing I have done. I felt very vulnerable.

(2006)

Others agree that strict regulations about what Bank staff members are permitted to do, and how the onus placed on them to represent the Bank, limit the kinds of things that they can do. Gavin points out:

There's only so much that the group can do here from the Bank and be seen as a Bank group. And then there's also the issue of what restrictions the group can do when presenting themselves as bank employees … I think it can be a sticky situation … because anything someone does in the country, it can come back to the Bank as "the World Bank is supporting this" as opposed to "the World Bank GLOBE" or "the World Bank member" is supporting it.

However, he also believes there still may be interventions that employees can pursue:

One of the things they try to do is contact the local groups when they are in the country, and give insight or recommend about how they can improve themselves, how can they develop as supportive organizations. I think that that's something that should be part and parcel of the group that's trying to build a bigger global community.

(2005)

But "even if they are doing something in their private life," he says, "they are seen as World Bank employees" (2005). Their engagement in activities not sanctioned by the Bank may put their careers at risk. Bank regulations also state that staff clubs must:

be recreational or professional in nature. Clubs/associations that are formed for political objectives are ineligible to use the Bank Group's name. The group cannot engage in lobbying, advocacy, or exertion of political pressure (e.g. pro or con gun control, abortion, animal rights, etc.).

Clubs that do not follow these guidelines risk losing status and related resources.

Despite the institutional limits placed on the kinds of impact GLOBE may have on development policy at the Bank and besides the individual championship of particular issues by Binswanger, there are still important ways in which GLOBE might champion "queer development." The group's existence and its HR achievements provide the space and rationale for broader application, and, through its challenges to social and cultural norms, creates opportunities for conversations and interventions about sexuality to emerge. Iliana points out that the existence of GLOBE within the Bank sends a direct message to countries that criminalize homosexuality. "GLOBE is a reminder to even those countries and governments for whom this exercise is not acceptable that even though for them it is not acceptable," she says, "when they are part of the entire world, they need to tolerate diversity" (2005). Binswanger also suggests, "the fact that the World Bank recognizes Gays and Lesbians is the bedrock for moving these issues into Operations" (2006). "How can you have double talk?" he asks. "Internally you acknowledge these are valuable people and outside you do not say the same thing?" (2006).

Contradictory messages about sexuality in the conception and implementation of development programs have often worked to multiply opportunities for advancing queer rights. As Lind and Share observe:

> An irony of the development field is that while sexuality has rarely been discussed other than in terms of women's reproductive rights and health, or in terms of social problems such as prostitution or the AIDS epidemic, funding from agencies such as USAID has helped to institutionalize and make visible Latin American LGBT movements ...
>
> (Lind and Share 2003: 56)

The visibility of GLOBE and the activities of its members may have also resulted in the production of more interest in and more research on sexuality in development, including work that begins to problematize the production of heterosexist norms and the exclusion of non-heterosexual people from analysis of development "problems" and participation in development programs. For example, a 2004 Africa region human-development-working paper series report, "Integration of Gender Issues in Selected HIV/AIDS Projects in the Africa Region: a baseline assessment," raised the specter of homosexuality and, notably, homophobia. The report's authors argued, "men's vulnerabilities and risk to HIV/AIDS are ... fueled by several factors," including "homophobia and taboo surrounding homosexuality (which forces men who have sex with men to keep their behavior secret and deny their risk)" (2). They observed that:

> notions of masculinity and femininity also influence ... vulnerability and risk factors. For example, the role-models for masculinity and the taboo surrounding homosexuality have a strong impact on homosexual behavior patterns, sometimes forcing men who have sex with men to demonstrate their "masculinity" by marrying and/or engaging in heterosexual sex, exposing their female sexual partners to HIV/AIDS".
>
> (5)

Similarly, a September 2004 report, "Targeting Vulnerable Groups in National HIV/AIDS Programs: the case of men who have sex with men – Senegal, Burkina Faso, the Gambia" provided a more comprehensive analysis. The report's foreword begins by posing a question: "In Africa, HIV/AIDS is spread overwhelmingly through heterosexual sex. Can, therefore, men having sex with men (MSM) be overlooked as a target group for HIV/AIDS programs without a significant negative impact on the programs' overall effectiveness?" (v). The study gives two main reasons why this is not the case: "First, MSM are much more prevalent in African societies than generally thought. And second, MSM are not an isolated group, but are in fact intensely and extensively sexually linked with the heterosexual members of African society" (v). It goes on to explain:

> The large majority of MSM do not identify themselves as homosexuals, and furthermore, most of those MSM that were interviewed for this study acknowledge having had sexual relations with a woman during the last month preceding this survey. As a result, even if homosexual activity is practiced by only 5% of adult males, any HIV infection acquired by this group will not be contained within the group, but can be spread to the rest of the population through heterosexual acts. The homosexual and heterosexual circuits are closely interlinked, and therefore, the cost to society of maintaining the taboo of same-gender sexual practices, and marginalizing people engaged in same-gender sexual contact, is very high.
>
> (vi)

Other initiatives are also under way in other sections of the Bank. The Latin America/Caribbean HIV/AIDS programs' coordinator has been particularly successful in getting MSM populations recognized in countries' National AIDS Plans.

Queer beyond AIDS? Queer beyond development?

These advances in research and policy on HIV/AIDS are important, but further evaluation of GLOBE's probable influence on the World Bank's development program reveals some striking limitations to its "queering" potential. The way in which questions and arguments about queer sexualities are being taken up, and the fact of GLOBE's situation as a collective of staff members invested in promotion of the World Bank's particular development agenda result in a very narrow critique.

As is clear from this discussion, almost all of the ways in which GLOBE or its members reference queer issues in analysis of development issues or in programs are tied to HIV/AIDS. That discussions of sexuality would first emerge in the Bank's operational work through HIV/AIDS is not surprising; as I have argued elsewhere (Gosine 2004, 2005a, 2005b), this pattern is common among international development actors. One of the implications of the prioritization of HIV/AIDS as a development issue has been the creation of space to engage in conversation about sexuality – conversations that could potentially lead to a more elaborate "queer analysis" of development. Referencing his own work at the Bank, Geir observed "sexuality doesn't come up when you talk about gas pipelines or trade, or conflict, even if it is relevant; with AIDS, you have to talk about sexuality. It's forcing people to talk about sex" (2006). However, there are important drawbacks to the configuration of discussions on sex and sexuality within a limited HIV/AIDS framework, for "queering development." In "Stumbling into sexualities" (2005), I identified four key features of this approach which reveal its critical limitations: the assumption of a Western model of sexuality as universal; the confinement of sexuality matters to HIV/AIDS policy discussions only; the invisibilization of women, particularly queer women; and the racist representation of Third World people.[19] Characterizations of gay men as promiscuous, irresponsible, and dangerous are also implicitly reproduced in the association of homo-sex with HIV/AIDS.[20] Within the work on HIV/AIDS, few questions are raised about the articulation of sexual practices and identities through heterosexist and Western frameworks, and fewer questions yet are being asked about the experiences and lives of sexual minorities and/or dissidents outside of this work. The explicit and implicit institutionalization of heterosexuality through development practices are not being problematized; the promotion of heterosexual models of family, inscription of heterosexist male and female gender roles, etc. are not even under consideration.

There is, too, the fact of GLOBE's operation as an instrument of the World Bank. While staff clubs are not mandated to promote particular positions, regulations forbidding organized resistance to any of the Bank's policies achieve that result nevertheless. Moreover, as employees engaged in formulation and implementation of World Bank policies and programs, GLOBE members are necessarily invested in the pursuit of the institution's vision of growth-led development. Any "queering" project pursued by GLOBE will likely not include critical opposition to but instead adhere to the neoliberal economic philosophy of the Bank, and continue to prioritize capitalist expansion as the ultimate priority of development.

Conclusion

People engaged in dissident sexual practices and/or who have adopted queer sexual identities have been so completely written out of development theory and practices that the mere recognition of queers' existence or non-heterosexual sexual practices in development institutions represents a significant challenge to heteronormativity; just as the claim for space made early in North American gay movements – epitomized in the popular proclamation *We're queer! We're here!* – was an important and, at the time, radical gesture, so too must the mere presence of GLOBE be appreciated for its insistence that the existence and equality of gays and lesbians be recognized. The group's efforts toward the creation of safer and more comfortable workspaces for Bank employees, and its attendance to questions about sexuality in policy and program discussions also set the pace for similar innovations in other development institutes, while valuing the involvement of queer men and women. But – as others also similarly observed about gay movements[21] – its failure to engage critical race, gender, and class analysis in the pursuit of sexuality rights may leave gains out of reach for the most marginalized queer men and women at the Bank.

The participation of gays and lesbians in the institutional processes of development opens up space for analysis of the regulation of sexuality but also provides no guarantee of resistance to heteronormative ideals in its implementation. Besides its contribution to fostering a more receptive climate in which to raise questions about sexuality in development theory and practice, there is no evidence that GLOBE is committed to pursuit of the broad interrogation suggested in Lind and

Share's notion of "queering development." Indeed, the fact of GLOBE's institutional location underlines important tensions about this project. Does "queering development" seek to merely provide recognition for and inclusion of gays and lesbians in the processes of ongoing development projects, similar, for example, to the recognition of women as "economic agents," as advocated in "women in development" frameworks? Is it enough to problematize the regulation, naturalization, and institutionalization of heterosexuality – or must such a project also emphasize contestation of the term "development" as well? That is, in revealing and working toward the disruption of heteronormative claims in development theory and practices, should we not also insist upon a critical interrogation of "development" that recognizes its successor relationship to colonialism, its often racializing and orientalist interpretation of culture and civilization, and its investment in capitalist economic growth? In other words: is "queering development" about making space for queers or about achieving more choices, greater freedoms, and more secure and pleasurable futures for queer men and women, through a radical rethinking of development?

Notes

1   The policy stated: "Harassment on any basis – including, but not limited to race, gender, religion, nationality, colour, sexual orientation, disability or age – is unacceptable ... staff should be aware that all forms of harassment may constitute misconduct, providing a basis for disciplinary action, up to and including termination of employment" (cited in "Building a Positive Work Environment," World Bank 2001a: 3).
2   Binswanger submitted an announcement of a meeting for gay and lesbian staff to the Bank's "Weekly bulletin" in early December 1992. His home telephone number was listed as the contact information. When the next week's bulletin was published, however, no listing appeared. Queries led him to a conversation with the Vice-President of Human Resources, who was persuaded by arguments that the organization of a gay and lesbian staff club did not contravene Bank Policy. He decided to allow its publication, on one condition. Binswanger remembers, "I was told, 'Yes, you can have it, but you have to put your name to the announcement'." (2006). He also learned of one group that attempted to pressure the senior management into adopting stricter regulations for staff clubs operating in the Bank, but that initiative failed because many other existing clubs would have been in violation of the proposed rules. Binswanger's name was added to the listing, and the announcement was published.
3   The term "heteronormative" references work by Sedgewick, MacKinnon, Ingraham, and Rich, among others, to describe the process whereby heterosexuality is normalized and naturalized.
4   A quick search elicited names for several gay and lesbian employee organizations at major multinational corporations, including: Xerox's GALAXE (Gay and Lesbian At Xerox), IBM's EGALE (Employee Alliance for Gay and Lesbian Equality), Microsoft's GLEAM (Gay and Lesbian Employees of Microsoft), AT&T's LEAGUE (Lesbian, Bisexual, Gay and Transgendered United Employees), and GLOBEs at the Ford Corporation and Intel.
5   Although GLOBE's "socializing" mandate is not well represented in this statement, it has remained an important aspect of the association; indeed, some of its members have suggested that with its main human resource battles won, the organization of social events (bar evenings and parties) by its lead and assistant "Cruising Directors" has become GLOBE's primary purpose.

6   As numerous queer critics have pointed out (e.g. Sinfield 1998, Alexander 2005), liberal approaches are also premised on essentialist notions of sexuality/sexual identity, and privilege dominant Western metropolitan models of sexual organization.

7   At the time of writing, efforts were being made to change this policy.

8   The United Nations GLOBE, for example, has for years struggled unsuccessfully to achieve parallel benefits.

9   This feeling is not uncommon among queer workers; as reported in a 1992 survey conducted by *Out/Look*, "28% of gay men and 38% of lesbians who responded said the need to hide their sexual orientation was a constant source of stress on the job" (cited in Davison and Rouse, 2004: 35).

10   A 1999 survey of GLOBE members reiterates this position; of 30 respondents who had partners, 16 said they registered themselves as domestic partners primarily "to make a political statement" (12).

11   A proposal to screen *Fire* set off a storm of debate and resulted in several postponements, but the film was eventually screened on February 18, 1999. Three hundred audience members attended the show, held at Preston Auditorium, on Bank premises.

12   The only data I could access on harassment came from a 1999 survey of 47 members of GLOBE, which included two respondents who claimed to have been harassed in the previous two years because of their sexual orientation.

13   Crisafulli: "When we started there was only a BCC list, which means that it's a blind copy and that the recipient sees only his or her own name and not the full list. Progressively over time ... It was actually when I came in, I suggested having a CC list and switching people over to that, and going back periodically and asking people if they want to switch over to the CC list. It gives us more of an open feel, it's not something that people are trying to hide. And ... a growing percentage of our members are on the CC list which is open and visible to everybody" (2005).

14   Requests for gender-disaggregated information about the pay or professional status of employees were denied.

15   Ravi also believes that local patterns of racial segregation in DC may influence the operation of GLOBE: "D.C. is a very segregated place – if you go to a bar, it's always choosing between all-white or all-black bars. The gay movement adopted the metaphors of the civil rights movement, but race clearly works [in the movement]."

16   For example, see Robert Young's *Colonial Desire* (1995) or Ali Rattansi's "Western racisms" (1994).

17   There are now numerous examples of queer-identified men and women actively engaged in organizing against homophobia in the Third World. Some better-known groups include: Naz and Bombay Dost in India, JFLAG in Jamaica, and the continent-wide All Africa Rights Initiative.

18   Binswanger first became concerned about HIV/AIDs as a development issue in 1996, 1997. He had just been appointed Director of Rural Development for Africa (Env/ Social/Health). Binswanger subsequently founded a Charity organization in Zimbabwe, the Community and Enterprise Development against Stigma, AIDSETI. The group covered the costs of education and health (including AIDS treatments) for a group of children orphaned by AIDS. In 2006, 22 children and ten adults were funded through this program, with financial support divided between a trust set up by Binswanger and a personal financial contribution.

19   The reductive focus of development discourse about sexuality on "fighting AIDS" takes up the same view of all Third World peoples as espoused in previous population-control and family-planning projects: that they are one-dimensional organisms led only by raw desire (whether for survival, reproduction, or sexual fulfillment), and do not experience the full range of emotions so readily associated with love and sex in the First World, and among white people in particular. The limited focus is also a racist characterization that makes non-white people appear to be less full humans who do not engage in as complex (and as intelligible) negotiations about matters of the heart (and body).

20 In some of the Bank's publications, calls to recognize sexual minorities in HIV/AIDS prevention work have emphasized one persuasive argument: since studies show that most men who have sex with men in developing countries also have sex with female partners, HIV/AIDS in sexual minority/dissident communities may infect the whole society. This position is articulated in the foreword of the 2004 World Bank funded study "Targeting Vulnerable Groups in National HIV/AIDS Programs":

> In Africa, HIV/AIDS is spread overwhelmingly through heterosexual sex. Can, therefore, men having sex with men (MSM) be overlooked as a target group for HIV/AIDS programs without a significant negative impact on the programs' overall effectiveness? First, MSM are much more prevalent in African societies than generally thought. And second, MSM are not an isolated group but are in fact intensively and extensively sexually linked with the heterosexual members of African society ... Even if homosexual activity is practiced by only five percent of adult males, any HIV infection acquired by this group will not be contained within the group, but can be spread to the rest of the population through heterosexual contacts.
>
> (2004c: v–vi)

While this approach may be effective in getting support for HIV/AIDS support and prevention programs, it also places responsibility for the disease on men not exclusively engaged in heterosexual relationships, and in so doing defines appropriate moral codes for sexual experiences and behaviour.

21 For example, Sinfield (1998), Alexander (2005), Julien and Mercer (1991), Manalansan (1997).

5 NGOs as erotic sites

Ara Wilson

Trafficking in NGOs[1]

In the mid-1990s, I volunteered as a rapporteur for an international conference in Thailand on trafficking in women, which was staffed and attended mostly by women. During the day, technical and emotional reports about various dimensions of trafficking placed the sexual and economic exploitation of women in a context of migrant labor issues, women's rights, policing, and enforcement concerns (including the testimony of a former sex worker who stressed women's agency). During the evenings, the flirtatious energy was so thick in some quarters you could cut it with a knife. A young American working on trafficking in Asia (then heterosexual) offered other women massages and suggestive banter. The former sex worker fielded her own admirers. A Thai activist demonstrated something called a Thai kiss to a married woman from Eastern Europe, igniting a long-term relationship that, in turn, sparked interesting cross-region organizing between women who love women in the global South and transitional societies like the former Soviet Union.

This trafficking gathering illustrates the basic element of the erotics of NGOs: the quite simple observation that, over the past two decades, NGOs and their ilk have served as locations for an unprecedented range of national and transnational interactions that can often include (and, arguably, foster) erotic dimensions. Others have remarked on the ways that increased funding for HIV/AIDS has globalized the identity of gay and its corrective MSM category, prompted the expansion of what become defined as local identities, and provided spaces for male same-sex gatherings (Wright 2000; Altman 2001; Adams and Pigg 2005). My observations of more than a decade of participation with NGOs in Thailand, the US, and international fora, as well as second-hand reports, suggest that female-to-female flirtatious energy, affairs, and long-term romances are hardly uncommon to the world of women's NGOs.[2] Obviously, this is not true equally or everywhere. But in particular during the intense build-up of meetings and exchanges that characterized preparations for the 1995 Fourth UN World Conference on Women in Beijing (which included some of the earliest uses of the Internet to produce links of connected women's groups worldwide), erotic energies were a part of many encounters. This includes the "local" and national groups in some countries as well as mobilizations in such regions as Latin America and Southeast Asia. It also includes the kind of organizing that occupied the spaces of the transnational, the cadre of women who regularly attended international fora, the class whose full-time job at the UN or with international organizations, including donors, placed them in globe-trotting circuits.

This essay is predicated on this anecdotal observation, that there was an erotic component to the unprecedented scale of female homosociality within the 1990s to 2000s boom in NGOs. What to make of the erotics within what has been called "the NGOization of feminism" (Alvarez 1998)? One answer might be that NGOs offered spaces for lesbians to engage the public sphere, where they found some degree of acceptance (Swarr and Nagar 2004). Self-identified lesbians, often already embedded within national feminist movements, took part in the emergence of NGOs in many contexts. The flowering of women's intimate relations in the context of homosocial spaces of women's politicized public participation is not new. Leila Rupp has traced women's romantic pairings in early twentieth-century international women's movements, noting that, "[W]omen-only organizations offered an appealing haven for those who made their lives with other women, whatever the nature of their ties" (Rupp 1997b: 583). It seems true that the proliferation of women's organizations through targeted funding, the expansion of NGOs, and the expanded networks these facilitated offered a relative haven. But the concept of "haven" suggests pre-existing desires that find realization through a particularly safe venue.

Whether or not self-identified lesbians participated in the transnational NGO boom, it is also possible to view NGOs as a new mode of political practice (or governmentality) that generates social relations, desires, and practices. The flirtations I have known about – or the broader flows I am calling erotic – were hardly confined to, nor dependent on, self-identified lesbian participants. Certainly the erotic energy of the trafficking venue did not emanate from encouragement from the top. The main Thai organizer, while not herself virulently homophobic, had required some persuasion over time to transform her outlook on lesbianism and the place of sexual politics in feminist projects in Southeast Asia and internationally. Indeed, the demonstrator of the Thai kiss, an able organizer in her own right, was instrumental in nudging this leader and Thai women's organizations more broadly along this path. In this chapter I consider the erotics of women's NGOs by considering the spaces, scales, operations, and practices of NGOs. The predominantly homosocial space, the political nature of the event,[3] and its part in an ascendance of transnational women's organizing all produced a climate for these energies.

In studying the realm of NGOs, I have found it hard to avoid replicating established modes of analysis, versions of social movement theory (in which I have no training), or political critique. For this exploration, I bracket the question of the explicit politics of NGOs, their political ends, or an evaluation of their function within global governance, structural adjustment, or colonial discourse. The period I address, particularly the 1990s, saw the formulation of sexual politics as "sexual rights," particularly for women, for those associated with HIV/AIDS (e.g. sex workers and gay men), for gays and lesbians, and other "sexual minorities"

(Wilson 2002). One could evaluate NGOs in terms of their intentional political agendas, which engage sexuality although often in encoded ways. Yet in order to consider NGOs as social sites, I have found it necessary to introduce a pause between discussing these erotics and evaluating its political meanings or effects. I do not explore the relationship between articulated claims for sexual rights with the erotics of relations among those making the claims. The essay draws ethnographic directions that explore "global assemblages" (Ong and Collier 2005), networks, and the intersection of practice and space to address the erotic–politic linkages found in liberal modernist political projects such as NGOs or others addressed in this volume. To explore the erotics of contemporary global politics in this way is not to claim that NGOs are hotbeds of queer possibility; nor that they are inherently liberatory sites for sexual freedoms; nor is the presence of eroticism a claim for open-ended sexual liberties. NGOs, like broader modernist developmentalist projects, have their own regulatory regimes, as those working on HIV/AIDS organizing have noted (Wright 2000). Rather, it asks about the social life produced within the operations of a new political mode. My reference points are the NGO arenas I know best, supplemented by literature and reported anecdotes: national-level NGOs I have observed in Southeast Asia and transnational circuits of NGO workers, UN staff, and funders (and the scholars who study this world) in regional formations particularly in Latin America and Southeast Asia and at international formations, such as UN fora.

Actually existing

NGOs represent a particular organizational form, typically characterized by formal funding, paid workers, and volunteers, and advocacy role rather than a member organization (Alvarez 1998), and often by formal registration with governments or the United Nation (e.g. to obtain observer status or attend meetings). NGOs are characterized by the professionalization of political and social claims. They are predicated on and expand a sense of expert knowledge, formal norms, and state and inter-state politics, alongside an emergence of global governance. NGO networks are also produced by funding: "bilateral, multilateral, and private funders have all thrown their support behind efforts of global and regional coalition building" (Mendez 2002: 218).

The non-governmental organization has been heralded as the prevailing institutional manifestation of post-Cold War civil society. It allows translocal political relations outside of state and market,[4] a development that has been particularly pronounced for transnational feminist advocacy (Keck and Sikkink 1998; Merry 2006). For some, it represents the internationalization of new social movements (Sreberny 1998: 212). NGOs' capacities for networks are elements of a horizontal politics: international feminist organizing "is built upon grassroots organizations, which combine into networks, build networks of networks ..." (Sreberny 1998: 219). For Castells, new transnational networks "are the actual producers, and distributors, of cultural codes" (1997: 362).[5]

In contrast to the recognition of NGOs as a progressive expansion of civil society, critical perspectives stress NGOs' collaboration with governmental and capitalist projects. NGOs, with their experts, social services, and articulation with the state and United Nations, represent one facet of the global regulation of populations (or governmentality). In the case of feminist politics, the "NGOization" of feminism refers to the transformation of feminist movements (where they existed) into institutionalized forms (Alvarez 1998) as well as the proliferation of an NGO form of gender politics (where distinct feminist organizing may not have existed much at all). This process has been criticized as a manifestation of the logic of neoliberal modernity (e.g. Spivak 1996), a part of the "anti-politics machine" (Ferguson 1994). Speaking of large, well-funded NGOs in *Empire*, Hardt and Negri write, "NGOs are completely immersed in biopolitical context of the constitution of Empire" (2000: 36). They argue that "their legitimacy resides ultimately in the ends of their political design, that is, at the most basic level, the project to establish a liberal order for the global capitalist market" (Hardt and Negri 2004: 175). These criticisms elaborate on those that fault NGOs for professionalization and co-optation of movements by "femocrats" (Booth 1998), donor-driven goals, and distance from the grassroots.

Such critiques are examples of the political evaluations of NGOs that inform virtually all discussions of this arena. Whether heralding or bemoaning, the prevailing discussions of NGOs are conditioned by comparative contrasts, stated or implicit, with other modes of articulating social claims, whether unformed publics or dramatic radicalism. "Both agree," writes Anna Tsing in *Friction*, "that when liberalism spreads, it is completely successful in creating the subjects it conjures, for better or for worse. Liberalism's dreams are no different than liberalism's practice in these accounts" (Tsing 2005: 214).

Bracketing the comparative "doing good" question about NGOs' political effects (Murdock 2003), I focus on NGOs as actually an existing sphere comprised of sites and practices that are fostering subjectivities which may or may not bear relations to liberalism's dreams. Part of this direction represents an empirical issue, that is, the complex variation of NGOs as a field. Much of the critiques of NGOization focus on larger organizations of the sort that receive funding from USAID or the World Bank. Most of the NGOs I have known have been much smaller. A lesbian group from the Philippines, CLIC, for example, first registered as an NGO in order to attend the 1995 Beijing conference. The Thailand trafficking conference was organized by moderately sized Thai and European NGOs and led to the formation of another transnational NGO. A great deal of analysis treats NGOs "as essentialized categories" (Fisher 1998; see also Mercer 2002; Murdock 2003). For the social analyst, it is important to recognize that NGOs represent vastly different sizes – from CLIC to UNIFEM (United Nations Development Fund for Women). Moreover, transnational women's organizing does not have the centralized model of Greenpeace (Sreberny 1998: 213). Networks present a complex phenomenon: they are a means but also an end, which is already steeped in reflective awareness of the value of networks (Riles 2000: 51). The term also describes relations between people – grassroots activists, advocates, state actors, and donors, who are connected to and through NGO structures.

The approach to NGOs as erotic sites is not only an empirical claim but also an analytical move. As Tsing writes, "[u]nderstanding the spread of liberalism requires getting outside of liberalism's self-portrait" (Tsing 2005: 289). It is possible to recognize NGOs as part of neoliberal modernity and still inquire about interesting possibilities (or contradictions) emerging within and through them. To do so, it is not Hardt and Negri's critique of NGOs in *Empire*, but rather their "method of the tendency" in *Multitude* that provides a guide: "social theory must be molded to the contours of contemporary reality" (Hardt and Negri 2004: 140–1). NGOs, their offices, meetings, and networks, represent a current form of actually existing politics, sociality, and norms, as well as normativity.

Taking this perspective, we can consider the intimate relations within the operations of global governance. Indeed, we might see relations within NGOs as located in the articulation of non-governmental spaces with practices and logics of governmentality. The erotic energies of the trafficking conference in this view can be linked with funding networks and the realignment of state and non-state functions. Their relation to the stated politics – to NGOs' own ends or to projects of global governance – is an open question. At the same time, by not expecting coherence, uniformity in different registers of governmentality, we can see different articulations of the erotic in this arena.

Such articulation is perhaps easiest to see in the realm of discourse. Development policies are "secured upon social networks that constitute interpretive communities for projects and programmes" (Mosse 2005: 231). The UN-NGO orbit presents an interpretive community (or several communities). The NGO arena is also embedded in globalizing discourses about gender and sexuality. The growth of the homosocial spaces of women's NGOs, as with international women's organizing in the early nineteenth century, intricately involved commentary about participants' sexuality and women's sexuality in general, including ideas considered modern and enlightened and their counterparts (Rupp 1997b). The 1975 UN Conference on Women in Mexico City, for example, attracted critique for the presumed focus of northerners and feminists on "lesbians and prostitutes" (Olcott 2007). Women's NGOs are quite conscious of sexualized evaluations of women's organizations and often regulate their activities – at least in public – accordingly (Rothschild 2000). NGOs have also been critical in helping to shape transnational discourse about sexuality, including sex education, HIV/AIDS, and women's reproductive rights. The erotics of NGOs is produced by reflexive actors (Ong and Collier 2005; Tsing 2005) within and through these discourses (Adams and Pigg 2005).

Ethnographies of modernity

Recently, NGOs, like human rights and development organizations, have become the objects of research and critical analysis. The erotics of transnational liberal projects can be illuminated by ethnographic work that considers the investments and meanings for participants in globalizing forms of institutions and rhetoric.[6] A growing body of work makes modernist liberal projects of development, human rights, or NGOs, the object of analysis, and suspends the question of whether NGOs "do good" or an evaluation of the meanings or realization of their intents (e.g. Fisher 1997; Riles 2000; Murdock 2003; Choy 2005; Mosse 2005; Tsing 2005). Their focus is on the social world, social relations, and practices. Such work takes as given, but not necessarily as interesting, the well-known gap between rhetoric and action, or lofty goals and obvious failures. Nor is their main aim to chronicle the expanse of liberal global governmentality.

If we "consider nongovernmental organizations as one specific form of collective action and human community" (Fisher 1997: 459), we can ask, what erotic relations does this form allow, foster, or curtail? The quotidian operations of actually existing NGO projects present both normative erotic alternatives and queer possibilities.[7]

One way to cast the erotics of NGOs is to view them as modern social spaces on par with other sites of modernity – factories, malls, or dorms. (The conference on trafficking in women took place in a university and so we were housed in dormitories, representing a convergence of modern arenas for same-sex sociality.) Scholars of Thailand have noted same-sex relations and the presence of tomboys in the modern venues of the factory and the shopping mall (Sinnott 2004; Wilson 2004). New forms of collectivity, like factories, have generated modes of intimacies that may seem apart from regulatory disciplines, and often underwrite resistance to it, but the social relations are shaped by the simultaneous liberties and constrictions of those new spaces.

The proliferation of NGOs introduced national and transnational homosocial spaces for women on an unprecedented scale. This is particularly true at the transnational level of regional and international meetings, where tens of thousands of women met across national borders. Few, if any, other auspices allow so many women to be abuzz together in one place. The proliferation of NGOs and international events provides new sites for – and generates – relationships among women. Thirty-thousand participants, mostly women, attended the NGO forum outside Beijing at the 1995 UN conference. In quasi-public spaces away from kin, religion, and conventionally defined community, women form relations with each other in relation to political goals. As a venue for interactions, international NGO gatherings are particularly salient among those from the global South. Activists from Thailand, for example, rarely encounter their counterparts in the Asia-Pacific outside of such regional and international occasions. Although they are profoundly shaped by Western-based powers, NGOs provide spaces for relations among non-Western women.

The social relations produced through NGOs and these international fora do not necessarily relate to, nor even necessarily match with, the purported rationale of the institution. There are hostilities and competition. The modes of interaction of many NGO workers can manifest classism or racism or, minimally, betray a democratic spirit with quite hierarchical or charismatic operations. But in conjunction with the hierarchies and regulations of the NGO arenas, as I have suggested, are erotic flows. The social relations of these events, and of the imagined and enacted networks, are not all asexual. The large projects of neoliberal modernity have unintended consequences: "the most important political effects of a planned intervention may occur unconsciously, behind the backs or against the will of the planners" (Ferguson 1994: 20).

The tacit politics of NGOs

Let me return to the trafficking conference, and other places of its ilk, where women have had occasion to erotically engage other women, under the roof of, though not necessarily under the political auspices of, non-governmental organizations.

Gay, lesbian, and queer geography has considered how nominally neutral spaces are shaped by, and structure, sexuality as either heteronormative or as dissident sexual sites (Binnie and Valentine 1999; Hubbard 2001). A number of case studies have shown how otherwise asexual or heterosexual spaces have been reconstituted to allow or signify same-sex sex, particularly male–male sexual encounters, for example in restrooms or public parks.[8] In Asia, tomboys (*tom*) and their feminine partners (*dee* in Thailand) use shopping malls or karaoke bars as spaces for romance and sociality (Sinnott 2004; Wilson 2004). Applying such feminist/queer ethnographic and geographic modes to NGOs means viewing these institutions as complex social sites that are shaped by their contexts but that also enable, or generate, erotic relationships, practices, and imaginings. NGO offices, as spaces for work, are spaces for identity, community, and pleasure (e.g. Jonsson 2001).

As the trafficking in women conference shows, some of the relations, practices, and identifications that unfold within their venues are homoerotic. I could chronicle other examples of female–female erotic exchange – flirtatious banter, short-term affairs at conferences, or long-distance relationships facilitated by meeting at international conferences. Some NGOs offer relatively safe, comfortable, or accepting spaces for queer women, butches, lesbians, or women who remain unmarried past the expected age. International feminist meetings offer one of the major ways to meet other women-loving-women, or lesbians,[9] or partners for flirtatious banter, from outside of one's country. The significance of the new NGO arena as an alternative translocal public arena is particularly weighted for women, who typically lack spaces comparable to men who have sex with men, gay men, or male-to-female transgenders in Southeast Asia or Latin America. In this way, NGOs offer counter hegemonic spaces, not by their stated political aims, but by virtue of being a modern, but non-corporate and non-state site. Here they resemble other spaces of modernity that have been used for erotic life, like factory dorms or public bathrooms.

At the same time, NGO spaces differ from so much of the public sphere that queer life has employed, which neoliberal capitalism has enclosed into private commercial structures.[10] NGOs' humble offices, adorned in earnest realist décor, lie beyond the contained commercial realms through which much of metropolitan queer life forges community, whether in Rio, Bangkok, or Manchester (Altman 2001). Especially when we consider the broader contexts for female–female sex or romance in terms of dominant economic, state, and sex/gender systems, NGOs can be read as sites of queer possibilities. Through them, the bolder women might be acting to "reterritorialize public spaces as sites of sexual diversity" in a way that asserts "that sexual 'others' have claims to citizenship alongside 'good' hetero-sexual subjects" (Hubbard 2001: 62). However, such public claims are more often confined within the spaces of accepting NGOs: one does not proclaim a pro-sex lesbian identity in the corridors of the UN. From a geographic perspective, how-ever, NGOs might be read as "ephemeral sites of freedom and control which could be used to create fleeting but transitory identifications out of which new identities and citizenship could emerge" (Hubbard 2001: 66).

The spaces of ephemeral freedom, the haven for same-sex intimacy, are also a site of regulatory norms. Women's NGOs are hardly free from homophobia or sex/gender norms and exclusions. One Filipina woman was fired from her organiza-tion when they learned she was a lesbian (Rothschild 2000). As a class process, professionalization recognizes certain forms of sexual expression as more accept-able than others. Arguably, where lesbianism is valued in the world of NGOs, it is most often the same-gender form of women loving women, as opposed to those forms that involve transgender identities or butch–femme relations (let alone sig-nifiers of dissident sexual practices like s/m). Whatever the attitudes of individual workers, women's NGOs claims to legitimacy often balance on the issue of sexual norms, whether for promoting lesbianism, abortion, promiscuity, or prostitution. Gay/AIDS organizations could be unwelcome to transgender m2f and uninvit-ing to heterosexually identified men who have sex with men (Wright 2000: 101). Some critics of international sexual rights organizing suggest that it imposes a heterosexual–homosexual binary on other cultures or shores up colonial discourse (Massad 2002; Hoad 2007).

Many have made the observation that NGO workers are often relatively privileged by class and social capital, as well as by race/caste/ethnicity within countries, and by national identities at the transnational level. The reproduction of social inequality involves sexuality as well: not only is the overall climate of the UN-NGO orbit heteronormative – as is most civil society (Hubbard 2001) – but where homosexuality is accepted, it is particular, classed and perhaps nationally recognized forms of erotic identity that are granted membership in this political sphere (Puar 2007). Other forms are excluded, even when they may be among the targeted populations of NGO projects.

NGOs' cosmopolitan class

I want to take the question of NGO class identity and its articulation with sexual identity in a different direction. Most NGO staff can be positioned in relation to a global economy oriented to service sectors and financial flows in systems of modernity that rely on flows of knowledge.[11] Read through the lens of global politi-cal economy, NGOs are expressions of this increased reliance of expert knowledge (or immaterial labor more generally). What is decried as the professionalization of radical activists is also the creation of a transnational sector of credentialed knowl-edge workers, part of a professional-managerial class whose alliances cut across private and public sectors.

Policy work is the labor of rhetoric, text, and representation. Many have bemoaned the endless textual productions of the NGO arena, like the development field. NGOs traffic in documents, representations, and rhetoric. The practices of representations of advocacy networks – including more conventional left movements like the organization of farmer/peasant groups, La Via Campesina – and practices of representation include "submitting proposals, organizing [sic] meetings, publishing newsletters or websites, drafting 'action platforms'" (Edelman 2003: 214) and, of course, fundraising. Rather than see such representational effort in a binary opposition with action, it should be understood as a crucial part of the struggle for the legitimacy and reproduction of policy work and NGO existence rather than concern with implementation per se (e.g. Riles 2000; Mosse 2005: 238).

As a vast sector, knowledge work represents a diffuse class that is a crucial part of contemporary capitalism and governance. Immaterial labor, according to Hardt and Negri:

> tends to transform the organization of production from the linear relationship of the assembly line to the innumerable and indeterminate relationships of distributed networks. Information, communication, and cooperation become the norms of production, and the network becomes its dominant form of organization ... This is indeed the key characteristic of immaterial labor: to produce communication, social relations, and cooperation.
>
> (Hardt and Negri 2004: 113)

They add, "[i]mmaterial production ... tends to create not the means of social life but social life itself" (Hardt and Negri 2004: 146). Speaking broadly, Hardt and Negri point to pervasive shifts in the production of subjectivities in relation to hegemonic power. To return to the specifics of NGOs, what their broad strokes suggest is that NGOs represent a mode of labor, regulation, and subjectivity that hinges on "information, communication, and cooperation."

What are the implications of the knowledge economy for sexuality? As I suggested above, part of the knowledge that NGOs traffic in concerns gender and sexuality, and expertise on gender-sensitive trainings or gender mainstreaming, incorporates sets of knowledge about sexuality as well. As reflexive actors, seasoned participants in international women's conferences themselves reflect on sexual knowledge in their work and identifications (or, one could argue, interpolate themselves in a globalizing sex/gender regime).[12] Their position as knowledge workers – engaged in a specific political milieu – generates a kind of sexual subjectivity.

The transnational NGO arena, including a globe-trotting set of advocates who frequent, or work at, international venues, best illustrate the sexual culture of the immaterial economy, because many of them share information and networks and attend the same meetings, which are complex events of overlapping formalized and informal domains. NGOs' knowledge workers are cosmopolitan: they "are not only at home in other cultures but seek out and adopt a reflexive, metacultural or aesthetic stance to divergent cultural experiences" (Featherstone 1990: 9). Throughout the conferences and meetings that punctuated the 1990s for internationally oriented

NGO workers, women who had not had relations with visible lesbian identifications learned to enact expressions of acceptance. Participants knew that this American women's rights advocate was partnered with this UN worker. International women's conferences created some sense of acceptance of visible lesbians or women's sexual relations with women, including affairs for heterosexually married women. The experiences in these international fora produced an epistemic community among progressive feminists characterized by at least a modicum of tolerance for or even a celebration of lesbianism or female–female sexuality. The class position of the immaterial NGO laborer entailed cosmopolitan erotic attitudes.

What I am suggesting is that an anti-homophobic stance in this transnational feminist arena be read not only as a function of explicit politics – as a result of struggles for sexual rights (though it is that, too), but also as a consequence of global class formation. Feminist organizing at the NGO-UN milieu fostered a climate that made identification as a lesbian possible – a certain kind of lesbian – at least within the NGO world, not necessarily when articulating with the governmental or UN circuits. Knowledge about sexuality, including both expert knowledge and everyday assumptions about the meanings and cultural capital of the erotic, are part of the global governance.

The erotics of NGOs

This NGO boom of the 1990s, associated with the rise of global governance, also represents the generation of new social spaces particularly for (usually elite) women. These spaces not only hosted, but also generated, relations along a spectrum of intimacy that traverse public/private divides. Same-sex relations have been produced in NGO offices, practices, networks, and meetings. Bracketing the NGOs as a political site in terms of enunciated political projects, this chapter has considered NGOs as sites of actually existing political praxis shaped by the tacit practices of modernity.

Let's be clear: NGOs are not sexy. Non-governmental organizations are an institutional form of the post-Cold War reformulation of state powers, social services, and political struggle. Circumnavigating the orbit of the United Nations, NGOs partake of the UN's language, full of short-lived acronyms and borrowed corporate terminology, and the particular bureaucratic logic, all expressed in the venue of the UN conference. Many NGO workers would be considered middle-class professionals, not an inherently sexy category. The aesthetic of the posters adorning the NGO office, or the newsletters or T-shirts, might be best described as earnest realism. The politics of NGOs, which is something more have written about than their aesthetics, lack the erogenous zeal of revolutionary struggle or electrified radical movements. In these ways, the explicitly political nature of NGOs mitigates their possibility as queer sites. In their day-to-day operations, NGOs lack passion. NGOization has been criticized for professionalizing grassroots activism, for working collaboratively with states and multilateral agencies, in ways that are seen to betray feminist principles and limit the prospects for social change. NGOs represent a loss of radical vision consonant with the more widespread perception that the possibilities of radical revisioning of society diminished in the post-Cold War period. If one were to think about queer politics as a form of radical aspiration, NGOs probably muster little enthusiasm.

At the same time, *because* of their progressive auspices, NGOs do not even offer the frisson of transgressive sex in an authorized institution or bureaucracy, like cruising the art gallery or a tryst in a storage room. Yet, almost because of this difficulty, I am interested in mustering energy to consider the queer prospects of NGOs, as a major expression of progressive politics worldwide. In some ways, this is about recognizing the diverse pleasures at play in political projects.[13] This is a way to ask about the queer possibilities of existing political spaces and institutions, especially transnational feminist ones, which means trying to identify queer possibilities in projects that are generated and constrained by the neoliberal or security-oriented new world order. Queering NGOs thereby critically engages the critiques of these projects: the "NGOization" of feminism, the expansion of human rights as an international, some say imperialist, regime, or what has been called a Gay International (Massad 2002).

I should note the risk this argument runs. Saying that women's NGOs might facilitate lesbian relations only confirms what homophobic conservative commentary has implied, whether in alarmist journalism about the invasion of lesbians into the UN World Conferences on Women,[14] or in voice pieces for politicized religions (i.e. fundamentalism). A report published by the International Gay and Lesbian Human Rights Commission, *Written Out*, has compiled evidence of how right-wing forces deploy sexuality to contain feminist and progressive efforts (Rothschild 2000). But is the assertion that feminism results in non-heteronormative sexuality actually wrong? Conservative fears that opening up opportunities for women, and dismantling patriarchal power structures, will result in women's greater sexual autonomy are, in fact, well founded. Moreover, the modernist spaces of schools, factories, and NGOs have often expanded the range of women's erotic intimacies.

I want to be clear that I am not trying to salvage the politics of NGOs.[15] Rather, I consider the social life within the actual existing sites of NGOs. Rather than evaluating their radicalism or lack, or argue for their function in global governance, this chapter asks, what kind of social life is liberal modernity generating? What is the place of erotics – particularly female–female intimacy – within and through the operations of global governance? This discussion just examines a different kind of sexual politics within transnational feminism.

James Ferguson argues that outcomes of development schemes that:

> at first appear as mere "side effects" of an unsuccessful attempt to engineer an economic transformation become legible in another perspective as unintended yet instrumental elements in a resultant constellation that has the effect of expanding the exercise of a particular sort of state power while simultaneously exerting a powerful depoliticizing effect.
>
> (Ferguson 1994: 20–1)

NGOs produce the unintended consequence of erotic female sociality. The rise of NGOs opened delimited sexual possibilities for (some) women. Thus, NGOs have at times realized – and possibly generated – political ideals in an unintended fashion, as existing spaces for sociality that offer conditions of pleasure for some.

Notes

1   A seed grant from the Ohio State University helped fund research on a different project – transnational sexual rights organizing – that provided much of the materials I draw upon here. I would like to thank Amy Lind for her interest in the piece. I have also benefited from presenting preliminary thoughts at the Gender Institute of the London School of Economics, the Cultural Studies conference at University of Arizona, and Rethinking Marxism Conference at University of Massachusetts-Amherst. Thanks to Kate Bedford, Suzanne Bergeron, Mary Margaret Fonow, and Yukiko Hanawa for comments and to Alexis Pauline Gumbs for help with the bibliography.
2   Although this paper is predicated on observations, ethnographic details will be sparse. Given the nature of this subject matter, concerning women's erotic relations with women, in quasi-public institutions, and sometimes concerning figures prominent on UN or national stages – in some senses, this material is not much more than a mode of gossip – I refrain from providing revealing information or revealing details. While this limits the vividness and concreteness of the cases, it is necessary for confidentiality. Moreover, the discussion I present here was formulated after the research, meaning that I did present questions about personal relations or sexual identity as central to my participation in this milieu at the time.
3   Some have suggested a link between the content addressed by the conference, trafficking, and the erotic energy I witnessed, suggesting a voyeuristic pleasure that has often been ascribed to regulatory sexual politics. It is possible and certainly women's NGO work is usually implicitly or explicitly connected with sexual knowledge: the link between sexual knowledge and desire is an interesting one (Adams and Pigg 2005). But this hypothesis that trafficking advocacy incites erotic desire does not match my experience of the event (which did not dwell on the sexual dimensions of trafficking) and moreover seems to suggest a repression hypothesis, where actors' political focus on a transnational system of exploiting female labor is reduced to sexual frustration.
4   Sreberny writes, "networks prefigure a global civil society, occupying a space ... between global markets and transnational corporate activity and the formal organizations that represent global political interests" (Sreberny 1998: 209).
5   The idea of the network as a pregiven reality to be discovered has been criticized by Annalise Riles, who suggests that knowledges of and aspirations for the network produce it (Riles 2000).
6   See Tsing 2005; Riles 2000; Jackson 2005.
7   This essay has not described the practical norms of transnational feminism. How are sexual norms produced through quotidian operations of NGOs, of banter over meals, decorating a new office, marking life events, and salutations? More attention to this informal dimension would reveal not only more examples of flirtation and sex – more gossip – but also a sense of the production of tacit norms and ideals about sexuality in progressive politics.
8   The geography of sexuality is a growing subfield of cultural or human geography and others working in queer studies have also taken up geographic perspectives (Bell and Valentine 1995; Binnie 1997; Hubbard 2001; Wilson 2004).
9   In the context of 1990s transnational feminist organizing, many NGO workers operating at the international level used the term lesbian to refer to themselves.

10 As places of employment, NGOs do not always require the nationalist or heteronormative identifications that employment in the state can. For example, in Thailand, work
for civil service (including teaching) as often in the corporate sector requires women
to dress in skirts or dresses, while NGOs do not have a gendered dress code.

11 For example, geographers have described the "role of worldwide social networks of
knowledge-based experts who have the resources and power (or access to power) to
impact on decisions in such arenas as foreign policy, economic policy" (Olds 2001: 26;
see also Castells 1989: 348).

12 Reflexivity in anthropology has shifted from a focus on the privileged position of the
researcher or ethnographic representation to the analytical attention to the ways that
anthropological knowledge is already embedded in the domains ethnographers are
studying (e.g. Riles 2000; Ong and Collier 2005; Tsing 2005).

13 For example, Mary Beth Mills has written about the pleasure of union organizing for
long-term activists in Thailand (Mills 2005).

14 Similar representations of the actual or presumed presence of lesbians occurred at the
UN women's conferences were present at the 1975 meeting in Mexico City (Olcott
2007) and in 1985 in Nairobi and 1995 at Beijing (Wilson 1996). For the transformation to concern about sexual deviance (from concern about heterosexual deviance to
lesbianism) in international feminism in the 1900s, see Rupp 1997b.

15 While I do not intend to be a defender of NGOs, I am sympathetic to accounts that insist
on the complexity of power and action even in the context of "global governmentality": recognizing, for example, that "a discourse of control may also be a discourse of
entitlement" (Mosse 2005: 238; see also Murdock 2003; Tsing 2005).

6 Promoting exports, restructuring love

The World Bank and the Ecuadorian flower industry

Kate Bedford

Introduction: development and heteronormativity

This chapter seeks to explore the sexualized nature of international development policies by utilizing the concept of heteronormativity. Heteronormativity refers to institutions, structures, and practices that help normalize dominant forms of heterosexuality as universal and morally righteous (Berlant and Warner 1998: 548). Proponents of the concept recognize that normative forms of heterosexuality change across time and space, and become hegemonic through profoundly political interventions. They also argue that use of sexuality as an analytic concept must be extended beyond LGBTQ people, and beyond interactions already marked as erotic, to consider the currently "unmarked" status of heterosexuality and the ways in which it is (re)produced in changing forms by political actors. Although much research has focused on states in this respect (Cooper 1995; Carabine 1996; Cohen 1997; Phelan 2000), many scholars recognize that the norms, institutions, and structures through which sexualities are reconfigured are also transnational in scope (Wilson 2004; Adams and Pigg 2005; Alexander 2005). Thus a key imperative of current research is to take international policy actors seriously as agents involved in the production, reproduction, and alteration of normative heterosexualities.

In this spirit I explore the sexualized policy impacts of the World Bank, the world's largest and most influential development institution.[1] This may initially seem a curious choice of institutional case study. The Bank can appear, to itself and many development critics, as a technocratic, economistic, passionless institution with narrow growth concerns – an organization wherein the "mess and goo" (Binnie 1997: 228) of sexuality seems manifestly absent. This (self-)perception belies the fact that the Bank is a leading international lender in reproductive health, and is increasingly involved in HIV/AIDS work. Rather than focus on such obviously sexual sites of policy engagement, however, I seek instead to elucidate the sexualized nature of the Bank's more mainstream economic activities. Specifically, I trace the connections between export promotion and the restructuring of intimacy as evident in Bank gender and development conversations about the flower industry in Ecuador. Using interviews with gender staff and flower industry promoters, along with analysis of Bank documents, I examine the sexualized claims made about floriculture, showing how export promotion activities are seen to generate multiple changes in men's and women's intimate behavior. In this way I seek to both queer conversations about exports, and to connect discussions of heteronormativity to the grounded loans, projects, and research activities of major development institutions.

Export orientation, floriculture, and gender

A tiny South American country with an unenviable reputation for recent economic and political chaos,[2] Ecuador's economy has been export-dependent for several centuries (Kyle 2000). However, emphasis on export promotion increased in the early 1990s, in line with broader neoliberal shifts involving critique of import substitution policies and renewed faith in export-led growth. Exports became regarded as, to use the Bank's terminology, one of the "Foundations of Ecuadorian Development" (Hachette 2003: 168). Trade reforms undertaken since that point have eliminated export taxes and licenses, reduced tariffs, and increased the role of private industries in export sectors such as petroleum.[3] Such reforms were heavily reliant on Bank pressure. Structural adjustment loans throughout the 1990s included pro-export measures as conditions (World Bank 1997a, b), and the Bank lent extensively to Ecuador to promote export diversification. In 1995, for example, it proposed the Export Development Project (later renamed the International Trade and Integration Project), lending US$21 million to increase international competitiveness through export promotion and trade reform (World Bank 1997a, b). Currently, the Bank is urging further reform of the petroleum sector, which constituted 40 percent of total exports in 2003 (Fretes-Cibils and López-Cálix 2003: 115). Non-traditional exports such as broccoli, software, and "Panama" hats – which originated in Ecuador – are also being actively encouraged (Fretes-Cibils and López-Cálix 2003, Ministerio de Relaciones Exteriores del Ecuador/CORPEI 2004); this sector grew from 8 percent of Ecuador's total exports to 29 percent between 1991 and 2001 (Hachette 2003: 165).

The flower industry has been one of the key beneficiaries of this restructured economic environment (Mena 1999; Palán and Palán 1999; Breilh and Beltrán 2003). Ecuador has become the world's third largest exporter of flowers, specializing mostly in varieties of roses. Plantations are concentrated in the mountainous areas north of the capital Quito, chosen for their conducive climate and good transport connections. This region is poor, and (not an unrelated fact) ethically diverse.[4] Rural areas are demographically dominated by Quechua-speaking indigenous people, and Afro-Ecuadorians from coastal areas are increasingly migrating to the urban centers of Highland provinces to seek work. When the milk industry – in which large landowners first sought out agro-industrial investment opportunities – suffered declining prices in the late 1980s, interest grew in flower production, and the industry expanded rapidly after Colombian producers began shifting location due to internal disruption. Between 1985 and 1997, the value of Ecuadorian flower exports grew from $0.5 million to $120 million, and the number of people directly employed by the industry rose from 6,700 in 1993 to 36,000 in 1998

(Colloredo-Mansfeld 1999: 11; Ministerio de Relaciones Exteriores del Ecuador/ CORPEI 2004: 21).[5] In 2003 exports of fresh flowers were valued at US$207 million (SICA 2006).

World Bank policies have greatly aided this sector, one it regards as "an excellent example in Ecuador of successful export entrepreneurship" (World Bank 1997a: 3). Floricultural industries were listed as one of the main beneficiaries of the funds given by the Trade and Integration Project to promote competitiveness and quality certification, for example (World Bank 2003a: 9, 13). The Bank has also aided floriculture through its more recent SICA project, which promotes agro-businesses in part through advisory councils giving producers, exporters, and investors a forum in which to discuss concerns and present recommendations. Floriculture has its own advisory council under this program.[6]

Moreover, the efforts of Bank macroeconomists to promote floriculture in Ecuador intersect with the institution's gender and development activities, on the grounds that exports generate women's employment and thus promote women's empowerment.[7] For example, the *Ecuador Gender Review* – the Bank's most important policy text on gender and development in the country – identified a link between export orientation and women's employment in rural non-farm activities, since "men have predominated in traditional industries, whereas women have concentrated in new sectors such as agriculture for exports" (Correia 2000: 37; see also Newman 2001: 2; Newman, Larreamendy, and Maldonado 2001: 11). This is particularly true of floriculture. In the late 1990s women accounted for two-thirds of employees in flowers (Newman, Larreamendy, and Maldonado 2001), and although this proportion has dropped, in some plantations women still constitute at least half of workers in flowers; in contrast women make up just 36 percent of employees in the modern sector overall, and 30 percent of employees in the agricultural sector (CONAMU 2003). The relative over-representation of women in flowers is due to lower wages, male migration from the area,[8] and a "nimble fingers" discourse familiar to feminist scholars of export orientation (Ong 1997; Talcott 2003) in which women are seen as better suited than men for delicate planting, weeding, and packaging operations. In contrast, men are over-represented in tasks considered dangerous and physically demanding, such as the construction of greenhouses and irrigation channels, and in fumigation (Newman, Larreamendy, and Maldonado 2001: 16, 28).

In short, then, floriculture is regarded by Bank gender staff as a key site for intervention, and it has been the site for important research into gender issues. For example, in 1999 the Bank undertook a quasi-experimental study in two similar regions of Northern Ecuador, one with flower plantations (Cayambe) and one without (Cotocachi), to ascertain the impact of women's work in floriculture. These areas are roughly 200 kilometers apart from each other, and, as the Bank's data description framed them, "are similar ecologically with each containing peri-urban centers in a main valley and disperse rural populations in the surrounding hillsides" (Newman 2001: 7). Two publications resulted from this research – an English language Bank discussion paper written by a Bank consultant entitled *Gender, Time Use, and Change* (Newman 2001) and a Spanish-language report, *Mujeres y*

Floricultura: Cambios y Consequencias en el Hogar (*Women and Floriculture: Changes and Consequences in the Home*) written by the consultant and two specialists employed by Ecuador's state feminist agency, CONAMU, and associated with Bank gender efforts (Newman, Larreamendy, and Maldonado 2001). The former report has more formal institutional weight than the latter, and was used to formulate *Engendering Development*, the Bank's most important DC text on gender policy to date. However, the two documents can be usefully read alongside each other, since they illuminate different elements of the research. For example, Newman's discussion paper relied heavily on economic argument and statistics, while more space existed in the CONAMU–Bank report for incorporation of interview data.

I wish to concentrate here on the links made in these texts between work in flowers and changes in the intimate sphere of sexual and intimate relations. I draw attention to four particularly salient claims about flower employment in this respect:

1   that it enhances women's sexual and intimate autonomy
2   that it makes women more attractive to men
3   that it strengthens families, through giving wages to altruistic women who share money with loved ones
4   that it domesticates and tames men, making them more loving partners and more willing to share in unpaid household labor.

I address these purported links between floriculture and sexuality in turn, explicating the Bank's position and exploring some of the empirical messiness involved therein. In this way I seek to demonstrate not only that Bank discourses about sexuality and export promotion are varied and sometimes competing, but also that the evidence on which they are based is, in places, seriously flawed.

Women's emancipation through intimate autonomy or happy couplehood?

The Bank's claim that women gained power in their intimate lives through work in flowers rests on standard neoclassical models of household bargaining, whereby self-interested individuals navigate personal relationships using available resources to press for preferences. On this basis employment empowers women simply because it gives them access to wages which improve their bargaining power. Thus the CONAMU–Bank report repeatedly affirmed the link between "economic autonomy and changes in status" (Newman, Larreamendy, and Maldonado 2001: 40), or between earning money and increased self-esteem and power as women gained independence from families and husbands. This position is nicely articulated in the text box on women in the flower industry contained in the Bank's 2004 poverty report on Ecuador, which concluded that "employment in the flower sector allowed women to view themselves, and their relationship with men, in a different light" (World Bank 2004c: 87). The CONAMU–Bank study included several quotations from workshop participants to reinforce this connection, such as: "a woman who is earning money can now impose her conditions, because she has become a little more independent," and "Now I earn money, and I command, and I do what I want" (Newman, Larreamendy, and Maldonado 2001: 41). The implications of this increased bargaining power were understood to extend to sexuality. The report claimed that women in the flower region were more likely to demand "respect" from men, by which they meant the right to have sex when they wanted to, rather than as an obligation (40). These women were also identified as having more control over contraception and fertility (81), and as being more likely to confront traditionally sexist behavior and to refuse to tolerate violence (83).

Put bluntly, the Bank does not have evidence for many of these claims linking economic to erotic autonomy. For example, the argument that women in the flower region assumed more control over their contraception and fertility – repeated in the conclusion to the CONAMU–Bank report as a finding of the study (Newman, Larreamendy, and Maldonado 2001: 81) – was speculative, since the research did not measure control over fertility. The authors also conceded that some women in the flower region lied to their male partners about their use of birth control because they were scared. Likewise the report stated merely that women in the flower regions were less likely to refuse to tolerate violence "at least in principle" (83), since they had no evidence linking lower abuse to wage earning.

These data confusions aside, however, what is most interesting about the Bank's comments on flower employment leading to intimate autonomy is their contested status. Were the Bank an unambiguously neoclassical institution, conversation about sexuality would be dominated by the claim that paid work led to individual erotic empowerment. However, that claim is a partial one, existing in unresolved conflict with a parallel discourse regarding the positive effects of the industry in generating loving partnerships and happy families. In part, this latter argument is a response to the fact that flower production is commonly associated with a range of negative sexual-social consequences in the region, including drugs, gangs, family problems, and brothels (Newman, Larreamendy, and Maldonado 2001: 30). Women employed in flowers are often locally viewed as sexually promiscuous given the mixed labor force in the plantations, leading to assertions that the industry is no place for women "of good manners" (respectable women, in other words) (31). Likewise plantations are seen by many as a cause of divorce and separation, facilitating affairs which destroy marriages (43). Mothers are also seen as overburdened with work such that their ability to properly raise their children is compromised (60). In these ways, flower employment is understood to undermine normative family formations and sexual moralities, by granting women excessive autonomy.

Bank gender staff have a complex relationship to these critiques. In some respects, as noted above, their research supports women who pursue their own destinies, and Bank staff can act as a corrective to some conservative critics of floriculture who endorse almost hysterical visions of imminent social collapse stemming from women's work. I never heard from a Bank employee that employment in flowers caused abortions or prostitution; that the industry was destroying the family; or that work in the industry caused women to throw their children in the rubbish – those discourses were limited to critics of the industry. Moreover the CONAMU–Bank report was concerned to disprove the belief that there is more infidelity in flower regions, showing that separation rates are the same for both areas (Newman, Larreamendy, and Maldonado 2001: 44).

That said, however, concerns about family breakdown certainly caused unease among Bank gender staff, such that policy-makers offered two counter-discourses: first, that the flower industry stimulates partnerships because women who work in it are attractive to men in the community; and, second, that it keeps families together. In a one-page discussion, the CONAMU–Bank report (with less formal institutional weight than Newman's Bank discussion paper) claimed that women working in flowers became more attractive to men because they mixed family love and independent wage earning. It argued that young men in the flower region: "have higher esteem for women who work for money (and) contribute to the house", and that they like "the appeal of having a stronger and more independent woman" (79). Men are thus enthusiastic to "court" such female workers (79). This clearly reinforces the sense that the autonomy on offer to women in floriculture is one that relies on, and reproduces, their commitment to male partners and thereby shores up normative intimate relations.

That said, however, more central to the Bank's gender and development conversation about flowers is the argument that the industry keeps existing families together. This argument rests partly on the claim that floriculture reduces male out-migration and enables poor people from other regions to move with their families intact (Newman, Larreamendy, and Maldonado 2001: 16). Most importantly, however, floriculture is understood to help families for the same reason that any industry employing women helps families – because women, always already connected to those families, will act altruistically to maintain them now that they have access to wages. Herein lies the core tension in the Bank's vision of empowerment through employment: between on one hand regarding women as self-interested autonomous actors enabled through wages to pursue their own destinies, and on the other regarding them as necessarily attached, by enduring love, to specific others with whom they will altruistically share their income. Thus the CONAMU–Bank report noted that women's wage earning in flowers has improved food availability and altered family spending habits, with more resources devoted to house repair, education, saving, and investing for the future (76). Conflict disappears in these conversations. The study argued that although most family members were opposed to women's work in the industry, "once they were working, the family discovered the importance of their economic contribution" (29) and became supportive. The family benefited from the increased resources, while women got more independence and strength (81); in essence, everyone won. Similarly, the study claimed that in Cayambe (a flower region) family planning "is a shared and consensual decision" (Newman, Larreamendy, and Maldonado 2001: 70). Assertions of women's increased power to control their fertility, and to have sex when they want to, hereby morphed into conflict-free assumptions regarding shared male–female decisions about intimacy. Incompatible preferences disappeared, replaced by a notion of negotiated bargaining that privileged notions of harmonious complementarity.

Again, empirical support for these claims can be tenuous. For example, the fact that more money is spent on clothes and desirable personal items for women in the flower region is underplayed, despite the challenge this poses to assumptions regarding women's loving altruism and its ability to diffuse objections about their employment. Most importantly, however, the Bank's research underplayed conflict in the home, a key consequence of women's work in flowers identified by many respondents. The CONAMU–Bank study included more references to conflict than the Bank discussion paper, acknowledging for example that marital discord could result from "the rapid change of relative power in the home" (Newman, Larreamendy, and Maldonado 2001: 78, also 11), and that industry could cause family strife through its long hours during peak demand periods (28). However, these conflicts were subsequently minimized. The chapter devoted to the effects of wages on women's status and the family included only one quote from a workshop participant relating to the negative effects of the industry, for example; eight were included for positive effects.

In addition, the Bank focused disproportionate attention on married women in flowers, wrongly assuming in many cases that all women in the industry are married. Consider, for example, Newman's claim that:

> As in more developed countries, married women's participation in paid labor has risen rapidly around the world, especially in export niches like that of Ecuadorian flowers. In Ecuador, the flower industry is only ten years old. Before it developed, women in these same rural areas had little if any paid employment.
>
> (Newman 2001: 3)

This slippage between married women and women in general helps the case that employment empowers women, because Newman's research found that while men are paid more than women in flowers, married women actually earn more than married men. However, the slippage is empirically suspect, and may conceal a key effect of floriculture employment on intimate relations – that it stops women from marrying. Notably, marriage rates are lower in the flower region, in part due to the generally younger age of the population, but as the CONAMU–Bank study recognized, "marriage rates are even lower for women who work in flowers. In addition there are more single women in Cayambe, and more working in flowers" (Newman, Larreamendy, and Maldonado 2001: 19). Neither study asked why, perhaps because the prevalence of single people would reinforce ideas regarding the undesirable consequences of the industry in undermining normative attachments. Furthermore, neither study explored the challenge this finding posed to the assumption that access to a wage leads women to share their income with those they love, hereby empowering their families in addition to themselves.

To reiterate, then, the Bank's vision of women's intimate emancipation through flower employment is a profoundly confused one. References to women going against family wishes, controlling their own fertility, and choosing their own erotic destinies exist in unresolved tension with a notion of women's autonomy resting on necessary attachments to specific intimate others. The Bank also frames the industry as a dating service *par excellence*, and working women as linchpins of family stability and survival. This tension is indicative of a deep unease within the Bank, and in floriculture regions more generally, that the industry may undermine normative relationships, one that is also evident in discussions about the sexualized impact of floriculture on men.

Flowers and the market generation of modern masculinity

In many respects, Bank gender staff foreground men in their work on flowers, arguing that "the presence of flower employment opportunities has had more of an impact on men than on women" (Newman 2001, 22). Specifically, they argue that the flower industry has increased the involvement of men in housework, a fact that should be celebrated as a solution to long-standing tensions between paid and unpaid labor. Feminist political economists have argued for decades that mainstream economics in general, and Bank development activities in particular, discount the importance of the unpaid caring labor done disproportionately by women. Thus many have argued that women are overburdened when they are forced into the labor market through economic necessity in the absence of policies to provide for the realities of human dependency (Waring 1988; Benería and Feldman 1992; Folbre 1994; Sparr 1994; Elson 1996; Léon Trujillo 2001; Peterson 2003; for specific critiques of the Bank in this respect see Kuiper and Barker 2006). That the Bank's research on flowers found men shifting time-use patterns to pick up the slack of care needs previously met by their wives was thus a startling one. In fact, this was the most important finding of Newman's research, emphasized in the opening summary, the abstract, and the overview of the report provided by the Bank in publication materials (Newman 2001, np – abstract).[9] For example, the first finding mentioned in the conclusion to the related discussion paper was as follows:

> The most compelling evidence of the industry's impact (on gender relations) is on married men's increased participation in housework. Married men in the treatment group (the flower region) spend double the time in housework, and this is clearly related to women's increased participation in the labor force.
>
> (24)

Specifically, the study found that men with working wives in the non-flower region worked 32 minutes a day in housework, while men with working wives in the flower region worked one hour (12). Moreover:

> Married male household heads who work in flowers do more housework than married male household heads who work in other sectors, 69 compared to 47 minutes … *Married and working male household heads do the most housework of any group of men when they work in flowers and their wives do*

too, 77 minutes. When men work in flowers and their wives work in another sector or not at all, their time in housework goes down to 36 minutes. When married male household heads work in another sector, but their wives work in flowers, their housework time is up to 69 minutes. *Overall, these data suggest that participation of either one or both of the spouses in flower employment increases men's time in housework significantly more so than work in other sectors of the economy.*

(12–13, emphasis added)

The CONAMU–Bank report repeated all of the above figures. It also included quotations claiming that men help more in flower regions, to wash clothes, to care for children, and so on; that young children in flower regions do not consider domestic labor women's work because they see their fathers doing it (Newman, Larreamendy, and Maldonado 2001: 58); and that social norms defining men as the family provider have been changed by women's employment, leading women to question their home obligations and leading men to start to share, "little by little," in domestic work (82–3). In these ways Bank staff assert that floriculture helps generate responsible men, and new types of gendered partnership involving two-worker, two-carer couples.

While this celebration of how floriculture produces loving family men merits wide-ranging critique, I focus here on just two areas of concern, regarding the model of masculinity upon which the claim rests, and the dangerous policy implications of the argument. First, the approach reinforces some troubling assumptions about poor masculinity. Poor World countries in general are framed as more sexist than Rich World ones, since market integration is understood to promote more egalitarian gender relations. Newman argued, for example, that "while it is true that roles in many developing societies are more narrowly defined for women, pressures from modernization are provoking swift changes" (Newman 2001: 3). In particular, men in poor countries are understood to contribute less to domestic labor than men in richer nations (Newman 2001: 10; see also Newman, Larreamendy, and Maldonado 2001: 52). Shifts in gender roles, and in normative forms of couplehood wherein men share caring work, are hereby framed as a result of modernization and the market, closing gaps that mark less developed societies.

Moreover, poor men within all countries are framed as more sexist than their better-off brothers. This is a key reason why involvement in floriculture is understood to generate changes in intimate attachments: because it offers poor women jobs and thereby alters the attitudes and familial behaviors of poor men, a group already seen by Bank gender staff as in particular need of change. Although the men and women who work in flowers are, as one Bank employee emphasized, hardly the poorest of the poor from the worst land in the mountains, they are nonetheless subject to the pathologizing perceptions about rural people, indigenous people, and the poor held by many development professionals. For example, I was repeatedly told that flowers had a positive impact in the region by giving money to women, crucial because men there drank their money rather than invest it lovingly in the family. As one floriculture specialist put it:

> ... and what is interesting is the subject of gender, is how when the woman receives the salary she shares it with the family, because another problem in the lower classes is that when the man receives it he simply wants to get himself drunk, (going) drinking ...

Although this individual did not work with the Bank I heard similar framings of poor male irresponsibility from people who did, and several Bank staff expressed interest in projects working with poor men to reform their alcoholism, violence, and fathering practices.[10] The Bank's work on flowers thus involved a series of negative assumptions about backward masculinities being linked to levels of development, ones central to the argument that floriculture would help produce more caring men through modernizing their attachments to their families.

Given these claims about poor men as particularly lazy, sexist, and uncaring, it is important to note that the Bank's research on flowers proved exactly the opposite with respect to caring labor – that men in richer families did *less* housework (Newman 2001: 21). Likewise, the report found that:

> single men in the control group (non-flower region) do more housework on average than single men in the treatment group (flower region), so the average housework for men as a whole is slightly lower in the treatment than in the control. This is probably due to the fewer job opportunities in the control group.
>
> (14)

Unemployed poor men were *more* likely to participate in domestic labor here, a finding that should not surprise mainstream economists. Any consistent application of neoclassical principles of utility maximization will predict that, with wives' employment held constant, richer men (whose time is more valuable) will be less likely to give it up to engage in unpaid domestic labor and more able to shirk responsibility by passing it off onto servants. The expected relationship here between development, wealth, and failure to care for one's family should be precisely the reverse of what the Bank predicted – a reversed reality that was in fact supported by the data.

Second, the focus on floriculture's reframing of masculinity endorses an extremely troublesome solution to tensions between paid and unpaid labor, one which decenters discussions about public policies and reinforces the (re)privatization of caring work. According to the Bank, the fact that married women earn more than married men in floriculture encourages their husbands to divert activities to domestic labor, since "as their wives' paid labor becomes more valuable, the men shift some of their own relatively less valuable time into housework" (Newman 2001: 13). Thus, tensions between paid and unpaid work do not actually require concrete policy solutions, since once married women's labor time is made more valuable, their husbands will automatically pick up the slack resulting from women's move into employment. Although this "little by little" process is acknowledged to be very slow, the only mention of policy interventions to deal with the problem is footnoted.

In a reference to a study on domestic labor in Finland and Australia, Newman recognized that Rich World gender differentials in housework are declining *so* slowly that "a complete re-negotiation of the division of domestic labor is not realistic in the short term, and that public policies are needed to redress the gender imbalances" (Newman 2001: 3). No further discussion is provided. With conversation about public policy interventions hereby silenced, responsibilities for caring labor are in effect (re)privatized into a model of the family that relies upon two working/loving partners integrated into both the productive and reproductive spheres of the economy. To reiterate, the partners are not *equally* integrated into such spheres – women's altruistic love for dependents is still assumed to outweigh men's. But nonetheless the resolution of tensions between paid and unpaid labor, between productive employment and family survival, rests on the fact that floriculture is seen to produce sharing couples consisting of altruistic women and newly domesticated men.

This imagined resolution merits contestation in part because it is not true. The Bank's own research showed that floriculture regions are home to disproportionately high numbers of single people and female-headed households. The institution's focus on how floriculture reinforces normative family attachments is thus a partial one reliant on the erasure of non-normative people. Space is hereby curtailed for examination of floriculture's more complex effects on sexuality – on how it may generate sex workers, divorced women, single mothers, and (even) gays and lesbians, for example. Considerable research points to the varied and contested effects of women's employment on their intimate attachments in this respect, confirming that global capitalism can reshape family bonds in complex ways (D'Emilio 1983; Wilson 2004; Mills 2005). The Bank's unidirectional tale is thus a simplified one belied by its own data.

Moreover, the Bank's celebration of floriculture and family is troubling because it reveals how heavily some feminist visions of emancipation rest on investments in sexual normativity. Happy, sharing couples are held up as the epitome of gender and development success, and this is an extremely dangerous policy for all those committed to securing individual rights to control their intimate lives. What, one may ask, happens to single people in this model? How are they to juggle paid and unpaid labor demands? What happens to those who choose non-normative intimate attachments? What happens when those *in* normative partnerships are widowed, divorced, abandoned, fired from their jobs, or abused? How can policy-makers frame efforts to enhance women's autonomy by enabling them to break coerced intimate attachments in this environment, one in which people's survival is understood – *by gender specialists* – to be legitimately contingent on their adherence to a purportedly empowering model of heteronormative partnership? That floriculture may not actually produce the intimate rearrangements celebrated by these Bank texts, then, is in many respects beside the point; the Bank's desire for this outcome is a troubling one that warrants contestation. Specifically, enthusiasm for the industry's generation of normative intimacies undermines arguments for concrete policy interventions to resolve caring labor dilemmas, and instead champions privatizing solutions that further narrow space for alternative sexual possibilities. Reimagining queer development futures will require a very different approach.

Conclusion and further implications

This chapter sought to explore the intersections between export promotion and sexuality in development by examining how World Bank gender staff understand the role of the Ecuadorian flower industry in the reformulation of normative heterosexuality. Their research argues that floriculture employment empowers women in highly intimate ways, yet it rests on a conflict-ridden approach to autonomy and is inconsistent in its framing of women's loving attachments. Most often, however, straightforward neoclassical arguments about individual empowerment through wages are less prominent than arguments celebrating the role of floriculture in strengthening families, with women's love as the crucial conduit. Bank staff also link flowers to the market generation of modern masculinity in which caring, loving men are reattached to their families. Sharing couplehood is hereby valorized as the ideal solution to the crisis of caring labor provoked by women's entry into paid employment, a definition of success that is not only immune to data, but which reflects some troubling investments in (re)privatization agendas and the celebration of normative sexualities.

Aside from concerns about the Bank, exports, flowers, Ecuador, or gender policy, however, I wish to close by considering how this case study may relate to the broader project of queerying development. First, it clearly confirms (along with many other chapters in this anthology) that multilateral development institutions are important policy agents involved in the reformulation of normative forms of heterosexuality. One does not need to (only) look to institutions that are explicitly targeting sexual minorities here, and neither does one need to (only) examine lending in sectors that are always already marked as sexual sites. This discussion has focused on women's employment and export promotion, not HIV/AIDS or reproductive health, and (in-jokes about gay men and flowers notwithstanding) queer folk are considered absent in this Bank research. Yet seeking out these unmarked policy sites where multilateral institutions address people they assume to be straight people may be a key component of queerying development. As many scholars interested in state projects of heteronormalization have noted, social policies aiming to reinforce normative arrangements of intimacy are rarely marked as sexual interventions precisely because they deal with normative expressions thereof. As Davina Cooper notes, they are thus "naturalized into invisibility" (1995: 69), or seen as simply commonsensical. This is a key reason why the Bank's celebrations of loving partnership generate so little comment or criticism, their reliance on apparently uncontestable appeals to normative family formations and loving couples rendering them simply unremarkable. While this reality should not eclipse the crucial role of research on self-identified LGBTQ populations, it does confirm the importance of looking beyond marked minorities to generate a comprehensive discussion of queerying development.

Second, the research confirms the importance of looking at men in a project oriented to queerying development, particularly at those men who the Bank are interested in changing – the poor, straight men who are persistently framed as lazy and unreliable, as drunks, as violent policy problems, as needing to work harder to generate the gender equality being sought by multilateral institutions. Again there is a common-senseness to this framing that warrants closer interrogation. For example, some recent anthologies have drawn attention to troubling representations of poor men in gender and development policy discussions, and to the colonial resonances of those portraits (Jackson 2001; Cleaver 2002). However, these investigations have not typically been linked to sexuality studies literature, or to the way in which heteronormativity is (re)imagined in relation to men's bodies, desires, and responsibilities. In this respect, then, in looking at how development can be queered, it is helpful to keep in mind Sharon Marcus' insistence in a recent overview of queer theory in *Signs* that "the sexualities we consider normal and think we know best are ... those we understand the least" (2005: 213). She thus demands attention to male heterosexuality, in order to contest "its status as universal, normal, homogeneous, predictable, and hence immune from investigation" (213). Looking at the World Bank confirms the value of looking at how men's ideal sexuality is being re-thought by one of the world's key development policy actors – and how that process of gendered heteronormalization requires some queer disruption.

Notes

1 The "World Bank" refers to the two most prominent agencies in the World Bank Group: the International Bank for Reconstruction and Development and the International Development Association.
2 Ecuador had five different presidents between 1988 and 1999, and its two most recent leaders were overthrown in coups – one of them after announcing (without consulting the US Federal Reserve) that the country would dollarize in the midst of an economic crisis. See North 2004 for a concise overview.
3 I trace this process, and the role of the state therein, in Bedford 2005a, but see also World Bank 1997a; Treakle 1998; Carriére 2001; Ferraro 2000; Cox Edwards in World Bank 1996; Beckerman and Solimano 2002.
4 The 2001 census claimed that 7 percent of Ecuadorian people were indigenous and 5 percent were Afro-Ecuadorian, but indigenous organizations claim that they represent a third or more of the population (World Bank 2004a; Collins 2004: 39). While 46 percent of Ecuadorians are poor according to recent national poverty measures, indigenous poverty rates are around 86 percent (World Bank 2003b: n.p.), and "indigenous and afro-Ecuadorian people have the worst living conditions, the lowest schooling levels with inappropriate educational systems, serious unemployment levels, minimal access to health services, and (face) severe social and economic discrimination" (Government Implementation Completion Report in World Bank 2003b: n.p.).
5 Flowers also generate indirect employment through transport needs, infrastructural requirements, and so on. ExpoFlores, the industry's export association, claims that 500,000 workers are associated with the industry in these ways.
6 SICA is the Servicio de Información y Censo Agropecuario (Agricultural Census and Information System Service). One can access the project's reports and advice on improving competitiveness in flowers at http://www.sica.gov.ec/agronegocios/consejos_consultivos/consejos/flores/principal.htm
7 This trope of paid labor as empowering to women is central to the Bank's current gender and development efforts; see Bedford 2005a. On this issue within gender and development theory see Zein-Elabdin 2003, Charusheela 2003; Barker 2005. Feminist scholars also highlight the gendered nature of many export industries; see Barndt (1999) and Méndez (2002), for example.

8 Some estimates suggest 25 percent of the country's total population has emigrated in the last two decades, most frequently to Spain, Italy, and the US (North 2004: 203). Male migration is particularly common in the Sierra; for example, I was repeatedly told that microenterprise projects in the region were directed at women by default, because all the men had left.

9 Institutionally sensitive reading practices should direct attention to the abstracts, summaries, and conclusions of Bank documents, since these are often the only parts read by busy staff.

10 I trace these initiatives elsewhere (Bedford 2005a, 2005b; 2007). They are less relevant in flowers because floriculture is essentially seen to have made them redundant, having generated changes in masculinity through market mechanisms.

7 "Headless families" and "detoured men"

Off the straight path of modern development in Bolivia[1]

Susan Paulson

The millennium has dawned on a new kind of revolutionary era in Latin America, an era in which new forms of organization and civil society are challenging the modern development visions and neoliberal policies that dominated the late twentieth century. This chapter analyzes select development initiatives that imposed normative models of family and sexual identity; describes practices and sites of everyday non-conformity that have been largely ignored by these initiatives; and links these local practices to emerging social movements.

Development policies and projects pursuing a variety of ostensibly unrelated goals have disseminated certain family models that – in a nation made vulnerable by widespread poverty, political instability and foreign interests – have impacted Bolivians' most intimate practices and relations. This chapter highlights mechanisms through which normative assumptions have worked to discriminate against a significant part of the population, as well as ethnographic descriptions of alternative forms of affection, affinity, and domestic collaboration among two non-normative groups. First are women who manage households that are variously labeled "headless," "incomplete," "single-mothered," or "broken" because the dominant male is perceived to be missing; and second are men who sexually desire other men, and who are sometimes labeled "detoured," "alone," "sissy," or "inverted" because they have not achieved the role of patriarchal heterosexual head of family.[2]

The idea that monogamous heterosexual marriage marks the zenith of civilization, culminating in a development path begun long ago by promiscuous hordes, is no longer embraced by most anthropologists, who tend toward more relative and contextualized views of sexuality and kinship. Yet public discourse and policy about marriage and family in the United States and Bolivia indicate that not everyone has made this shift. Forty-one US states have recently passed laws and amendments that narrow the definition of marriage (Chronicle of Higher Education 2005), expressing a desire to curb variation and codify an ideal family model constituted by one man, one woman, and their legitimate children, even though less than one-fourth of US households are constituted by such families (Schmitt 2001).

In Bolivia, constitutional revisions approved in 1994 established a "new" multicultural and pluri-ethnic nation, and consequent media campaigns and educational reforms worked to raise awareness about cultural and linguistic diversity. Yet the homogenizing idea that "*la familia boliviana*" is based on a married couple with children continues to be advanced by surprisingly diverse parties including national family law, catholic catechisms and sermons, indigenist movements that idealize "Andean complementarity," feminist organizations that locate gender-based oppression in conjugal relations, and national and international development programs that use the nuclear family as the principal unit of analysis, benefits, and accountability. This image is reinforced via what Appadurai (1996) calls "mediascapes," as billboards, consumer products, television stations, and school supplies broadcast images of families ranging from the stone age *Flintstones* through the contemporary *Simpsons* and futuristic *Jetsons*, all constituted by monogamous heterosexual matrimony and legitimate children, living in private uni-family homes, protected by a faithful dog or dinosaur. These mass messages eclipse realities of most Bolivian households, two-thirds of which (67.6 percent), according to the most recent census, are not constituted by nuclear families (INE n.d.: 64).

In recent decades, some of the same forces have disseminated a complementary model that has also come to be applied as if it were a descriptive category. Starting in the mid-1980s, international development funds were directed to the Bolivian Ministry of Health for HIV/AIDS awareness and prevention campaigns that worked with gay rights organizations and international media to bring new ideas about sexual relations and identities into social consciousness. Among them is the notion of a kind of man called "homosexual" or "gay," an independent entity with a fixed sexual nature defined by preference for same-sex partners that (in a modern society) should correspond with a marked social identity. This category is expedient for bureaucrats responsible for counting and managing target sectors of the population. And, like versions of strategic essentialism embraced by indigenous and women's movements in Bolivia and elsewhere, the idea of "gay" as a distinct and inherent type of being can facilitate a sense of natural community or motivate joint political action. In practice, however, the notion has not resonated readily with the ways in which Bolivians experience sexual desire or organize social behavior and relations.

The problem is that development initiatives do not present categories of "family" and "gay individual" as *heuristic devices* used to make a culturally diverse population more legible and manageable for development purposes, nor as *prescriptive* visions used to promote the global expansion of certain cultural ideals. On the contrary, they are widely portrayed and understood as *descriptive* models useful for extending services, rights, and benefits to existing populations. This chapter strives to highlight contradictions between heteronormative and homonormative development models and the actual practices and meanings of people in Bolivia, where the need to understand "alternative" identities and relationships is particularly urgent in light of Bolivia's restless civil society and rapidly changing political scene, marked by the demise of traditional bastions of social organization, including political parties, unions, and conventional families. In this context, non-normative, or queer, forms of organization and affinity are gaining new relevance and impact, bolstering Lind and Share's (2003: 57) call for efforts to "queer development" by rethinking models and places of sexuality and gender in development practices, theories, and politics.

Queer analytical framework

Before presenting the cases studied, we set the scene with a brief discussion of this chapter's unconventional analytic approach, some key anthropological concepts, and historical context.

It may seem queer to include in the same analysis rural women who head households, urban men who sexually desire men, and development initiatives from different decades. These phenomena are rarely addressed in the same studies or policies, and tend to be relegated to different academic realms and literatures (women's studies, homosexuality studies, development studies). My unconventional framework is inspired by Bolivia's remarkable social movements, where creative collaborations across difference are advancing intersectional critiques of conventional models and forging new kinds of proposals. Later in this chapter, we explore ways in which expressions and actions of "headless families," "detoured men," and others contribute to what Guillermo Delgado (2006: 18) describes as "transcommunal approaches" in which diverse ethnicities, feminisms, sexualities, and subaltern classes draw from their own positions and environments to articulate responses to related histories of invisibility and exclusion and to threats from the homogenizing bulldozer of modern development.

The situations of women heads of households and men who sexually desire men are not parallel, nor are they two sides of a coin. I ask how exclusion from normative models of identity, sexuality and relatedness, as well as participation in alternative forms of the same, are experienced by people of different gender and sexual identities and varied locations in the nation. At the same time, I consider how these experiences are connected as parts of a Bolivian landscape shaped by colonialism, inequality, and poverty, and by an ongoing push for modern development common to many parts of the world. In order to illuminate connections in this multi-sited and cross-time framework, I draw from a series of ethnographic studies (Paulson 2000 and 2007; Paulson and Bailey 2003).

Anthropologies of relatedness

Amid public debates on family and sexuality, anthropologists are questioning the paradigmatic status that marriage has held in scholarship as well as in policy. John Borneman argues that a tradition in which "anthropologists have read 'marriage' backward in time and across the universe" (1996: 219) has contributed to empirical neglect of people who are not married and of other forms of affinity, and has hindered our ability to theorize human sociality. Roger Lancaster (2005: 23) argues that a search for human universals has driven ethnographers to see marriage everywhere, observing that "Lévi-Strauss thought that if he could isolate the most 'primitive' or 'elementary' form of kinship, he would capture, like a fly in a bottle, what was most 'universal' about the subject."

Redressing a fixation on marriage that has caused scholars and policy-makers to misread or neglect other forms of culturally organized intimacy and relatedness requires theoretical as well as empirical work. Borneman draws from queer theory to destabilize dualisms (married–unmarried, hetero–homo, civilized–uncivilized) that have structured scholarly analysis, while Judith Butler (2002: 15) forges a new conceptual approach in which kinship is no longer seen as an autonomous institution, distinct from community, friendship, and state regulation.

Whereas kinship theorists had narrowed "affinity" to refer almost exclusively to relations established through heterosexual marriage, recent ethnographies generate new ways of looking at this basic concept. Kath Weston's landmark study *Families We Choose* (1991), describes ways in which lesbian and gay families build kinship networks through choice and love, while Ellen Lewin's books on lesbian mothers (1993) and on lesbian and gay commitment (1998) situate non-heterosexual families in the context of US cultural values and practices. Reviewing ethnography of "woman-headed" Afro Caribbean households, Evelyn Blackwood found forms of affinity similar to what I see in Bolivia: "Feminist researchers documented households shared by two adult women (sisters or mother and daughter) and their children (Barrow 1986), by consanguineal units of related kin (González 1984), and by adult kinswomen with kinsmen and close women friends who were regularly present (see Monagan 1985; Bolles 1996)" (2005: 8).

Recent thought on masculinities also help move beyond marriage as the defining institution. In the rich volume *Changing Men and Masculinities in Latin America*, Matthew Gutmann (2003: 3) emphasizes that male roles and expectations are not simply expressions of marriage/family relations, but integral to institutions and ideologies built into unequal structural foundations of local and global society. By exposing the trope of the "patriarchal heterosexual male" whose desire and power are widely (albeit implicitly) understood as fundamentals of all marriage and kin systems, Blackwood (2005) reveals that the prominence of this figure has blinded us to empirical realities of other men and families, such as those she studied in the Caribbean.

> Men in these kin networks cooperated with and assisted in the economic and social lives of their kin, but they were neither dominant nor decision makers. Few stories have been told about these men's lives because they have been viewed as failures, as men who did not attain the patriarchal norm. Consequently, anthropology's study of men and masculinity has yet to attend to the diversity of men's gender relations.
>
> (Blackwood 2005: 9)

Assumptions about the primacy of male desire seem to contribute to serious contrasts in the literature I consulted for this study. Whereas sexual desire and pleasure are central to scholarly writing on male homosexuality, they are virtually absent in literature on woman-headed households, in which economic need and child survival are driving factors. Jolly (2000 81) observes that the absence of sexuality from development agendas conveys the assumption that, while people in the global North need sex and love, people in the global South just need to eat, and explores vital challenges of addressing sexual issues in international development without imposing Western concepts and agendas, be they heterosexual, homosexual, or queer. While cross-cultural scholars scorn the universalizing assumptions about marriage and family that dominate US politics, surprisingly little critique has been voiced about teleological tales of socio-sexual evolution in which people in all societies should develop a certain type of homosexual identification, lifestyle, and rights.

These new efforts to see and theorize kinship and gender help us to rethink the ways and meanings through which Bolivian women and men build relatedness. One feature that emerges as notable in these studies is the importance of culture-specific forms of commensality, and specifically *compadrazgo*, a sacralized system of affinity common in many parts of Latin America (which anthropologists used to call "ritual kinship"). Another is the context-specific identification among people with parallel experiences of marginalization.

Making nation through normative men and families

Like those in other postcolonial societies, Bolivia's leaders strove to make certain models of gender and sexuality compulsory through public education and extension programs (Larson 2005) and military service (Gill 1997). After World War II, new kinds of international policies and programs worked to disseminate and normal-ize certain family and sexual relations among populations around the world. The 1948 Universal Declaration of Human Rights helped to spread marriage as a global ideology and legal category;[3] starting in the 1970s, anti-discrimination initiatives advocated women's rights to voluntary and equitable marriage;[4] and beginning in the 1990s, HIV/AIDS prevention programs advanced the relatively new category "homosexual/gay" as an alternative identity and set of rights. Implicit in these ini-tiatives is a teleological vision of history in which diverse peoples and resources in countries like Bolivia evolve into modern capitalist nation-states; multiform kin groups transform into legally registered nuclear families; and hidden unnamed sexual desires and practices are replaced by either heterosexual marriages or open gay identities. These efforts to drive Bolivia forward on the path of modern devel-opment have made deep, and deeply uneven, marks, while indigenous people in the Andean highlands and Amazonian lowlands have resisted, appropriated, and/or resignified elements of these "universal" models (Arnold 1998; Canessa 2005).

In spite of this stubborn diversity, Bolivians in all kinds of life situations and relationships have been seen, counted, and dealt with *as if* they were heads or mem-bers of normative families or, more recently, *as if* they were gay individuals. These purportedly universal categories, used to make the processes and reports of national and international agencies more efficient, accountable, and comparable throughout the world, have seriously influenced the success of development initiatives, or lack thereof. Here we analyze two national/international initiatives that used globally dominant models of family and sexual identity to map Bolivian society: an agrarian reform and peasant union system that institutionalized a male-head-of-household model in rural Bolivia starting in the 1950s; and an HIV/AIDS prevention and awareness campaign that promoted a gay individual model in Bolivian cities starting in the 1990s. Because these initiatives ignored relevant cultural realities, they not only fell short of their stated goals, but produced unintended impacts that exacerbate problems originally addressed.

Land reform and agricultural modernization: moving resources away from Bolivia's "headless households"

For decades national governments and international development agencies have promoted the expansion of individual land rights with the stated goal of improving livelihood and food security for the rural poor. By favoring legal titling for men defined as "heads of household," many of these schemes worked to institutionalize hierarchal marriage and family models, outcomes rarely identified as goals of land reform. Recent research in Africa, Latin America, and Southeast Asia provides evidence that land titling policies have sometimes jeopardized access to resources for local women, exacerbated economic inequality within communities, and/or contributed to ecological degradation (World Bank 2005).

In the wake of Bolivia's 1952 revolution, the National Revolutionary Movement moved to overcome social exclusion that limited national development by extending land tenure, education, and voting rights to poor and indigenous people, and by purging the word "*indio*" from official documents. Predictions that racial distinctions would fade as a modern mestizo nation emerged have been negated by recent surges of indigenous activism, and by the stunning 2005 election of indigenous president Evo Morales. Yet the revolution's remarkable success in institutionalizing new forms of gendered recognition and exclusion has advanced largely unheralded.

Bolivia's 1953 land reform law defined beneficiaries as all Bolivians over 18 years old who farm the land, *regardless of sex*.[5] Yet during official titling procedures, nearly all the names inscribed were men's. Similarly, "male heads of households" were called to participate in unions overseen by the Ministry of Peasant Affairs. Both arrangements failed to capture the richness of existing cultural systems for land management, decision-making, and collaborative labor in which men and women play active, albeit distinct, roles. James Scott points to long-term implications of this kind of "abridged maps":

> They did not successfully represent the actual activity of the society they depicted, nor were they intended to; they represented only that slice of it that interested the official observer. They were, moreover, not just maps. Rather, they were maps that, when allied with state power, would enable much of the reality they depicted to be remade. Thus a state cadastral map created to designate taxable property-holders does not merely describe a system of land tenure; it creates such a system through its ability to give its categories the force of law.

(1998: 3)

Let us take a look at some secondary outcomes of these processes in Cochabamba valleys, where I carried out 18 months of fieldwork between 1988 and 1990, and returned a dozen times since to continue research through participant observation, household surveys, life histories, institutional analyses, focus groups, and other methods. During this period, the impacts of family models applied in the agrarian reform and union system were multiplied by projects implemented by development agencies that chose to work with official peasant unions and to link technical and financial support to land ownership, thus bypassing more inclusive local forms for organizing labor, decision, and access to resources.

One internationally funded project that I studied in detail promoted the expansion and intensification of commercial wheat production on private agricultural plots through certified seed and equipment extended on credit to land-owners, and through technical training and organizational support provided to peasant unions. For over a decade, the project strengthened wealthier and more normative families through their male heads (Paulson 2004). Ironically, a "women and development" initiative appended to this project in the mid-1990s exacerbated the inequitable distribution of benefits and costs. The extension agency formed an association of women wheat producers, distributed inputs on credit, and provided technical training to female members. Those who participated were married women from families with the greatest access to land and other resources, in which both spouses obtained improved seed packages. These women valued the opportunity to receive institutional support, converse with extension workers, and generate income. One declared, "With the proceeds from the wheat, I've begun selling chicha. Now I have cash all the time and can do what I want to." Yet the extension of benefits to select women was linked to increasingly inequitable distribution of natural, financial, and technical resources within the community. The access of certain couples to a double quota of seed, credit, and training allowed their families to consolidate control over greater extensions of land and water, thus diminishing communally managed resources. This affected poorer families, many of them organized around women, who earned a livelihood by pasturing other people's livestock, gathering and selling fuelwood, and doing other activities that depend on open-access resources.

While development efforts to expand commercial wheat production on private plots helped to enrich normative families with titled land, it also reduced resource access and jeopardized the well-being of other families. An unmarried mother of five explained:

> It's not worthwhile to work on the hillsides anymore. There is no fuelwood left, not even grass for the little animals. Now mostly I wash clothes in the river; there are three or four women who pay me by the dozen to wash. And I had to send my daughter, the second one, to Cochabamba City to work as a maid.

By the 1990s, this type of outcome was so widespread in Bolivia and elsewhere that it provoked a whole new wave of development initiatives aimed specifically at vulnerable and resource-poor women. Unfortunately, in the absence of queer critique, the artisan cooperatives and micro-loan projects that typified this women-and-development wave focused more on helping marginalized individuals than on interrogating the development models that helped shape that marginalization.

This example is one of many cases in which assumptions built into development projects have led to economic and political benefits for people in certain sexual relationships and family arrangements, while degrading or diminishing resources and forms of participation available to others. One might think that, after decades of such tangible incentives, people would comply with the norm. However, in an in-depth survey of 55 households in the Municipality of Mizque, I found that about a third of the households surveyed were female-headed; one-third consisted of families comprised of a man, a woman, and their children; while the rest included a wide variety of relations and arrangements (Paulson 1996). Nationwide, the 2001 census found that 30.8 percent of households were headed by women (Maletta 2005: 5).

The fact that some of the poorest and most marginal households in Bolivia are run by single women reinforces the assumption that non-normative family and sexual status is the cause of their troubles. Yet women without male partners, often excluded from direct benefits of programs such as those described here, do find collaboration, resources, and sexual and emotional intimacy in a variety of ways, some more, some less accepted by society. Profiles of two households in the Mizque survey offer insight into some of these strategies.

Tomasa, 42 years old, lives in an adobe and cement house together with her two children, two grandchildren, and her widowed mother Sabina. Tomasa's 10-year-old son goes to school and helps tend their 28 sheep and five cows, and her 20-year-old daughter, Beatríz, lives at home with her two small sons. Tomasa says that she was desperately attracted to her common-law husband, with whom she lived for several years, bearing two daughters, of whom only Beatríz survives. However, his temper caused trouble and he moved away. For over a decade, Tomasa has maintained an off-and-on relationship with a man in another community. Beatríz also has a male partner, who stays in her room between trips to Santa Cruz where he works as laborer in commercial agriculture. Tomasa's house is on the edge of a hectare of land that Sabina inherited from her husband, most of which is cultivated by sharecroppers. The three women plant a little corn, and earn most of their living through commerce and raising animals. Beatríz buys candy, toys, and other commodities from her mother's compadre in Cochabamba, then goes to markets and fiestas where she spreads out her carrying cloth and sells them.

Sisters Miguelina and Angela, both in their forties, live on the edge of a small rural town in adjoining houses. They spend most of each day in a shared back patio where they work, cook, and socialize, telling stories and laughing with friends who stop by, and with clients who come to consume the soft drinks and *chicha* (fermented corn beverage) that the sisters make and sell. Over 15 years, I have enjoyed many hours of shared work and conversation in this patio, and watched Angela's two children grow up in this affectionate home. Now in her early twenties, the eldest daughter is devoted to both Miguelina and Angela, and stays with them when she and her male partner are not away working in the city. Angela's sociable teenage son collaborates with his mother and his Tía Miguelina, who together attend the school performances and soccer games in which he is involved. Unlike most of their neighbors, the sisters do not own or farm land, nor do they participate in the peasant union. In 1994, Miguelina and Angela served as co-hosts for an important patronal feast. The sisters received the *cargo* (ritual responsibility) the year before from a mature married couple; together they saved and planned for the major feast and, side by side, they carried out the hosting duties in a celebration that gave them great pride and pleasure. Without access to farmland, the sisters drew on compadrazgo relationships and other forms of exchange to obtain the massive quantities of produce needed to host the festivities.

Women heads of household in this study find identity, intimacy, and relatedness in a variety of sibling, friendship, and intergenerational ties, often consecrated through compadrazgo. These ties, clearly vital in developing diverse economic strategies as well as human solidarity, might be reinforced in a new kind of development initiative designed to support a wider range of the population.

AIDS education and prevention: limiting connections with Bolivia's "detoured men"

During the past few decades, people in many cultural traditions have adapted cosmopolitan models of gayness in a process that Dennis Altman (2001) calls "global queering." Media frequently represent this change as progress toward a more advanced social order where homosexuals finally gain the right to express their "natural" desires and identities. Yet ethnographic research in postcolonial and developing societies suggests that people who may not find gay identity any more natural than the missionary position are adopting new identities and lifestyles for all kinds of reasons (Stevenson 1995; Parker 1999).

Diverse factors influence ways in which Bolivian men connect or not with gay identity (cf. Tellería and Pers López 1996). Challenges of economic survival that make it difficult for many men and women to sustain the family model promoted by state and church also limit realization of the independent gay lifestyles presented in mass media. Some men, married or single, engage in homoerotic activities without perceiving themselves, or being labeled by others, as gay. Here we consider a group of men who sometimes and in some places self-identify as gay, most are not married, and their social relations are based partly on shared homosexual desire. I do not refer to these men as "gays" or "homosexuals" because many do not consistently embrace, nor do their lives correspond with, the type of social identity usually associated with these labels.

During the past 15 years, I have come to know a network of Bolivian men who are sexually attracted to men. I have carried out interviews and life histories with a number of them, and have done participative observation in a variety of settings. I also draw on transcripts of life histories of some men in this network recorded by my colleague Tim Wright. These men recount diverse homoerotic desires and experiences, as well as life collaborations and forms of relatedness, played out in varied contexts. Their narratives reveal the influence of cultural roles and rules common in many parts of Latin America, including the distinction between a masculine-identified *activo* who penetrates and a feminine-identified *pasivo* who receives in homosexual intercourse; the derogatory term *maricón*, applied to boys and men who do not fulfill certain masculine social expectations and to men who are perceived as effeminate or *pasivo*; and a constellation of time/spaces, postures, gestures, and understandings called *el ambiente*, a semi-secret world that flows through and around straight geography. Today these meanings and practices coexist with cosmopolitan terms and ideas about homosexual identities and relations that began to make a mark on this landscape in the late 1980s, later than in other parts of Latin America.

El Proyecto Contra el SIDA (Project against AIDS) was founded in Bolivia in 1993 with funds from the USAID, and implemented in collaboration with Centers for Disease Control and Prevention in Atlanta (CDC) with the goal of education and prevention of HIV/AIDS among men who have sex with men. Researchers sought to identify a Bolivian population that would allow them to measure incidence and prevalence of the virus, and to document a baseline and changes in knowledge and practices. In order to help make the elusive target group more visible, a gay center and activities were developed in the city of Santa Cruz. Some men did gather at the center, see safe-sex films, and get free condoms; however, only a small portion (and by no means a cross-section) of men who have sex with men participated in project activities. Planners on various levels had assumed the existence of a hidden homosexual population whose members could – with the right approach – be identified, gathered, and educated. However, as I analyzed the initiative together with its first coordinator, Tim Wright (2000), we came to understand the project as a struggle to establish a new sexual identity group against a landscape deeply engraved by class, racial-ethnic, and gender differences.

As a dozen or so working- and middle-class men began to gather at the gay center, poor and/or indigenous men were not embraced by the nascent community, and wealthy Bolivians preferred to connect at private parties or on trips to Rio or Miami. Men who perceived their heterosexual manliness to be enhanced by sex with other men declared the idea of identifying socially with homosexuals repulsive. Meanwhile, effeminate or transgendered individuals were not welcomed for fear that association with them would soil the group's image. In sum, this chapter of gay genesis left out many men who were too poor, too rich, too white, too indigenous, too masculine, or too feminine. Retrospection reveals limitations of the homonormative assumptions of international professionals who expected men whom they perceived as closeted homosexuals to "come out" and embrace a new gay identity that would lead to healthier emotional lives and greater social rights, as well as curb the spread of HIV/AIDS. One result of this disconnect between professional expectations and local realities is that many Bolivian men who have sex with men have been left out of sexual health education and disease-prevention campaigns.

This case pushes us to stop treating sexual identity as an independent variable, and instead address sexual desires and practices in the context of cultural realms through which Bolivian men build identity and relatedness (Paulson 2007). Some Bolivian men who establish manly identities and relations through work, family, and/or homosocial bonding engage in a range of homoerotic behaviors without being labeled – or identifying themselves – as deviants. Others – including men in disadvantaged economic and racial-ethnic positions; men who do not enjoy healthy family or homosocial relations; and sex workers or transvestites with marked appearance and location – are more vulnerable to being labeled according to their homoerotic practices, and to being treated in degrading, sexualized, and violent ways (Wright 2006).

Like women heads of household discussed above, non-normative Bolivian men draw on long-standing cultural forms of organization and relatedness to create identities and bonds across differences of social place and power. The men with whom I have interacted over the years have developed elaborate traditions to celebrate cultural/religious rituals together, including an annual all-night celebration of San Juan (winter solstice), and an homage to the Virgin of Urkupiña each August, complete with religious mass, music, and feasting. The generative use of compadrazgo relations in the context of these events can be seen at a dinner party hosted by a friend named Efraín with the goal of organizing the Urkupiña celebration. The 33 guests were drawn together partly by shared same-sex desire: most were single, middle-aged, middle-class Bolivians who have known each other for years; others included several Brazilian students, two mature US expatriates, and a couple of men from rural backgrounds. After dinner, our host took out a leather book, from which he read the names of those who had held ritual responsibilities for the previous year's celebration, including Godmother of new clothes for the Virgin, Godfather who sponsored the priest who blessed the Virgin, and Godparents of food, beer, and music. As Efraín called out the cargos amid abundant laughter and teasing, people commented on the grandness with which certain tasks had been carried out in previous celebrations, offered to take on specific responsibilities for the upcoming event, and volunteered others for roles. For nearly a decade, now, co-participation in Urkupiña celebrations has helped consolidate shared identity and enduring relations.

To sum up: in spite of sustained financial support, neither the project discussed here nor parallel initiatives developed into strong or sizeable LGBT organizations in Bolivia, posing a notable exception to Lind and Share's (2003: 56) observation that "In the 1980s and 1990s in virtually every Latin American country, small [LGBT] groups transformed into well-established non-governmental organizations (NGOs), thanks to support for HIV/AIDS outreach and support provided by international agencies, ministries of health, and private foundations." Yet, although internationally funded organizations and global media messages have failed to trigger the formation of a new sexual identity population visible and legible to researchers and bureaucrats, Bolivian men described here have built alternative spaces and communities. They have also engaged with other non-normative or subordinate individuals and groups in a remarkable range of social and political initiatives and expressions.

Emerging movements and identities: transcending hetero and homo normativities?

Bolivia's emerging social movements are forging creative alliances that fuse activism for sexual/gender rights with struggles against racism, patriarchy, and neoliberal capitalism, seen as interwoven barriers to a more equitable society and full human expression. A broad sense of "justice" rather than "just us" was foregrounded by the 11 organizations and networks participating in the 1999 "Congress of Gay, Lesbian, Bisexual, Transvestite, Transsexual and Transgendered People of Bolivia" and later collaborated with a variety of women's organizations to advocate for Law 810 on Sexual and Reproductive Rights. In 2002, Bolivia's Gay Pride Parades were re-conceived under the more inclusive banner "Marcha Orgullo de la Diversidad Sexual," and by 2007, Cochabamba's principal newspaper described "March for Gay Pride and Sexual and Gender Diversity" as "overflowing with glamour, joy, luxury, color and respect among participants and viewers who lined the Prado" (Los Tiempos 2007).

Two spirited movements have gained high visibility and popular impact in Bolivian cities and media. First is the militant feminist-anarchist collective *Mujeres Creando*, founded in 1990, whose members work through graffiti, street installations, workshops and other participatory methods, in addition to publishing and television. In conscious contrast to sophisticated government discourses on women's rights, *Mujeres Creando* has launched a feminism of the streets aimed to politicize people to fight battles about tangible issues such as access to resources, work, and land. In efforts to build relations with women like the semi-literate indigenous farmers discussed above, *Mujeres Creando* created and distributed a "spoken book" on CD with messages about "feminism for women who are mothers." To advance their work with male sexual and gender identities, they published an accessible book supporting freer expression of men's sexuality (Galindo and Paredes 2002). Moving beyond "women's issues" narrowly defined, they have initiated and supported action including anti-poverty efforts, attacks on racism, and mobilization of debtors.

Second is the *Familia Galan*, a transvestite community of over 30 members who, during the past decade, have used street performances, theater and humor to advance intersectional critiques of multiple forms of oppression and repression. La Familia's energetic public outreach has ranged from collaborating with the Gregoria Apaza Women's Center in theater performances for indigenous youth in El Alto to joining Bolivian women's organizations in Sucre in a public act for abortion rights supported by the Latin American Network of Catholics for Choice. In a BBC interview (Atkinson 2005), Galan member David Aruquipa eloquently addressed their goal of facilitating new ways of seeing beyond conventional identities and family models.

> The concept of "trans" is very important to us. By opening up the world of trans, we are calling into question what people consider to be normal or politically correct. We want to challenge the accepted values that try to impose rules

on our bodies. These bodies, that bring our politicised mandate out into the open, are "trans" bodies.

The whole idea of the Family Galan is to challenge the notion of the traditional nuclear family. We are a family with love, fights, disagreements and tender moments like any other family. We are bonded by a philosophy that diversity is essential to family life.

During 2006 and 2007, gender and sexual identity advocates participated in constituent assembly processes to rethink Bolivia's constitution from the ground up, and found unprecedented access to official politics, as recounted in an e-mail that Danna Galan sent to me in March 2006:

We are participating in some initiatives of Evo Morales' new government, with myself representing the trans/gay movement, with great success. We launched the debate about sexual diversity from the valuable standpoint of cultural diversity. We prepared a proposal for public action by the government, and they invited me to implement that proposal from within the administration! So, now I am working as an official, with good possibilities of impacting public policy in this country.

Both the great promise and the formidable challenges of these initiatives are rooted in their zeal to replace conventional vertical mechanisms for categorizing and controlling Bolivia's people with more equitable and inclusive, if yet uncharted, means.

On a parallel path, Bolivia's President Morales and collaborators have diverged from genealogical and essentialist understandings of indigeneity dominant in many parts of the world. Bolivians in and out of political power are invoking an indigenous positioning informed by historical consciousness, relative place in the nation, and ideological solidarity. This approach entails a sense that, because indigenous people have been marginalized and exploited in processes of colonization and globalization, they are in unique positions to develop critiques of neocolonialism and globalization. And, by experiencing exclusion from full participation in the nation state, indigenous people have developed unique capacities to understand other marginalized people, ranging from exploited and unemployed workers to women and men in non-conventional families and relationships.

This chapter draws attention to less-recognized cultural practices and meanings, evidenced in organizational strategies of unmarried rural women and urban men, that appear to be vitalizing these emerging forms of identity and relatedness. Álvaro García Linera (2004), now Vice President of Bolivia, notes that as unions are undermined by fragmentation of the production process, and rural and urban community organizations and family structures are weakened by migration and employment instability, pre-existing forms of cultural and territorial organization are gaining new relevance.

Conclusion

National and international development initiatives, together with state policies and legislation, have brought normative family models into diverse Bolivian lives, and have presented the gay individual as an alternative to the family. Yet census, survey, and ethnographic data presented here show that the practices and meanings of a significant portion of Bolivian households and of men who sexually desire men do not correspond with these official models. This chapter traces the impacts of normative global models on local realities: an agrarian reform designed to improve the conditions of rural peasants empowered men via private property titles, reducing the relative power and resources of peasant women; a productive project for women widened the breach between women who are married or resource-wealthy on the one hand, and women who are single or resource-poor on the other; and a project designed to support gay identity and to educate gay community provoked rifts among men who have sex with men, and reached only a small portion of them.

This study finds that cultural forms of organization and identity that do not correspond with globally dominant norms are deep and widespread in Bolivian life, and that policies and programs that ignore or undermine these rich forms of belonging and collaboration can be counterproductive to stated goals of national development. Programs that strengthen certain types of families and individuals in ways that jeopardize others limit success in improving community well-being and in fighting poverty and disease.

Another key finding here is the importance of commensality and context, relative to biological and legal-institutional factors, in building identity, affinity, and commitment. Bolivians invest great effort to consolidate relatedness and identity through ritualized celebration of food and drink. The generative power of compadrazgo is exemplified by Miguelina and Angelina co-hosting the feast of their town's patron saint; and by male friends joined as co-parents in celebrating the Virgin of Urkupiña each August. Groups in this study might be understood as a vanguard of a Bolivian move away from the fixed roles and vertical relations that have characterized party politics, farmers' unions, and conventional family models, and a rejection of patron–client relations described by Albro (2007). This move foregrounds solidarity among actors and groups who share marginal socio-historical positions and experiences, and forges creative collaborations across difference to develop intersectional critiques and to advance new kinds of proposals. Development visions and programs would do well to recognize and support such vital culturally embedded practices and forces.

Notes

1 I express my gratitude to the Bolivian men and women who shared their life stories to advance this study. Thanks to John Byers, Linda Farthing, and Chaise LaDousa for motivating me to think and grow with this material, and to Tim Wright for involving me in his early research and analysis, as well as his recent dissertation on homosexual lives and issues in Bolivia. I would like to thank editor Jack Rollwagen for insightful comments on a paper that explored some aspects of this study in *Urban Anthropology*

and *Studies of Cultural Systems and World Economic Development* (36(3): 239–80) and for facilitating fruitful interaction with papers by Albro (2007), Canessa (2007), and Rockefeller (2007).

2 Common terms in Bolivia include: sin jefe de familia, familia incompleta, madre soltera, familia descompuesta, and desviado, soltero, maricon, invertido.

3 Article 16 of the Universal Declaration of Human Rights proclaims the right to marry and found a family, equal rights to and in marriage, and consensual marriage, and states that, "The family is the natural and fundamental group unit of society and is entitled to protection by society and the State."

4 As one example, see the 1979 Convention on the Elimination of All Forms of Discrimination against Women, Article 16 on Marriage and Family Life.

5 Decreto Ley de Reforma Agraria, #3464, 2 agosto 1953, Capitulo 1 articulo 77. "Todos los bolivianos, mayores de 18 anos, sin distinción de sexos, que se dediquen o quieren dedicarse a las labores agrícolas, serán dotados de tierras donde existan disponibles de acuerdo a los planes del Gobierno, y siempre que en el término de dos anos implanten trabajos agrícolas."

Part III

Resisting global hegemonies, struggling for sexual rights and gender justice

8 Spelling it out

From alphabet soup to sexual rights and gender justice[1]

Sangeeta Budhiraja, Susana T. Fried and Alexandra Teixeira

In August 2004, in Kathmandu, Nepal, 39 metis – self-identified "cross-dressing males" – were arbitrarily arrested and held in custody without food or water for 13 days. The International Gay and Lesbian Human Rights Commission (IGLHRC) was called on to work with the Blue Diamond Society (BDS) – a sexual rights organization providing information, advocacy, and resources to men who have sex with men, metis, people living with HIV and sex workers in Nepal – to prepare an Action Alert[2] to mobilize international protest denouncing the arbitrary arrests and unreasonable detention of the 39 metis, and to demand their release. The director of BDS drafted the majority of the Action Alert, and described metis as "cross-dressing males." Since IGLHRC's work rests on respecting the identities and expressions that local activists use in their own contexts, they defined "metis" in English using his language. However, when IGLHRC staff in New York sent the Action Alert to their office in Argentina to be translated into and circulated in Spanish, they were met with the difficulties of translating identities across boundaries: In the Argentine context, the use of "cross-dressing males" refers most often to heterosexual males who on occasion wear women's clothing. In Argentina, this terminology can be seen as inaccurate to transgender and travesti activists and organizations who demand to be understood on their own terms rather than in reference to their departure from traditional masculinity or femininity – in this case, gendered dress codes.

The process of translating this Action Alert in order to mobilize international support illustrates one of the challenges of cross-national organizing around fixed-identity categories. In contrast to travesti and transgender-identified activists in large parts of Latin America, many metis involved with BDS do not necessarily identify as part of a trans movement. Rather, they make rights claims based on violations that are perpetrated against them when they "cross-dress" – i.e. as a result of their gender-transgressing behavior or gender expression rather than their (gender) identity.

This example raises important questions for collaborative work *within the human rights system*: How do we organize around multiple forms of identity shaped by various cultural contexts and spaces? How do we name and identify our common ground in order to foster effective organizing strategies and international public policies? How do we frame or translate these conversations in the languages of rights and/or development? In this chapter, we will make the case that rights-based organizing strategies and development interventions around sexual orientation and gender expression need to shift away from common categories of identity toward a broader context of struggle. First, we lay out an argument for why an "alphabet soup" approach to demanding human rights (i.e. adding more and more letters of the alphabet to the acronym GL, then GLB, then LGBT, now LGBTQI and more) masks more than it reveals about the diversity of sexual and gender expressions and practices, as well as the myriad forms of coalescing across common interests and common struggles. Next, we introduce and explore the concept of "sexual rights" as an alternative framework for advocacy and "border crossing." Finally, we propose a pairing of *sexual rights* with *gender justice* as a useful, and potentially liberatory, framework for human rights organizing and development strategies.

In our understanding, *sexual rights* or *sexuality-related human rights* entail affirmative claims about the gendered right to exercise citizenship in all its manifestations as self-determining agents, as well as demands for protection against the use of our bodies as sites of, or excuses for, human rights violations. As many activists and scholars have noted, women's sexuality or sexual autonomy, in particular, carries enormous symbolic significance as well as material consequences – for fundamentalists and religious extremists as well as for feminists and women's rights advocates.[3] Given the core (but often unarticulated) significance of women's (and others') sexual autonomy and bodily integrity in struggles for and against women's ability to exercise all of their human rights and to live lives of dignity, we borrow Chandra Mohanty's (1997) concept of a *common context of struggle*. Those who challenge traditional norms of gender and sexuality – among them feminists, sex workers, lesbian/gay/bisexual, and transgender people – are situated within such a *common context of struggle*. As Mohanty suggests, it has become urgent to articulate this *common context of struggle* in a manner that is built on the many differences among us, noting especially that "sexuality" is always locally, historically, and culturally embedded.

This leads us to one of the persistent challenges that arises when we try to define what *sexual rights* or *human rights to sexuality* mean in the context of broadly varying cultures – the boundaries of socially and culturally appropriate *sexuality* (as well as the parameters of *culture*, itself) are formed within its specific historical and local context. Thus, while both *sexuality* and *culture* are often presented as fixed and immutable, in fact they are fluid and variable. Moreover, the borders of *culture* or *cultural practices* (as well as "appropriate" *sexuality*) are neither transparent nor uncontested. Often, the borders of *culture* are written on, enacted via, and patrolled through women's bodies and lives – as well as men's and most certainly on the bodies of trans persons. Often, but inconsistently, women are regarded as the bearers of protectors of culture. Indeed, at the level of policy and practice (including healthcare and services), women are reduced to their child-bearing roles.[4] And yet, women are also feared as the potential destroyers of culture, especially when their sexual identity, expression, and/or practices run counter to social and cultural norms of appropriate femininity.

The regulation of sexuality in service of social and cultural norms, as well as political imperatives and development priorities, often operates through systems of force, constraint, and punishment – sometimes explicitly, sometimes implicitly. Within the context of development practice, where sexuality has been integrated into interventions, these generally address sexuality as instrumental – i.e. in service of other, more "pressing" development goals, such as population control, HIV/ AIDS prevention or treatment, or violence prevention. As the report of the Expert Group on Development Issues' conference "Making the Linkages – Sexuality, Rights and Development" puts it, the focus within development "has been on encouraging people to say no to risky sex, rather than empowering them to say yes to, or ask for, safer and more satisfying sex" (Jassey 2006: 3). From the imposition of "ABC" (Abstain, be faithful, use condoms) policies to the persistently dominant use of the "household" (read: heterosexual family, at best inclusive of single-parent and extended families) as the primary unit of development strategies, heteronormativity[5] remains the assumption in most development and rights interventions.

Identity politics: the alphabet soup approach

Both in national and international legal systems, identity categories are successfully used to make rights claims based on protections from discrimination and the basic principle that everyone can claim certain freedoms by virtue of their common humanity. Where rights are based upon protected categories of identity, this framework has a long history of success; the Dalit rights movement in India, indigenous rights movements in Brazil, and civil rights organizing in the United States are but a few examples.

Grounded in this tradition, what started as the "gay rights" movement in the United States became the "gay and lesbian" rights movement, followed by the "lesbian, gay, bisexual, and transgender" (LGBT) movement and, recently, we have seen the banner of collective identities expand to different permutations that include questioning, straight allies, two-spirited, intersex, queer.[6] Throughout the trajectory of these expanding and historically situated identity constructs – increasingly referred to as an "alphabet soup" of identities – successful organizing at national and international levels has largely been the result of advocacy grounded in traditional models of identity politics and "minority rights" or "civil rights" frameworks. The ever-expanding list of identities that lay claim to the "sexual minority" banner represents a diverse range of practices and desires that define themselves in contrast to social standards of heteronormativity and binary gender.[7] Common ground is thus defined as identities that do not conform to the specific social and cultural structures governing gender and sexuality.

Within the specific context of the United States, the collective-identity model of LGBT organizing is a product of cultural and historical necessity, or, as sociologist Joshua Gamson points out: "interest group politics on the ethnic model is, quite simply but not without contradictory effects, how the [US] American sociopolitical environment is structured." Although sexual orientation and gender identity and expression are not explicitly protected categories under federal law, various state and city ordinances now recognize these collective identities and provide (often imperfect) defense from discrimination.

Similarly, four countries – South Africa, Ecuador, Fiji,[8] and Portugal – have now passed constitutional protections that include sexual orientation as a protected category of identity. Yet, while these formal protections are a requisite structure for human rights protections, the recent brutal murder of Zoliswa Nkonyana, a lesbian killed by a mob in a Cape Flats township in South Africa, makes clear that constitutional protections are not enough.

The construction of categories that are based on behavior rather than identity have also fallen victim to "alphabetization." Take, for example, the category of "MSM" (men who have sex with men). Emerging from the public health lexicon that focuses on behavior (and behavior change), the term MSM was intended to capture the fact that many men who have sex with men do not consider themselves to be gay/homosexual. In the context of HIV/AIDS responses, interventions targeted toward gay men, therefore, will not necessarily encompass many men who have sex with men. These have been important corrections and expansions of our understanding of sexual practices outside social and culture standards. However, at a recent conference on MSM and HIV/AIDS held as a satellite to the International AIDS Conference 2006, some attendees proposed modifying "MSM" to "MSMW" in acknowledgment of the fact that many men who have sex with men also have sex with women. Other attendees contested this move, arguing that adding letters of the alphabet only pointed out the potential absurdity of our effort to "fix" sexual practices into nameable categories, rather than taking on the fluidity – indeed the messiness – of sex and sexuality. Along these lines, a study of *The Sexual Networks and Behaviours of Men who have Sex with Men in Asia* finds a distinct lack of coherence in the term "men who have sex with men" and urge attention to:

> the dangers in assumptions that are often made in many studies about easily accessed or familiar populations being the or the main MSM grouping. There was no singular MSM population in any of the four countries reviewed and nothing remotely approaching the possibility of being the major grouping that might mark the tip of any single main MSM iceberg. While there are MSM who identify as gay men in these countries to differing degrees [they] cannot be regarded as the core MSM grouping in any country.
>
> (Dowsett, Grierson, and McNally 2006: 105)

In the larger context of international human rights activism and cross-national advocacy – where the range and diversity of identity constructs that claim this same "common ground" are countless – the criteria for evaluating the success of organizing strategies can be said to be twofold: Does this strategy lead to effective remedies and responses? Does it change the conditions that give rise to violations (Miller 2006)? In the case of "LGBT" organizing, we can ask more specifically, does the identity framework lead to effective rights protections? Does this framework transform the power structures that animate heteronormativity and binary constructions of gender?

Identities without borders

Emphasizing the oppression of marginalized communities by other more privileged communities, identity-based organizing strategies have successfully surfaced the inequalities faced by non-heteronormative people in a heteronormative world. What identity-based strategies have not adequately addressed, however, are the underlying structures of power that stratify people into categories of privilege and oppression and structured, in part, through sexual hierarchies.[9]

The number of LGBT organizations around the world is growing dramatically (Adam, Duyvendak, and Krouwel 1999), and many of them are increasingly exploring the value of applying a human rights approach to their work. Many of these organizations have been very vocal in making the point that sexuality is not simply a private matter. Yet, in many places, same-sex sexual behavior is not associated with a specific identity. In these circumstances, the terms "lesbian" or "gay" are not only misnomers, but they can obscure local meanings of sexuality. This reality is one of many that fuel the current tension between rights-claiming based on constructing politically viable identity categories formed by sexual orientation and gender expression and a growing political imperative to deconstruct and de-essentialize both sexuality and gender (see Gamson 1995).

Whether they claim the name "gay" or not, the reality is that people are often targeted for abuses because of their same-gender desire, attraction, and sexual expression. Often, this abuse is inextricably rooted in other hierarchies of privilege/oppression based on race, class, ability, nationality, age, and other markers of identity. The persecution of men who have sex with men and women who have sex with women is often justified by those in positions of power (which can include religious and even medical authorities) as necessary to purge a particular society of "Western," or "corrupting," influences. Many vehemently deny that lesbians and gay men even exist in their nations, cultures, or voting constituencies. This denial renders segments of a population both "deviant" and invisible, and also leads to heightened persecution. In turn, this stigma and increased persecution allow a climate of impunity for the perpetrators of abuses. After all, who will come to the defense of the indefensible?

In a panel presentation on the future of sexuality research and advocacy, Barbara Klugman, Program Officer for Sexuality and Reproductive Health at the Ford Foundation, suggests that the proliferation of identity-based rights claiming in the US has led to a "silo approach" to organizing and social justice work around gender and sexuality:

> When I came from South Africa three years ago, I was struck by how disparate thinking around sexuality is. [...] I realized that this [the U.S.] has become a country where people think of themselves in terms of identity groups, and organize in terms of social identity categories. [...] And what is most striking is that there do not seem to be many shared agendas. The U.S. is full of grass-roots and local level organizing with thousands of groups each working away at their specific concerns. But small silos of activity don't make a

social movement; they don't enable enough bodies, and more importantly, a broad-enough shared vision, to make claims for social justice that have to be heard by those with power.

(Klugman 2006)

While the alphabetization of organizing strategies around sexual orientation and gender expression is suggestive of a strategy that brings together a broad diversity of bodies and identities to make claims for social justice, the expanding recognition of diverse identities under the LGBTQI banner is simultaneously rooted in the need to expose the dynamics of oppression *within* the movement. In 1995, sociologist Joshua Gamson explored this tension in an article that asked: "*Must Identity Movements Self-destruct?*" In this article, Gamson explored the paradox inherent in most identity-based social movements: "Fixed identities," he argues, "are both the basis for oppression and basis for political power." (Gamson 1995: 391). While Gamson uses the article to affirm the logic of both the strategy to construct collective identities as well as the movement to deconstruct them, he points out that "most of the current theories take hold of only one horn of the dilemma: the political utility of solid collective categories" (Gamson 1995: 402). Gamson challenges organizers to question the content, viability and political usefulness of sexual identities "even as they are used and assumed" (Gamson 1995: 397).

Sonia Katyal (2002) takes up a similar question, with similar conclusions. Noting that same-sex practices have occurred in a vast array of communities and contexts through recorded history, "the emergence of a tangible gay and lesbian identity is an extremely recent development. As one author observes, in India, to commit a homosexual act is one thing; to be a homosexual is an entirely different phenomenon" (Katyal 2002: 97). On this basis, Katyal asks the question of whether "sexual orientation itself is a culturally specific concept" (Katyal 2002: 97). Along these same lines, Dennis Altman emphasizes:

the complexities involved in applying universal norms of both freedom and sexual identity to societies with very different cultural and social structures from those which produced the particular construction of "gay" and "lesbian" identities. Arguments around the tensions have taken place in recent years in most non-western countries, often with a conflation of "tradition" and the legacy of colonialism, with the result that post-colonial states such as India, Zimbabwe, and Malaysia defend the retention of anti-homosexual laws that are in fact legacies of colonialism.

(Altman 2004: 63)

At the same time and along with the abovementioned observers of same-sex sexuality across the globe, he also notes the emergence of explicitly named *gay* and *lesbian* groups "in most countries with sufficient political space for any sort of political organizing, and gay pride parades are now held in cities as different as Manila, Johannesburg, and Sao Paulo" (Altman 2004: 63).

Much of this organizing, as Sonia Corrêa and Richard Parker note, is increasingly anchored in rights-based approaches. However, rather than following the historical trajectory of focusing solely (or primarily) on rights violations, advocacy for sexuality-based rights engages positive as well as negative rights claims. Searching for "erotic justice" or sexuality as a practice of freedom, they call for "a positive approach to sexual rights that will ensure more than protection against harm and the achievement of the highest standard of health requires the re-thinking of private/public boundaries" (Corrêa and Parker 2004: 26). While affirming the importance of addressing sexual violence, especially as it occurs in the private sphere (in the home and/or by family members) they also follow:

> the analysis developed by Claudia Hinojosa ... [to] acknowledge that the sexual rights debate has matured enough to begin to openly advocate for sexuality as a practice of freedom, as a legitimate domain for the search for pleasure or a loving form of communication based on equality, responsibility and choice.

Considering what is non-negotiable, Corrêa and Parker identify a central challenge to be "devis[ing] conceptual definitions and political strategies that will effectively prevent and punish sexual abuses that occur in the private domain and, at the same time, enhance the possibility of pleasurable sexual experiences in privacy and intimacy" (Corrêa and Parker 2004: 26).

In the context of this dilemma, organizing strategies that have grouped lesbian and bisexual women with gay and bisexual men demand that we think through the costs of a unified banner and think strategically about the framing of our common ground. Cultural sources of oppression that target women demand advocacy and organizing that highlights and distinguishes this reality from those of gay and bisexual men. For women in general, abuses such as forced marriages and childbirth, "corrective rape," so-called "honor killings," or the perpetuation of beliefs that women, and particularly married women, are always available for sex – with or without their consent – are too often justified as securing social, economic, and cultural norms (Fried, Miller, and Rothschild 2007); women who have sex with women, whether they identify as lesbian or not, are specifically situated within this gendered context. Women's sexuality, in general, is regulated in all communities and maintained through particular legal responses, strict social constraints or severe punishment. As such, human rights abuses against lesbian and bisexual women are shaped and determined by particular gender prescriptions and standards as well as by sexual identity. Those who engage in same-sex practices are often the first to be targeted by organized efforts to consolidate or secure power and to maintain their control over "culture" and community. In such cases, it may quickly become clear that the concept of "dangerous" or "non-conforming" sexuality can stretch to encompass any acts that the government sees as threatening to its power – single women, men who are not "masculine enough," unmarried opposite sex couples and others. In this context, effective organizing strategies will therefore be those that not only establish protections for "sexual minorities" but those that aim to reveal and dismantle gender inequity.

It can be similarly argued that organizing strategies that have grouped lesbians, bisexuals, and gay men with a diverse group of transgender people have failed to adequately distinguish these realities and have therefore quite possibly even contributed to the conditions that give rise to violations: a persistent conflation of sexual orientation and gender expression. As a movement, the LGBT platform is yet to adequately address the intersections of sexuality and gender and articulate, in explicit terms, the convergence – and especially the divergence – of the separate but related agendas of lesbian, gay, and bisexual organizing, and transgender (and intersex) organizing. Instead, mainstream LGBT advocacy has, in practice, implicitly posited that "LGB's" have sex, while "T&I's" have gender. Riki Wilchins, a prominent transgender activist and theorist argues this point:

> [W]hile cultural sensitivity to gender has exploded in recent years, it has also been strangely limited and stunted. All that explosive force has been channeled into one area: transgenderism. So whenever gender is mentioned, it is inevitably written down – and too often written off – as only transgender, something only affecting a small, if embattled minority. [...]Oh, to be sure, we must all bow before the gods of inclusion. We must ensure no "LGB" issues forth without its trailing "T." But you and I, *we* don't have problems with our gender. All the men we know are tops, and all the women high-heeled femmes. While it's hard not to cheer the emergence of transgender as an important queer cause, confining the dialogue on gender to one identity [in the LGBT] has had the curious side-effect of relieving the rest of society – gay and straight – from examining its own history of transcending gender norms.
>
> (Wilchins 2002: 15)

As a movement, the LGBT community, as a whole, has neglected to take up the rights of trans people to transgressive sexuality, for example, by campaigning around homophobic sex-reassignment policies in places like Chile and Saudi Arabia where sex-reassignment surgeries have been legalized and new gender identities recognized in an effort to transform an individual from homosexual to heterosexual. Or the case in Argentina where an individual was given permission to have surgery and legally claim a change in gender identification if he agreed to never get married. We have similarly neglected to focus sufficient attention and strategy on lesbian, gay, and bisexual challenges to the binary construction of gender.

Given our criteria, we contend that spelling out each of the broad range of identity constructs that exist around the world cannot fully encompass the lived experiences of sexual and gender non-conforming people and communities. Therefore, using them as the source of claims-making, while already contributing to important social advancement, will not be enough to transform the underlying systems and conditions that give rise to human rights abuses on grounds of sexual orientation and gender expression.

Spelling it out: sexual rights

At the prompting of both domestic and international colleagues for whom the identities "gay" and "lesbian" failed to be accurate or meaningful, the staff and board of directors of IGLHRC changed the organization's mandate in 2002 to adopt a sexual rights framework for promoting the rights of all people whose sexual orientation and/or gender expression do not conform to social prescriptions. IGLHRC has since used *Sexual Rights* as an umbrella term that encapsulates a range of human rights principles as they relate to sexuality. Situating their advocacy within this framework – a framework that is rooted in the standards set forth in international human rights treaties, covenants, and agreements – they have used the discourse of sexual rights to address abuses based on sexual orientation or gender identity in connection to broader strategies of social control over bodies and sexuality in general.

For example, in 2000/2001 IGLHRC's revised mission statement changed from one that promoted the rights of "gay" and "lesbian" people to one that aims to secure the human rights of those who are subject to discrimination on the basis of "sexual orientation or expression," and "gender identity or expression." In addition to spelling out the grounds for abuse rather than naming specific collective identities, the significance of the change in wording of the mission statement included adding the word "expression" to "orientation" and "identity" as a way to signal their understanding, as the persecution of metis in Nepal makes evident, that people are often targeted for attack because of the *perception* of who they are and what they do based on their appearance or conduct – which may or may not be connected to the individual's own *identity construct*. Documented cases of police brutality against trans people in the United States provide additional examples of cases of persecution that are not tied to gender "identity" but rather gender expression and perceived sexual orientation (Cabral 2005a).

For many activists, adopting a sexual rights framework is grounded in the diverse realities, identities, and expressions of our colleagues, clients, or partners. As a result, some advocacy has shifted from organizing around common categories of identity to building a *common context of struggle*.[10] In the arenas of a truly *international* human rights movement, this shift more explicitly recognizes the various cultural contexts and spaces that shape sexual practices, orientations, and gender identities and expressions, while facilitating their translation into shared rights agendas that link not only travestis in Argentina to metis in Nepal, but also to sex workers, men who have sex with men, women who have sex with women, and single and widowed women all over the world who refuse to easily comply with the predominant social/cultural expectations for their sexual and gender comportment.

At the same time, as CREA (Creating Resources for Empowerment and Action, based in Delhi, India) notes in an introduction to their annual, *Sexuality and Rights Institute*:

> Few of those who work on sexuality are familiar with the conceptual and theoretical underpinnings. Even fewer are aware of the links between sexuality

and gender, health and human rights. Outcome – strategies are developed on unexamined models often at cross purposes with stated goals. Advocacy initiatives and programs do not further well-being or assertion of rights.

And, indeed, with or without such an anchor, the range of issues and concerns that are encompassed under what many human rights activists and scholars are referring to as "sexual rights" is broad.

As a human rights project, claims to sexual rights are claims to a range of protections connected to identities, expressions, and practices around gender and sexuality. It includes both positive rights to dignity, autonomy over one's body and sexual life, privacy (among consenting adults), free expression, assembly, liberty, and physical integrity.[11] It also encompasses traditional "negative" rights such as the right to be free from discrimination, torture, violence, and coercion on the basis of sexual orientation, and/or gender identity and expression. Claims to sexual rights are what one activist calls:

> the embodiment of an old and general goal: on the one hand, the achievement of substantive equality for all persons; on the other hand, the extension of protections for human freedom and dignity to include the most vulnerable groups, and to publicize and prevent even the least visible and most easily concealed abuses and violations.
>
> (HRW and IGLHRC 2005: 14)

In practice, engaging sexual rights frameworks has inspired a growing number of initiatives to be inclusive of, but not limited to, people who claim recognized identities based on their sexual orientation and/or gender expression. In other words, there is a push to conduct advocacy that is grounded in the right to construct identities – such as lesbian, gay, bisexual, transgender, kothi or any other – while rejecting the need to be bound by any identity in order to access rights and freedoms (see Miller 2004). In this vein, Corrêa and Parker comment that the struggle for sexual rights in its diverse and multiplicitous forms, "is among the most important forces of change in contemporary society, with key contributions to broader debates related to social development and human security in the contemporary world." They argue that on a global level, sexuality has become:

> a key contested domain or field of struggle. Whether at the local level or in international arenas such as the United Nations, sexuality and sexualities are being reformulated and reframed around the globe today. Highly "modern" sexualities are being constructed in societies throughout the world, just as diverse forms of fundamentalism and violence have been unleashed in response to such changes, combining today to make sexuality one of the key forms of social struggle and conflict … Concrete examples of these struggles are almost endless …
>
> (Corrêa and Parker 2004: 19)

As they note, a "sexual rights" framework is proving to be a meaningful tool for advancing the rights of people whose sexual orientation and/or gender expression do not conform to social or cultural prescriptions. People – whether they identify as lesbian, gay, bisexual, transgender, meti, woubi, hijira, all-sexual, travesti, women loving women, or heterosexual – have a right to control over their bodies, autonomy over decisions related to their sexual life, and the right to express and interpret that sexual life free from coercion or discrimination. From our perspective, this growing discourse is a bold challenge to heteronormativity and its corresponding and intersecting systems of privilege and oppression.

The sexual rights framework is therefore, by definition, a broad, multi-issue framework that serves to acknowledge the fluidity of identities across space – as in the case of localized identities such as women loving women, metis, and travesti – as well as over time – as in the case of people who take on or emphasize multiple or different identities across their lifespan, some of which may be rooted in their gender identity or expression, but may also be anchored in their sexual expression or conduct. It is also a framework that frees people from the (often unarticulated) expectation that identity and practice must always be externally coherent.

In addition to addressing emerging tensions of identity politics, the sexual rights framework presents a formal opening for broader coalition building. For example, as the visibility of "gay and lesbian rights" grew worldwide, women's health and human rights advocates were engaged in articulating a sexual and reproductive rights agenda that sought to assert women's rights to control over their sexuality as well as their reproduction, and for their sexual autonomy as well as protection from sexual violence. Momentum has now grown strong around a broad agenda that seeks to affirm the right of every human being to "pursue a satisfying, safe, and pleasurable sex life" (WHO 2002). The ways in which the accusation of lesbianism is used to attack women's human rights defenders and organizations, and the ways in which these women and organizations respond to these tactics is another important point of intersection between movements that are traditionally treated as "separate" (Miller 2004: 91).

Therefore, a sexual rights framework, which speaks to the rights of bodily integrity and sexual and gender autonomy and expression, provides for advocacy strategies which embrace a larger community. Working transnationally and/or in international arenas necessitates an organizing strategy that takes into account geographically and historically specific concepts of sexuality and gender and gives deference to local activists' preferred ways of thinking of and expressing any gender which falls outside of social and cultural norms; it requires modes of organizing that do not reify gender binaries.

Finally, a sexual rights framework also creates a space for cross-movement organizing, which is crucial for advancing the human rights of all people who are subject to discrimination on the basis of their actual or perceived sexual orientation – for hijras in India who have no right to housing, for metis in Nepal who are repeatedly abused by the police and arbitrarily arrested and detained, for travestis in Argentina who face daily discrimination in the workplace, for *baklas* in the Philippines who don't have access to accurate health information, for butch women in Guatemala who are targeted for rape, and for a transgender person in the US who is thrown into jail because she is assumed to be a prostitute or denied a passport because her gender expression doesn't match the sex on her identity documents.

Claims to sexual rights would, as formal rights do, require changes in law and policy, including health, education, and justice systems, to secure the promotion and protection of sexual rights, as well as to monitor, respond to, and provide redress for violations. Alice Miller reminds us that existing rights standards already allow us to conceptualize a state's duties in these contexts: "For example, rights protections around identity, such as religious identity, tend to be absolute protections: persons cannot be forced to change their identity, nor can they be restrained from changing their identity" (Miller 2004: 91).

Spelling it out further: gender justice

> Trans and intersex people's sexual and reproductive rights are different from the way we've been categorizing and conflating trans rights as sexual rights.
>
> (Cabral 2005a)

Current organizing around sexual rights by activists coming from LGBT and "sexual minority" movements are currently repeating mistakes of the past. As the LGBTI movement has been heavily criticized for doing little more than paying lip service to the T and I (and B for that matter), present day sexual rights coalitions are demonstrating a continued tendency to gloss over the conflation of sexual orientation and gender identity in a way that seems to posit that LGBs have sexual orientation while T and Is have gender identity and expression. When we say that sexual rights is an umbrella term for rights associated to *conceptually linked strategies of bodily control* (Long 2005),[12] we need to be self-reflective and ask whether we have carried old hierarchies, oppressions and blind spots into our reformulated banner of sexual rights. We need to ask whether we are sufficiently rooting out the system of oppression or merely giving it a new cloak. At the recent Beijing +10 meeting,[13] what was formerly the *lesbian caucus* was renamed the *diverse sexualities caucus*. Both the discourses of sexual rights and diverse sexualities which are emerging in international fora such as this one consistently use "sexuality" as an organizing principle for people and practices that are sexually non-conforming *and* gender non-conforming. *Gender* diversity has yet to be meaningfully integrated into the agenda beyond the inclusion of a sentence condemning binary gender and naming transgender communities. Rarely in these spaces are assumptions about binary gender meaningfully called into question. As we advance a discourse with the aim of changing the conditions that give rise to violations, it is important to ask whether *all* of the ways in which persecution and regulation of trans bodies and experiences are best served by a sexual rights analysis and advocacy framework. It is clear that, as a broad coalition, we need to be more deliberate in advocating for the rights of all gender-variant people to the full range of sexual expression and diversity, as well as the often overlooked reproductive rights of trans people. We must also more explicitly acknowledge that LGB and TI are not mutually exclusive categories and invisibilize gay trans men as well as lesbian and bisexual transwomen, and genderqueer people.

Similarly, wide-ranging advocacy efforts are pairing *sexuality* with *gender* to include the right to gender diversity beyond the binary. But, at this point, new questions emerge. For example, would it be more accurate to talk about the sexual rights of trans men, trans women, travesti as their right to sexual autonomy – so, for example, in the case of countries where sex-reassignment surgery is permitted in order to make someone heterosexual ... the right of trans people to be gay, to have sexual autonomy, to marry, to reproduce or adopt or abort? Which is the umbrella, sexuality or gender? LGB(TI) activists who are adopting the sexual rights framework say that it is sexuality. Riki Wilchins claims otherwise:

> The instinct to control bodies, genders, and desires, may be as close as we have to a universal constant. It is common to cultures rich and poor, left-wing and right-wing, Eastern and Western. [...] And here I mean gender in its widest sense – including sexual orientation, because I take it as self-evident that the mainspring of homophobia is gender: the notion that gay men are insufficiently masculine or lesbian women somehow inadequately feminine. And I include sex, because I take it as obvious that what animates sexism and misogyny is gender, and our astonishing fear and loathing around issues of vulnerability or femininity.
>
> (Wilchins 2002: 11)

Perhaps it is time for the sexual rights discourse to borrow strategies from one of its historical foundations and add a category to its banner: gender justice.

Conclusion: sexual rights and gender justice

Identity-based organizing and sexual rights advocacy are not necessarily opposing or mutually exclusive frameworks. Indeed, as advocacy tools, they each offer unique opportunities. Grounded in this broad agenda, sexual rights activists have been working in innovative coalitions to promote rights protections at the UN Commission on Human Rights, the UN Commission on the Status of Women and in national contexts and spaces. These coalitions are actively engaged in multi-issue organizing that links the agendas of activists working on safe migration, violence against women, LGBT rights, housing rights, HIV/AIDS, and the rights of human rights defenders, among others.

This multifaceted sexual rights approach to organizing supports the most basic principle of human rights, the inherent dignity of all people. As an international movement, there will always be issues of translating realities and contextualizing the conditions that give rise to violations (i.e. metis); the sexual rights framework does not solve this problem but it does help to name and identify common ground in ways that stand ready to animate effective remedies and responses.

Notes

1 This chapter is a significantly revised, lengthened, and updated version of an earlier piece drafted by the authors when they were staff at the International Gay and Lesbian Human Rights Commission (IGLHRC).

2 IGLHRC Action Alerts are sent via e-mail to alert member activists about cases and patterns of discrimination and abuse, and mobilize pressure and scrutiny in order to end discriminatory and abusive laws, policies, and practices, as well as advocate for progressive changes in laws, policies, and practices, by states and non-state actors.

3 For an excellent overview of the relationship between fundamentalisms and women's sexual and reproductive rights, see Berer and Sundar Ravindran (1996); Feldman and Clark (1996).

4 Take, for example, the case of HIV prevention programs that focus on preventing mother-to-child transmission. In some cases, these prevention programs seem to focus entirely on the mother as the vector of disease for the child rather than a patient/client in her own right. See Center for Reproductive Rights (2005).

5 We use the term "heteronormativity" to encompass the set of practices used to enforce "normal" (men as "masculine" – read assertive and in control, and women as "feminine" – read passive and docile). Cathy Cohen has defined heteronormativity as the practices and institutions "that legitimize and privilege heterosexuality and heterosexual relationships as fundamental and 'natural' within society" (2006: 24). Her work emphasizes the importance of sexuality as implicated in broader structures of power, intersecting with and inseparable from race, gender, and class oppression. See also: http://www.answers.com/topic/heteronormativity.

6 See for example, "Is gay over?" in *The Advocate* (June 20, 2006); the mission statement of the Audre Lorde Project at http://www.alp.org/mission/mission2.html; and the GLBT entry in Wikipedia at: http://en.wikipedia.org/wiki/GLBT.

7 The dichotomous social construction of gender as limited to the categories "male" and "female" is increasingly contested.

8 In Fiji this protection has been persistently threatened with repeal.

9 The concept of "sexual hierarchies" was broadly introduced by Gayle Rubin (1984) in her influential article "Thinking Sex: Notes for a Radical Theory of the Politics of Sexuality." This piece has also been reprinted in many other collections (e.g. Abelove, Barale, and Halperin 1993).

10 Chandra Mohanty argues that it is not racial identity but the "common context of struggle" that makes "women of color" cohere as a group. Here we use this "common context" more generally to make a broad distinction between identity-based organizing and organizing that is based on a "context of struggle."

11 For the most part we are referring to consensual sexual conduct among adults. The discussion is more complicated with children and adolescents, although we still advocate for a realm of young people's decision-making, calibrated to the evolving capacity of the child (as noted in the Convention on the Rights of the Child) and, wherever possible, in consultation with parents, guardians, and other trusted adults. Such rights include the right to age-appropriate sexuality education and the right to access to information.

12 Phrase borrowed from Scott Long, Director, LGBT Rights Division, Human Rights Watch, personal communication, 2005.

13 "Beijing +10" refers to the ten-year review conducted within the auspices of the United Nations of action by governments toward achieving the goals set out by the 1995 "UN World Conference on Women." For more information go to http://www.women watch.org.

9 Disrupting gender normativity in the Middle East

Supporting gender transgression as a development strategy

Petra Doan

In Western contexts there has been much discussion of "queering" space as a means of resisting the heteronormative patriarchal paradigm. There has been much less attention to the issue of how one might actually queer the development process. Changing deeply entrenched development practices is a time-consuming undertaking. It has taken a concerted effort to gain widespread recognition that development projects might have differential impacts for men and women. The broadening of this focus from Women in Development (WID) to Gender and Development (GAD) has taken additional effort (McIlwaine and Datta 2003), but even so, the focus remains on a largely heterosexist conception of gender. Jolly (2000) argues that this narrow framing of sexuality does not jibe with the multitude of sexual identities around the world.

This chapter will explore the ways that the expression of non-normative genders in the Middle East might be seen as a mechanism for resistance to rigid patriarchal structures. The focus on this part of the world is justified by the fact that this region has some of the lowest levels of empowerment for women and the prevalence of some of the most highly restrictive patriarchal systems. Ilkkaracan and Mack (2002: 760) argue that "[t]he collective mechanisms aimed at controlling women's bodies and sexuality continue to be one of the most powerful tools of patriarchal management of women's sexuality and a root cause of gender inequality in the region."

In this chapter, the Middle East includes what is known as the Arab world (the Maghreb and the Fertile Crescent) with two significant additions: Turkey and Iran. Each of the countries in this region shares significant Islamic history and long-standing trade and imperial connections that suggest a common patriarchal heritage with respect to gender relations. It is in this highly authoritarian patriarchal region, that Lockard (2005) suggests that "femininizing and queering the Middle East" may be a key vehicle for ensuring lasting democratization.

There are two possible avenues to "queer" something like the development process. The first, more straightforward, approach is to address the development practitioners and persuade them that programs should be inclusive of and in some cases oriented toward those individuals whose sexual or gender identity falls outside heteronormativity. The second, more challenging, tactic is to work directly to empower those people who are excluded from the direct benefits of development programs based on the heteronormative paradigm. If development is ultimately contingent upon the bottom-up empowerment of the disenfranchised, rather than a more top-down donor-driven agenda, then this latter strategy should be preferred. However, Western donor bias often reinforces existing local prejudice, making it difficult to identify, much less to empower, local queer populations.

This chapter accepts the Jolly argument that sexuality is more diverse than most development practitioners suppose, but adds the perspective that genders are also much more diverse than the heteronormative paradigm has suggested. People working in the field of international development need to be aware that differently gendered people have existed throughout history and in nearly every culture (Bullough and Bullough 1993; Feinberg 1996; Nanda 2000). Bornstein (1994) suggests that there may be a thousand or more genders, limited only by the power of our imagination. Wilchins (2004) argues that expanding from a dichotomous to a full spectrum of gender is an essential element of the queering process. Unfortunately, most Western efforts to develop "queer spaces" have seriously neglected gender, leaving the transgendered population at serious risk (Doan 2007). If gender variations are as widespread as these scholars have suggested, then one critical avenue for queering development would be to empower those individuals whose self-perception of gender is variant from the heteronormative paradigm and who embody their queerness in ways that unsettle and challenge fundamental gender norms.

This chapter considers some key examples of pioneering individuals who have dared to express a non-normative gender in this region. These individuals demonstrate with their bodies the difference between sex and gender in a region where the two have been synonymous, thereby undermining the patriarchal systems of power. The importance of these gender transgressions is considered in the context of the wider struggle for greater tolerance for sexual diversity as well as feminist struggles to oppose the patriarchy. Finally, this chapter will provide some suggestions for ways that development practitioners might acknowledge and include gender-variant individuals in the Middle East as a first step towards queering the development process and stimulating change on a broader scale.

Debates continue as to how gender variance is understood and experienced in the Middle East. In the case of transsexuals, some people feel that because transsexual surgery is a recent innovation in the West, any discussion of gender-transgressive behavior that uses Western terminology must be based on an "orientalist" perspective.[1] Other scholars have suggested that any description of LGBT activism must equally be based in orientalism. For example, Massad (2002) suggests that the International Gay and Lesbian Human Rights Organization has pushed a gay agenda so hard that it has created a right-wing backlash in the region because such international groups operate from a Western (orientalist) and not an Arab frame of reference. He argues that "the Gay International's imperialist epistemological task is proceeding apace with little opposition from the majority of sexual beings it wants to 'liberate' and whose social and sexual worlds it is destroying in the process" (Massad, 2002: 385). There is clearly an ongoing struggle over identity in the Middle Eastern region which raises difficult questions for the hetero-patriarchy. Whether these questions are "orientalist" (or something else) needs further discussion.

AbuKhalil (1997) argues that the broad condemnation of homosexuality within Islam is a relatively recent attitude of the twentieth century, when clerics and governments reacting to colonialist Christian morality began to condemn homo-sexuality. The current visibility of the LGBT rights movement in the West does seem to have sparked a responsive movement in the region, although Western freedoms may have simply prompted existing identities to speak up. In any case the more conservative Islamist clerics have seized this as an opportunity to label local LGBT activists "pawns of the West." For instance, AbuKhalil (1993: 34) notes that one cleric has written a pamphlet which argues that the spread of the VCR from the West "explains the practice of homosexuality among Arab men." Today it is probably more appropriate to blame the Internet. What is clear from this historical overview is that there is a long-standing tradition of gender variance and sexual attraction within the region that transcends the heteronormative, no matter what labels are used to describe them.

Liminal identities of modern Middle Eastern transsexuals

In spite of the critics of Wikan for her ethnocentrism in using the term "transsex-ual," in recent years there have been a number of influential transsexual women in the Middle East who have challenged the dichotomous gender categories embedded in religious beliefs and legal systems.[2] The first openly transsexual figure in the region is from Turkey, named Bülent Ersoy (Zuhur 2005). Ms. Ersoy remains a popular singer of classical Turkish music, who had sex-change surgery in the early 1980s. When she submitted an application to have her gender legally changed after sexual-reassignment surgery, she set off a lengthy debate in Turkey. This process eventually resulted in a change in the laws regarding transsexuals in that country (Atamer 2005).

Maryam Khatoon Molkara petitioned successfully for a similar change in status for transsexuals in the Islamic Republic of Iran. Ms. Molkara was given the male name of Fereydoon at birth, and tried several times during the 1970s to gain an audience with Ayatollah Khomeini to plead for permission to change her sex. In 1983 her persistence finally convinced the Ayatollah to issue a *fatwa* (religious ruling) permitting her to undergo sex-change surgery (Tait 2005). Today Molkara heads up a transsexual support group and continues her campaign for greater understanding for the increasing numbers of her sister and brother transsexuals (Fathi 2004).

Sally Mursi was given the male name Sayed at birth in her native Egypt. She was a student at the Al Azhar School of Medicine, when she realized that she needed to live her life as the woman that she knew herself to be. In 1988 she found an Egyptian surgeon willing to perform sex-change surgery, but upon completion of the surgery, the school authorities expelled her from the men's medical school. The authorities accused her of stirring up social instability and creating public disorder. Although the influential Sheikh of al-Azhar issued a *fatwa* in 1988 indicating that transsexual surgery was a matter best left to a doctor's discretion (Khattab 2004), the Al Azhar medical school refused to readmit her to the women's medical college in part because she had begun working as a belly-dancer in order to earn a living as well as pay for her legal fees. Ms. Mursi continues her legal battle for broader acceptance and understanding.

Another example of a transsexual woman whose liminality crosses both language and cultural barriers is Dana International (aka Sharon Cohen). In the early 1990s Ms. Cohen, a mizrahi or Israeli Jew with roots in Yemen, became something of an underground sensation in neighboring Jordan and Egypt. Because of her Yemeni roots, she sang some of her songs in Arabic, making them accessible to an audience beyond Israel (Swedenburg 1997). The fact that Ms. Cohen later won the Eurovision music contest performing as Dana International makes her something of a transnational mold breaker. One commentator notes that:

> It is fascinating in these increasingly fundamentalist, repressive times, as waves of terror sweep over the sands from Iraq to Algeria, that the voice that seems to unite so many disparate people is one that is banned in Egypt and Jordan as "shameful" in terms of sex rather than religion. Being a woman in the Middle East is shameful enough, but Dana International pushes the envelope of that definition.

> (Moriel 1999: 316)

Unfortunately, her popularity may have triggered a backlash by some fundamentalist clerics who view her as an Israeli cancer infecting the minds of Arab youth (Swedenburg 1997). In spite of this controversy, Ms. Cohen remains one of the most visible transgendered individuals in the region.

While initial recognition for transsexuals has been gained by individuals, wider acceptance requires a more concerted effort. Demet Demir is a transsexual activist from Istanbul who has demonstrated the effectiveness of coalition building to achieve more humane policies within an urban community (Kandiyoti and Robert 1998). In the early 1990s transsexuals were a well established part of the sex trade in the government-regulated red light district in Istanbul (Fleishman 2000) and as many as 70 transgendered women lived on a street named Ülker Sokak near Taksim Square (Demir 1995). In the preparations for the United Nations Habitat Conference held in Istanbul in 1995, the police began beating and arresting the transsexual residents in an attempt to clean up this neighborhood. Ms. Demir and her sister transsexuals protested this "neighborhood cleansing" and began a new era of public activism for the rights of trans people (Martin 2003). Although Ms. Demir has been beaten and imprisoned several times by the authorities for her activism (Demir 1997), she has maintained her membership in the Radical Democratic Green Party as well as the Turkish Human Rights Association, advocating for greater acceptance of LGBT people. Eventually, she was recognized by IGLHRC and awarded the Felipa de Souza Award for her activism.

The struggle for sexual freedom and gender justice in the Middle East

While transsexuals and other gender-queer individuals cannot single-handedly dismantle the heteronormative dichotomous gender system, they do raise a number of unsettling questions for more rigid authoritarian regimes about the fundamental differences between sex and gender, and the relative fixity of these concepts. The accompanying erosion of fixed boundaries between the sexes may permit a more open expression of the full range of gender and sexual expression. In both Turkey and Lebanon local organizations in support of LGBT rights have had some success in advocating for greater openness. In Turkey, Lambda Istanbul was formed in response to a crackdown on homosexuals in the early 1990s. Today this group provides an Internet site, organizes regular get-togethers, and has published the first AIDS guide (Martin 2003). This organization has also helped LGBT people to become more articulate about their needs as an urban community (Yenicioğlu 1997). In Lebanon, an organization known as Helem has been working to decriminalize homosexuality and struggle against homophobia (Torbey 2005).

In spite of some success in the struggle for LGBT rights, there is an ongoing religious backlash and a tendency to use homosexuality as a scapegoat and rallying cry for further Islamist reforms. Although homosexuality is formally illegal in most countries in the region, in some countries it has been tacitly tolerated in the past. In the more conservative states, this is no longer the case. As a graphic example, two teenagers were hanged for the crime of homosexuality in Iran in 2005 (Fathi 2005), and there have been repeated crackdowns in other countries.

In Egypt there has been increasing harassment of gay men exemplified by the arrest of 52 gay Egyptians in 2001 in what is now known as the Queen Boat incident (Massad 2002). Bahgat (2001) suggests that this action against gays is most likely a reactionary attempt by the Mubarak regime to burnish its image as a keeper of public morality, and thereby undercut the ever-present Islamist opposition movement.

Unfortunately, in the most conservative regimes, this backlash has been closely linked with gender variance.[3] For instance, in 2005 in Saudi Arabia 100 men were arrested and sentenced to imprisonment and flogging after state security police broke up a private party in a rented hall. The crime that they committed was that some of the participants were wearing dresses and behaving like women (Human Rights Watch 2005). More recently in 2006 a court in the United Arab Emirates jailed 12 men who were arrested after being discovered preparing for a gay wedding by donning women's clothing and make-up (Shoffman 2006a).

Even in more tolerant societies there is a fear of gender transgression. Certainly in the US the transgendered population is often the most vulnerable and most visible of all sexual minorities, triggering crimes of rage (Doan 2001, 2006). In the Middle East the response is no different. In Lebanon a young lesbian interviewed by the Women's Studies journal *Al Raida* indicates that while she is active in the lesbian community in Lebanon, she is afraid to come out in public as a lesbian. She writes: "With me people are very natural. I mean people aren't revolted by masculine girls. There are a lot of masculine girls around. I think it's harder on feminine guys. People can't stand that (Hamdar 2002: 94).

The case of Jordan is similar according to Zuhur (2005) because gays and lesbians are afraid of family retribution in Jordan. She suggests that lesbians may be victims of honor killings as well as beatings by family members with no legal recourse to such assaults. Assfar (1996) describes the fear of lesbians in Jordan which revolves around the notions of honor and shame.

Although Jordanian law contains no mention of the word *suhak* (lesbianism), widespread prejudice within Jordanian society is more powerful that any legal prohibition. Lesbians are afraid to be visible because they fear losing whatever freedom of movement they may have. Jordanian society is a closely knit, family- and religion-oriented one in which people know one another and there is little opportunity for anonymity (Assfar n.d.).

The situation in Iraq merits special attention. In 2005 Grand Ayatollah Ali Sistani released a *fatwa* in which he told his followers that homosexuals should be killed (McDonough 2006). Subsequent to this religious edict there were numerous killings of gays, including more feminine-appearing gay men and at least one transsexual, Dina Faiek, who was beaten and burned to death by the Badr militias on a main street in Baghdad (Shoffman 2006b). Regrettably, because effeminate gay men and transgendered people are so visible, they have been the most likely targets. Gay Iraqis reportedly feel that Sistani has unleashed what amounts to a pogrom against gays and lesbians (Gay and Lesbian Arab Society 2006). This is especially egregious because, as an occupying power, the United States is more than complicit in this action. Fortunately, after several months of killings the *fatwa* posted on Sistani's website against gay men was removed in May of 2006 (Shoffman 2006c).[4]

Finally, in Iran the situation is challenging for young women who identify as lesbian. An online report from Mona, a young Iranian woman who attends university in Tehran, presents a moving picture. She is terribly torn between her understanding of her own identity as a lesbian and her attachment to her family. In her words:

> Homosexuality is not accepted in Iranian society at all. Most people consider it evil. At best, they think it's an illness. Many parents, if they find out that their child is gay, will use violence against them, humiliate them, even reject them. If they are very open-minded, they might take their child to a psychologist. If someone finds out a friend is gay, they will stop seeing them. Some will be abusive. People who are understanding are very rare. You have to hide everything, even from your own family.
>
> (Mona 2002)

Lessons for development practitioners

In a region as socially conservative as the Middle East, some development practitioners may shrink from taking on culturally loaded issues such as sexuality and gender variance. It certainly might be difficult for some international agencies or

NGOs to make this an explicit focus of project and program work. However, this chapter suggests that rather than ignoring incipient local rights movements, development outcomes related to women's issues and basic rights would benefit from more broadly inclusive projects and coalitions for the following reasons.

1. *Undermining social-control mechanisms*: Those who visibly transgress gender norms may have some important lessons for development practitioners who wish to advocate for greater women's rights as well as greater sexual freedoms. The key mechanisms used to regulate gender-based inequality in the Middle East are honor (*sharaf*) and shame which ensure women's compliance with traditional expectations (Shukri 1996). Because women are told that their behaviors reflect directly on their family's honor, any behavior that deviates from traditional gender norms will bring shame on the family and tribe. In addition, women are controlled by restricting their mobility through the use of seclusion (*purdah*) and required veiling. Sexuality is equally controlled because any visible expression or performance of female sexuality outside of the marital home is seen as a serious violation of family honor.

Gender transgressors can undermine these control mechanisms in several ways. First, although the patriarchy tries to use honor and shame to regulate behavior of differently gendered people, with transgendered individuals these systems do not work as well. In Turkey, Janssen (1992) argues that people who live openly as transgendered or *köçek* do experience a severe loss of status with direct effects on the individual's family honor. However, instead of controlling gender-transgressive behaviors, for many transsexuals expressing their "true" gender identity is more compelling than family honor so they are willing to risk societal sanctions, thereby undermining this rigid system of control. Second, those who openly change sexes undermine the very basis of the mechanisms needed to control female sexuality. When men become women and women become men, the rationale for ensuring the rigid segregation of the sexes is weakened.

2. *Mitigating social control through international coalitions*: Development practitioners should be aware that an important means of alleviating shame is the development of coalitions both within national systems and across national borders. Moghadam (2005) suggests that transnational feminist networks are extremely important in developing the solidarity needed to achieve lasting change. Two groups that she cites which are active in the Middle East are Woman Living Under Muslim Laws (WLUML) and the Sisterhood Is Global International (SIGI), both of which have been resisting the trend toward increasing Islamic fundamentalism through extensive networking both within the region and outside the Middle East. Other groups such as Women for Women's Human Rights – New Ways (WWHR) is a women's and human rights NGO established in Turkey in 1993 which has been actively organizing conferences and seminars on women's issues and sexuality in the Middle East and in the Muslim world in general. Afary (2004) concurs that women's organizing for civil society is an essential step in improving the human rights situation.

Sandoval (2002: 25) argues that a new form of dissident global resistance is needed that "recognizes and identifies all technologies of power as consensual illusions" which are required for ensuring social justice. Sandoval further argues that such a dissident global resistance movement would carve out new spaces of resistance where "transcultural, transgendered, transnational leaps" can be used as stratagems for opposing entrenched power domains. For example, in Jordan, closeted lesbians have discovered that, despite the oppression, change is possible. Assfar (1996) argues that establishing connections with lesbians from other Arab countries has been a critical element in opening up possibilities for change.

> In the past five years, some individual lesbians have begun to network with lesbians from other countries within and outside the region. Contacts with two Arab-American groups, the Gay and Lesbian Arabic Society and the Arab Lesbian and Bisexual Women's Network, have been particularly important because their members share a similar cultural background. Lesbians in Jordan are without a mention, without recognition, very marginalized … YET WE EXIST.
>
> (Assfar 1996)

Middle Eastern women whose sexuality or gender identity does not conform to expectations continue to experience oppression. The response to this prejudice is a kind of sometimes quiet, and sometimes not so quiet, organizing throughout the region. Anissa Hélie (2006) provides a useful analysis of the importance of coalition building to withstand a patriarchal backlash. She argues that in this region:

> … leaders of politico-religious movements promote conservative, highly selective interpretations of religion and identity in order to gain or maintain power … The mythical "values" promoted are, in fact, those of nationalism, xenophobia, sexism and homophobia. Therefore it is not surprising that women, minorities, and LGBTI people are the most vulnerable to fundamentalist right wing politics.
>
> (Hélie 2006: 3)

3. *Strengthening local coalitions*: Hélie goes on to make the case for a coincidence of interest between these various progressive groups at the local level and suggests that "coalition building with other faith-based groups, or on an identity basis, allows for fruitful exchange of strategies and mutual support" (2006: 11). She stresses that what is needed is local coalition building that can at times be reinforced by international NGOs, but she is equally clear that local groups need to take a lead role.

Altman (2004) concurs and suggests that incipient homosexual movements in developing countries must also establish their own identities and activities appropriate to the existing cultural milieu. Such local network formation in the face of organized homophobia has been successfully used in Slovakia where the development of queer civil society (nine gay and lesbian organizations) was essential to creating a network for change (Wallace-Lorencová 2003).

Modest amounts of international support can provide useful sustenance for such domestic movements. In Lebanon and Turkey, local organizing has been reinforced by subtle support from international organizations. In Lebanon, Helem has been supported by the Heinrich Boll Foundation from Germany. In Turkey, Lambda Istanbul has been supported by the International Gay and Lesbian Human Rights Organization. If development practitioners from other international agencies provided similar support to other organizations in the region, who knows what might happen.

Conclusions

The task for development practitioners in the Middle East is to find ways to support the development of broad-based feminist coalitions that are able to resist the erosion of women's status and expand global human rights, including those of gender and sexual expression. While some critics may argue that "cultural" issues such as sexuality should be ignored by international development workers, to do so would also be to take a clear position that supports the status quo of an entrenched patriarchal system. The critical development task in this region is the development of an empowered civil society that is broadly representative of the diverse populations in this region, and is able to make claims for access to resources and recognition of basic human rights. In some cases, local NGOs are able to provide a locus for change within the larger social structure, as was the case in Turkey with the Turkish Human Rights Association's support for Demit Demir. However, other groups may be fearful of taking on work that challenges the existing system, and this is where development workers may be able to provide additional capacity-building and supportive linkages.

A case in point is the Egyptian Organization for Human Rights (EOHR). This group is governed by a Board with 16 members, only one of whom is a woman. After the Queen Boat incident discussed above, one of its employees, Hossam Bahgat, took a strong public stand in favor of the victims of the Queen Boat incident, yet was fired because the EOHR was afraid of taking on the complex issue of homosexuality (Bahgat 2001). A BBC news report quotes Hisham Kassem, Director of the Egyptian Organization for Human Rights, as saying, "What could we do? Nothing. If we were to uphold this issue, this would be the end of what remains of the concept of human rights in Egypt" (BBC 2002). And yet two years later with the support of international NGO Human Rights Watch, five other Egyptian human rights organizations (the Egyptian Association Against Torture, the Egyptian Initiative for Personal Rights, the Hisham Mubarak Law Center, the Nadim Center for the Psychological Management and Rehabilitation of Victims of Violence, and the Arabic Network for Human Rights Information) released a major report condemning the use of torture on homosexuals in Egypt (Human Rights Watch 2004).

Sometimes these kinds of broader coalitions can be the focal point for needed changes when a single group may not have the ability or the will to take a risk. Hélie (2006) argues that the task for development workers in such situations is not to set the agendas, but to encourage the inclusion of all voices so that real empowerment can take place. As Sonia Corrêa, coordinator of the Sexual Reproductive Health and Rights Program of Development Alternatives with Women for a New Era (DAWN), has argued:

> These are signs of how dangerous and complex the political landscape in which we move has become. We may panic and retreat. But we can also use these dangers and complexities to reconsider the reluctance in respect to queer theories, and to start exploring its potentialities, as a tool to respond to fundamentalist voices and a bridge towards renewed dialogues and alliances across gender and sexual identities.
>
> (Corrêa 2006: 12)

If some of those voices are differently gendered or oriented, this may not be such a bad thing since destabilizing the forces that dichotomize gender may be the key to forward movement for sexual minorities as well as for women in general.

Notes

1 The original use of the term orientalism referred to the "Western style for dominating, restructuring, and having authority over the Orient" (Said 1978: 3).
2 There is very little public presence of transsexual men in the Middle East or in the relevant literature. The only reference found cites the case of a Bahraini Princess who became a man, but lives in London because if he returns to his home country, he might be killed (Wynne-Jones 1999).
3 In the US, Riki Wilchins (1997) argues that many hate crimes against gays and lesbians are more often a function of their overt violation of gender norms than their sexual identity, which is not nearly as visible.
4 It is interesting that the *fatwa* against lesbians is still apparently in force. Since lesbians are often under the radar of the hetero-patriarchy, this may be simply an oversight.

10 Behind the Mask

Developing LGBTI visibility in Africa[1]

Ashley Currier

Contributors to this volume have presented valid criticisms of heterosexism, Eurocentrism, and the invisibility of queerness within development institutions, discourses, and practices. Instead of duplicating these arguments, I argue that negotiated partnerships between foreign donors with an explicit interest in funding and supporting lesbian, gay, bisexual, transgendered, and intersexed (LGBTI) movement organizations in the global South sometimes promote sexual and gender diversity. With donors' financial support, some LGBTI movement organizations in the global South direct their programs with relative autonomy and "have some advantages over more traditional development: their small scale, unofficial nature, and activist element" (Jolly 2000a: 86). However, these advantages do not negate unequal relationships between donors and LGBTI movement organizations.

Grassroots organizers operating unofficially or on a small scale usually require funds to sustain their efforts, and they market themselves to obtain funds. At a minimum, movement organizations must elevate donors' understanding of LGBTI issues and prove "there are benefits – or at least few risks – to potential supporters" (Bob 2002: 399). The onus of proving their need to European or North American donors reflects the unequal positions of donors and movement organizations. LGBTI movement organizations may have to work harder to market themselves to prospective foreign donors than anti-poverty movement organizations because many donors recognize poverty as a widespread problem. They may have to justify why donors should provide financial support, if sexual and gender diversity is a new concept for donors. Some organizations may alter their public visibility to match a donor's programs and ideals. Such strategizing around visibility may involve reframing the organization's message in a way that resonates with donors, for instance, by using language that equates LGBTI rights with human rights or by (over)emphasizing the local cultural, social, and political obstacles that organizations face.

Public visibility and invisibility describe more than the public presence or non-presence of LGBTI persons. They are strategies through which LGBTI persons and organizations evade danger (through invisibility) or manifest their numbers (through visibility). Though queer critiques converge in their assessment that LGBTI persons are absent from or invisible in development discourses and practices (Kleitz 2000; Jolly 2000a), the strategies that LGBTI movement organizations use to become publicly visible remain under-scrutinized. It is essential that development practitioners, donors, and activists grasp how visibility *works* because it can alter LGBTI persons' lives.

Public visibility is a basic concern for many LGBTI persons and movement organizations. Two cautions are in order. First, LGBTI persons' experiences of sexuality are as diverse as their experiences of visibility. In other words, experiences of visibility and invisibility are not the same around the world (Manalansan 1997, cited in Bacchetta 2002). Second, public visibility can have positive and negative consequences for LGBTI persons, which can differ depending on individuals' race, ethnicity, class, and nationality (Puri 2006). For instance, Black lesbians and gay men who reside in South African townships are at risk of homophobic violence, due to the public visibility of divergent gender and sexualities (Reid and Dirsuweit 2002). Sexuality and gender are "most definitely ... survival issue[s]" (Lind and Share 2003: 70). The choice for LGBTI persons to become visible may be a luxury in tolerant sociopolitical circumstances, a potentially positive consequence of visibility, compared to repressive circumstances in which sexual and gender minorities may mask their sexual and/or gender non-normativity for personal safety. In the latter case, invisibility may be a necessity and perhaps a negative consequence, as the choices for disclosing their alternative sexual and gender identities may be limited for LGBTI persons. Masking may be "exhausting or painful," as it requires constant vigilance, whereas unmasking can constitute a liberating process for individuals (Steinbugler 2005: 429). In this case, visibility is synonymous with individuals' public performances of their sexual and gender identities, whereas invisibility involves the opposite: the withholding of public enactments of divergent genders and sexualities.

Queer theory addresses such performative and political questions about public visibility. One aim of queer politics is to amplify LGBTI persons' public visibility by "establishing *safe space for public sexualities*" (Richardson 1996: 15, emphasis mine). Within this framework, creating safe spaces for public sexualities in South Africa – the country of focus in this chapter – entails demonstrating that divergent genders and sexualities are African. Establishing safe spaces may also involve challenging assumptions about LGBTI persons, such as: that gay men and lesbians are intersexed, or that gay men desire to be women and lesbians men (Swarr 2003). Visibility emerges as a fundamental question not only for LGBTI persons as individuals, but also for LGBTI persons as a social and political group who challenge homophobic and transphobic definitions and uses of public spaces (Epprecht 2005).

However, little research documents how LGBTI movement organizations try to establish "safe space for public sexualities" (Palmberg 1999; Richardson 1996: 15). In this chapter, I address this gap by illustrating how a South African LGBTI movement organization, Behind the Mask (BtM), attempts to generate safe spaces for sexual and gender diversity in South Africa and throughout Africa. Using ten interviews with staff members, ethnographic observations of the organization's daily operations between September 2005 and April 2006, and analysis of the organization's website content, I demonstrate how Behind the Mask's strategies of amateur journalism and marketing increase the visibility of the organization,

LGBTI persons, and LGBTI movements in Africa and facilitate the forging of ties with other African LGBTI grassroots organizations. After describing the South African LGBTI movement's history and the rise of Behind the Mask, I consider queer and social movement theories of visibility to understand the organization's visibility strategies.

The South African LGBTI social movement

The history of the South African LGBTI movement proves that racial and sexual politics go hand in hand (Nagel 2003). The South African gay movement emerged in the late 1960s in response to the apartheid government's police raids on white gay clubs and private parties in Johannesburg's suburbs. White gay male and lesbian activists sought to curb raids and persuade the state to decriminalize sodomy (Gevisser 1995). This manifestation of the movement dissipated in the mid-1970s, giving way to more discreet, separate social clubs for white gay men and lesbians, an example of the effect that state repression can have on the public visibility of sexual minorities. Black South Africans were not allowed to travel freely in urban areas without a pass that admitted them to white parts of town for certain hours for work (Mamdani 1996), making it difficult for Black, multiracial, Indian, and white gay men and lesbians to mingle in urban areas. The movement remained racially segregated in the 1980s until anti-apartheid and gay organizing intersected and resulted in racially mixed gay and lesbian (and eventually bisexual) organizations (Luirink 2000).

Since the ascendancy of a Black majority democratic government, led by the African National Congress (ANC), and the repeal of apartheid-era discriminatory laws and policies in the early 1990s, the LGBTI movement has won several major victories. Under an umbrella group, the National Coalition for Gay and Lesbian Equality, South African LGBTI movement organizations successfully lobbied to get a sexual-orientation non-discrimination clause permanently enshrined in the 1996 Constitution (Croucher 2002; Cock 2003). The Coalition and other LGBTI movement organizations fought to get the state to decriminalize sodomy (1998), extend adoption rights to same-sex couples (2002), and legalize same-sex marriage (2005) (Epprecht 2004: 212). Since these significant wins, LGBTI movement organizations have concentrated on the movement's many remaining grievances: the rape of Black lesbians; the (mis)representation of LGBTI persons and the movement as unAfrican; the provision of mental and physical health services for LGBTI persons, including those living with HIV/AIDS; and the offering of legal services to individuals who have been discriminated against because of their sexual and/or gender identity.

Theorizing public in/visibility

This volume considers queer theory's potential for subverting development discourses that crystallize sexuality in heteronormative terms, namely in reproducing sexuality as a heterosexuality that individuals experience strictly as "masculine" men or "feminine" women (Gamson and Moon 2004). Some queer theorists have embraced visibility as a way to upend heteronormative social institutions (Hennessy 2000: 37). Queer political tactics involve exposing, subverting, dismantling, and replacing heteronormative discourses and practices with fluid gender and sexual categories (Berlant and Freeman 1998). Visibility metamorphosed into a useful tactic and strategic orientation that has been unevenly diffused to countries in the global South (Chabot and Duyvendak 2002). Just as publicity functions differently in distinct political fields, LGBTI persons around the world experience visibility and invisibility in diverse ways. As such, processes of visibility become hybridized as LGBTI persons and movement organizations incorporate them into their own repertoires of action and activist cultures (Bhabha 1994; Phillips 2000).

Many scholars have examined the production of visibility of LGBTI persons as individuals and as a group in the global North. These processes include promulgating positive messages about LGBTI persons in the media, which "can prepare the ground for gay civil rights protection" (Hennessy 2000: 31–2). Much scholarship shows how performing sexualities publicly creates spaces that fluid social and sexual identities can inhabit (Butler 1990). Geographers, in particular, have studied how LGBTI persons in North America and Western Europe mask their sexual identities to avoid harassment or violence in heterosexualized public settings (Corteen 2002; Steinbugler 2005). Research on the queering of spaces in the Ivory Coast, Thailand, and Brazil expands research on the performance of LGBTI identities beyond North America and Western Europe, the use of public space by LGBTI persons and groups, and the processes by which LGBTI persons opt to become visible or to withdraw from visibility (Green 2001; Wilson 2004; Nguyen 2005).

Documenting same-sex relationships across time has been an important historical visibility project for South African LGBTI movement activists (Leatt and Hendricks 2005: 312–13; Morgan and Wieringa 2005). However, across sub-Saharan Africa and in South Africa, many state and religious leaders deny the contemporary and historical existence of LGBTI persons. At issue in claims that homosexuality is unAfrican and LGBTI rights activists' assertions to the contrary, apart from defining the sexual and racial boundaries of what is African, is whether these two groups are quarreling over whether LGBTI identities or same-sex sexual acts are foreign (Aarmo 1999; Phillips 2000). The tendency of LGBTI activists and their opponents to collapse identities and behavior together suggests that identities are easier to see than behavior – "[s]ex is no longer about what one does but rather what one is" (Nguyen 2005: 264). Part of the visibility project in South Africa involves establishing that homosexuality is authentically African, which "becomes fundamental in the negotiation of identity in the post-colony" (Mathuray 2000: 2).

Though these studies make important contributions to the burgeoning literature on LGBTI performances of identities, the conceptual opacity of visibility still beleaguers many studies of LGBTI publicity. What happens after LGBTI persons become visible? Does the performance of visibility end with a permanent state of visibility? Unless scholars address these questions, the assumption that after "coming out" publicly, LGBTI persons in the global North and South remain out, goes unquestioned. Visibility for LGBTI persons then becomes a default *outcome* or *accomplishment* dispersed across time and space, rather than an unfolding social process, strategy, or performance that takes place within a confined time and space. LGBTI public visibility may be a political victory in North America or Western Europe, but regarding the concept only as an accomplishment obscures the processes by which LGBTI persons elsewhere emerge publicly, the obstacles they face in so doing, and their decisions to become visible or to eschew visibility.

Just as scholars ignore the processes by which LGBTI persons become and remain visible, they also disregard how LGBTI movement organizations become visible. The "struggle to be seen" transcends movements for social change, yet few studies interrogate how social movements cultivate visibility (Guidry 2003: 493; emphasis removed). How social movement organizations manage their public visibility is a process that many scholars overlook, even though it is crucial to an organization's ability to broker relations between unconnected groups or to obtain funding or support from international donors (Bob 2005). Studying how social movement organizations cultivate public visibility or retreat from public view can shed light on how activists prioritize and tailor their messages for certain audiences.

A South African LGBTI movement organization is an excellent case study for examining how organizations craft their own visibility and that of LGBTI persons. LGBTI movement organizations are guarantors of "safe space[s]" because they "provide meeting places and ... answer the psychological needs of insecure and harassed gays and lesbians" (Palmberg 1999: 267). How, when, and why do LGBTI organizations deploy collective identities publicly? Does the deployment of markers of LGBTI public collective identities, if there are any, differ in the global North and South? If so, how? If scholars do not pose these crucial questions about the strategic nature of visibility, it risks becoming a flypaper concept, catching all forms of LGBTI movement publicity.

Behind the Mask

The name "Behind the Mask" refers to the cloak of social, cultural, political, and legal invisibility that many African LGBTI persons don every day. As an organization, Behind the Mask addresses issues of interest to African LGBTI persons, such as hate crimes, poverty, HIV/AIDS, and unemployment (Interview, staff member, January 13, 2006). Its website offers "a platform for exchange and debate for LGBTI groups, activists, individuals and allies" through an online chatting function and frequently updated news articles (http://www.mask.org.za/). Behind the Mask's website design allows for "anonymous" viewing; a staff member distinguished the website from other gay-themed websites. "It's not a gay site with pictures of naked men or pictures of women with [bare] breasts ... Our strength is we're able to give people information without it ... blaring on the screen" (Interview, October 31, 2005). In this sense, Behind the Mask eschews prurient visual content, such as pictures of unclothed men and women, to distinguish itself from commercial gay websites in South Africa.

In its early years, Behind the Mask was housed within the Gay and Lesbian Archives of South Africa. With donor funding, the organization secured office space and resources and has served as an incubator for a Black lesbian organization, the Forum for the Empowerment of Women (FEW), and a Black LGBTI youth organization, the South African Youth Liberation Organization. Due in part to its financial and geographical base in Johannesburg, South Africa, Behind the Mask dedicates most of its journalistic resources to reporting on LGBTI issues in the country, although it is developing a network of correspondents throughout Africa. The organization also works to strengthen bonds with and among other African LGBTI movement organizations.

Eleven people staffed the organization when I observed Behind the Mask from October 2005 to March 2006: the Dutch founder who served as a part-time paid consultant,[2] the director, the managing editor, the office administrator, the house-keeper, the webmaster, the part-time French translator, the junior reporter, the human rights researcher, and two temporary, unpaid interns from Germany and Uganda. All staff members sometimes wrote stories for the website, although the junior reporter and managing editor wrote regular feature stories as their primary duties. Apart from the Dutch founder, American office administrator, Burundian French translator, and German and Ugandan interns, the rest of the staff were South African. Reporters wrote in English, and some stories were translated into French. Behind the Mask also recruited correspondents living in other African nations to report on LGBTI social issues, increasing the organization's ability to gather first-hand information about what is happening in other African countries.

Most Behind the Mask staff members were, by definition, amateur journalists or "journalistic activis[ts]" (http://www.mask.org.za). At the time I conducted this study, apart from the founder and the current managing editor, both of whom were trained journalists, no staff member had formal journalism training, though the junior reporter was pursuing a degree in communication at a South African university. The organization did provide compulsory training and writing workshops for staff and foreign correspondents who wrote for the website, however, which I outline below. Addressing the lack of formally trained journalists, Behind the Mask recently overhauled its hiring policies to ensure that it recruited staff with professional journalism experience.

Aware of the widespread hostility to homosexuality, Behind the Mask framed stories to show LGBTI persons they were not alone and LGBTI movement organizations how groups in other African countries were fighting repression. Like activists from different social movements, Behind the Mask uses Internet amateur journalism to disseminate the LGBTI movement's claims and demands through-out Africa and the world. The Internet has enabled "amateur journalists" to inform interested audiences about what happens behind movements' closed doors in compelling, intimate detail (Atton 2003). Such accounts may strike audiences as more authentic than delayed, second-hand accounts that come from professional reporters who may only write stories about social movements protesting an egre-gious violation of the law or social convention. Additionally, amateur journalism may resonate with activists and audiences who feel that the mainstream media marginalize and misrepresent them (Atton 2003). It has been a valuable strategy of visibility for Behind the Mask. The organization crafted a distinctive way of communicating the message that "homosexuality is African" and cultivated credibility with donors and African LGBTI persons and organizations through its accurate representation of African LGBTI persons and organizing.

Promoting the LGBTI movement's visibility: homosexuality is African

Behind the Mask promulgated the message that homosexuality is African to counter rhetoric from conservative political and religious leaders who believe that homosexuality is unAfrican. In its mission statement, Behind the Mask claims that it aspires to "change negative attitudes towards homosexuality and same-sex traditions in Africa" (http://www.mask.org.za/). For the past decade, Zimbabwean President Robert Mugabe, former Namibian President Sam Nujoma, and southern African religious leaders have claimed that homosexuality is a byproduct of European colonialism and that decolonization will not be complete until governments and societies stamp out homosexuality (Epprecht 2004). Behind the Mask covers events and activism in Black LGBTI communities to prove that homosexuality is part of the African experience.

One momentous event involving Black LGBTI persons was the first-ever Black LGBTI Pride parade in Soweto in September 2005. Reporting on the parade, a special correspondent distances the event from the mostly white, gay male spectacle of the Johannesburg LGBTI Pride parade:[3]

> There was no rainbow flag in sight, no white men in g-strings and fake lashes or bare-chested white women with powerful machines between their legs. The dominant colour here was the bright orange of the parade marshals' pinafores and characteristic hats.
>
> (Malimabe 2005)

The author casts this parade not as a commercial spectacle typical of the mostly white marchers at the Johannesburg Gay Pride parade, but rather as a more somber, political demonstration as participants walked freely in Soweto "singing songs of freedom" (Malimabe 2005). The author implies that the Soweto Pride parade is an authentic image of African homosexuality and a throwback to the protest styles characteristic of anti-apartheid activists.

That the event took place in a township away from the Johannesburg commercial business district is also telling. The parade's location in Soweto and the lack of white participants confirms that most white South African heterosexual and LGBTI persons would not venture into Soweto due to the township's historic aura of political violence. The parade brought LGBTI politics to a Black township where many Black lesbians are targets for harassment, violence, and rape because of their sexualities (Muholi 2004). Soweto Pride reminded Sowetans and South Africans that LGBTI persons are proudly Black and African. Similarly, Behind the

Mask's stories "challenge the idea that homosexuality is 'unAfrican' … through a medium broadly in use to define post-apartheid African identities" (Spruill 2004: 106). Behind the Mask does not reject arguments about whether homosexuality is African on the grounds that whatever is African itself is a fiction used by opponents to persecute African LGBTI persons. Instead, Behind the Mask publishes varied images and stories of LGBTI persons to prove that a range of identities, viewpoints, and experiences are "African."

As evidenced by the Soweto Pride correspondent's rejection of white, apolitical Gay Pride, Behind the Mask reporters do not shy away from addressing racial politics within the South African LGBTI movement. The campaign for same-sex marriage was one debate that split many LGBTI persons along racial and class lines. Pursuing same-sex marriage to the exclusion of other issues, such as outlawing hate crimes and stopping the rape of Black lesbians, has sparked concern among Black South African LGBTI activists. A reporter writing about the Lesbian and Gay Equality Project's public rally in May 2005 in support of legalizing same-sex marriage calls on LGBTI movement leaders and activists to be honest about how race affects the movement's strategies and goals:

> [W]hy does it seem that the talking is left to a mainly privileged group of mainly white people, whilst the actual marching, singing and demonstrations are left to black people? … Changing the definition of marriage by common law is not going to put bread on the table, it is not going to provide life skills, and it is most certainly not going to provide any number of people with jobs. Did the [white] organizers really consider the debates before this undertaking?
>
> (Mathope 2005)

The writer notes that physical protest is the only activity in which Black LGBTI activists engage, or, more accurately, is the role that white LGBTI movement leaders have allocated to them. Political labor in the movement has been divided racially.[4]

This commentary suggests that Black LGBTI persons often face more pressing issues than obtaining the right to marry their same-sex partners because they struggle with poverty, homelessness, and unemployment (Oswin 2007b). By portraying the full range of experiences of Black LGBTI persons, Behind the Mask reporters help audiences to understand that the struggles of Black South African LGBTI persons, and, by extension, Black African LGBTI persons, are more complex than winning the right to marry whomever one wants. In addition, by portraying the realities and hardships that many Black African LGBTI persons face, Behind the Mask reporters insist that homosexuality is African, which is a larger, more diffuse aim of the African LGBTI movement. By questioning the motivations and actions of different LGBTI movement organizations and activists, Behind the Mask correspondents suggest that African LGBTI activists do not utilize Western forms of organizing without examining the implications of these organizing tools.

Promoting organizational visibility: Behind the Mask's national and international credibility

Though amateur journalism lends immediacy to the experience of LGBTI events, Behind the Mask's reliance on this strategy has hampered its ability to generate timely and original news stories. In a proposal to a Northern donor, the organization claimed that it worked in a "reactive" manner. "After news [has] been broken, brokered or reported by other publications, we post them on the [Inter]net." Reasons why Behind the Mask has not overcome this reactive tendency include the inability to "mainstream ourselves with the media in South Africa as well as the continent," the "lack of journalistic skills, i.e. sub-editing, hard-news and feature writing" among staff; "office-bound journalistic practices as *the organisation currently has no vehicles*"; no current "affiliation to professional bodies for mentoring and peer-review purposes"; and a "lack of input from staff which [sic] is indifferent towards current affairs and news" (emphasis original). Being transparent about the organization's practices and frankly admitting the organization's weaknesses have worked to Behind the Mask's advantage, as it consistently manages to obtain funding from foreign (Northern) donors.

To continue its work reporting on African LGBTI issues, Behind the Mask depends on Northern donors to fund its activities. Therefore, marketing its plans as innovative has been crucial to the organization's survival. Marketing and cultivating credibility can be important for movement organizations trying to gain international support or funding for their efforts (Bob 2005). Marketing as a means of cultivating a social movement organization's public credibility is a narrower strategy of LGBTI movement visibility, which, in turn, promotes the movement's visibility. Since its launch, Behind the Mask has received financial support from Mama Cash, Atlantic Philanthropies, Astraea Lesbian Foundation, Hivos, and the Netherlands Institute of Southern Africa (NiZA).[5]

Behind the Mask has promoted itself as a reliable source for news about African LGBTI persons and the movement through its sobering coverage of the political and social repression of LGBTI persons throughout Africa. The organization has achieved this reputation due to foreign correspondents' contributions to the website and journalists' access to LGBTI groups in different countries. In particular, the organization has tracked the Ugandan government's hostility toward LGBTI persons and activists. In 2005, Behind the Mask published first-hand accounts of a Ugandan LGBTI movement leader whom the police detained and whose house they searched. Due to a close relationship Behind the Mask forged with Ugandan LGBTI movement organizations, a journalist was able to obtain details about the police's unexpectedly "cordial" treatment of movement leaders. The journalist states, "With international lobbying looming amidst frantic around the clock strategising, including BtM's network of activists on the continent, … [activists] are on alert mode as they acknowledge that this may be a pacifying tactic to soften them up" (Ngubane 2005). The journalist alludes to international human rights bodies like the International Gay and Human Rights Commission and mentions Behind the Mask's presence in Africa and Ugandan contexts, boosting the organization's credibility with readers. An insider's look at how Ugandan activists interpret the police's behavior also enhances the organization's credibility with readers because they have unparalleled access to Ugandan LGBTI movement leaders.

Behind the Mask also fulfills an important bridging function in enabling local African LGBTI activists to access international human rights organizations, especially those interested in sexuality, much like Latin American LGBTI movement organizations that "are acting simultaneously on several levels – locally, regionally and internationally" (Lind 1997: 9). Because many international human rights organizations cannot tackle all reports of rights violations, a vacuum exists for many LGBTI persons who have no way to contact international organizations (Bob 2005: 17–18). The episode in Uganda enabled Behind the Mask to cement a formal working relationship with the International Gay and Human Rights Commission, whose staff aided detained Ugandan LGBTI activists. These ties raise Behind the Mask's international profile, in turn, allowing the organization to mention these accomplishments when they request future funding from foreign donors.

Despite Behind the Mask's ability to market itself effectively as an organization worthy of funding and as an example of how an LGBTI movement organization can marshal visibility positively, negative visibility hounds the movement in Africa. The myth that homosexuality is unAfrican has generated charges that some LGBTI activists are "gay for pay." In addition to suggesting that Africans only engage in same-sex sexual acts with foreigners for money out of financial necessity, this accusation extends to individuals who present themselves as sexual and gender minorities and apply for funding from donors. Behind the Mask has a positive reputation for handling money well; as a result, donors have consulted Behind the Mask about such fraud in Africa.[6] There is concern among southern African LGBTI activists that scam artists have referred to southern African LGBTI movement organizations in their fraudulent funding applications, sullying the names of these organizations without their leaders knowing that a scam was under way. Southern African LGBTI activists also worry that widespread fraud could result in cessation of funding of LGBTI projects in Africa, which would jeopardize their operations (Interview, February 22, 2006). In fact, in 2003, a Dutch donor, Hivos, informed its African LGBTI "partner" organizations in an e-mail message that it was difficult to work with LGBTI movement organizations in East Africa:

> On several occasions organisations did not show up for scheduled meetings with Hivos staff. Correspondence is often slow and questions raised are not answered or answered too late. Narrative and financial reports are sent too late and do not provide sufficient insight into the results of the project supported. When contract periods end no follow up proposals for further support are submitted. New proposals arrive very late. Meanwhile organisations are building up debt because office rent and utilities are not paid and subsequently expect Hivos to pay for these debts.

As a result of these experiences, Hivos opted to "discontinue" direct funding to African LGBTI movement organizations and explore indirect means of support such as "short courses or exchange meetings." Behind the Mask seems to have been an exception to this threat of funding termination.

LGBTI movement organizations' visibility, as sustained by international funding, has positive and negative consequences. Funding ensures that organizations providing much-needed services continue to function. On the other hand, organizations like Behind the Mask have difficulty transforming themselves into sustainable organizations, especially when they expend so much energy locating other sources of funding. Critics claim that when LGBTI movement organizations are totally reliant on international funding, they are little more than puppets of Northern donors (Epprecht 2001; Oswin 2005; Richardson 2005). Following this argument, these LGBTI movement organizations supposedly feed into the misperception that homosexuality is unAfrican because they obtain ideas and resources for political organizing from non-African sources. This line of thought fails to consider how local groups "indigenize" or hybridize Northern knowledge and mechanisms (Derman 2003). These arguments are premised on the assumption that social movement organizations import and consume social identities constructed elsewhere and uncritically deploy them locally, which, as I have demonstrated, is not the case with Behind the Mask (Richardson 2005). Behind the Mask uses Western sexual and gender identity categories that already circulate among African LGBTI activists.

Behind the Mask straddles many of these criticisms, but not uneasily. First, there is concern that highly visible organizations with international funding like Behind the Mask may put "more grassroots organisations, and those working for radical social change" at a disadvantage because donors flock to the former, enhancing organizations' public visibility while "contribut[ing] to the invisibility and/or the de-resourcing of less mainstream organisations" (Chasin 2001: 202, cited in Richardson 2005: 528). Behind the Mask staff do not believe that applying for funds from donors conflicts with the organization's commitment to helping struggling LGBTI activists and movement organizations elsewhere in Africa because if the organization ceases to exist, there will no continental watchdog for LGBTI rights. Second, it is true that Behind the Mask relies solely on funding from Northern donors. However, my analysis of the organization's style of amateur journalism, network of African LGBTI activists and movement organizations, and marketing efforts demonstrates that the organization remains firmly planted in African discourses about LGBTI issues. Third, Behind the Mask has evolved from a grassroots "[q]ueer initiative" into a professional organization with paid staff (Jolly 2000a: 86). Behind the Mask still retains its autonomy and dedication to disseminating information to LGBTI persons and organizations in need of it. Additionally, the organization picks the projects on which it will work. Behind the Mask's donors do not micromanage the organization's projects. Certainly, the organization tailors its projects so that it meets donors' guidelines, a telltale sign of its marketing strategy, but it does not undertake projects it cannot complete. In this sense, the organization remains vigilant about ensuring that Northern donors' agendas do not overtake its priorities.

Conclusion

At the moment, it may be easier for foreign donors to fund politicized LGBTI movement organizations than to integrate LGBTI concerns into existing development frameworks. While this benefits LGBTI movement organizations in the global South that continue to receive funding, lack of incorporation of LGBTI concerns may ultimately backfire. Since few donors may be willing to fund work on LGBTI issues, if donors hold social movement organizations to the standard of becoming sustainable or locating alternative funding sources, organizations may find themselves in an untenable position. LGBTI movement organizations' staff members in Namibia and South Africa I interviewed complained about having to spend time and energy identifying new sources of funding. This cycle of identifying and applying for funding sometimes kept them from reacting to political emergencies and from deploying strategies and tactics proactively.

With the exception of Behind the Mask's Northern donors and the Swedish International Development Cooperation Agency, donors and LGBTI activists and movement organizations dance nervously around one another. Some donors and development practitioners debate who should receive funding and why. Development practitioners' reluctance to fund projects and organizations that exclusively work on sexual and gender diversity and integrate these concerns in their work may have roots in utilizing criteria of material urgency in prioritizing responses to and support for development projects. "Many in development would argue that 'basic needs' are a more immediate priority than sexuality for those in economic difficulty" (Jolly 2000b: 3). Is this scenario better known as the "'Most Truly Victimized Pageant'" (Stevens 2004: 221)? Is it a matter of demonstrating how marginalized and fearful African LGBTI persons are? This form of visibility may garner funds for African LGBTI activists, but it reproduces dangerous images of the African continent as full of helpless victims, further dehumanizing African LGBTI persons, and consigning them to a victimhood that is difficult to escape (Oswin 2007). It seems more helpful to conceptualize the visibility of needs and persons within development discourses and practices as perhaps distinct from, but not incompatible with, the needs of other populations.

One way to begin integrating these different perspectives is to ask: "What does it mean to be LGBTI in Africa? What are the experiences of LGBTI persons in Africa?" By tracking the experiences and concerns of LGBTI persons and how LGBTI movement organizations respond to them, Behind the Mask plays an essential role in documenting the lives of African LGBTI persons. Such documentation is valuable to development practitioners who may be unsure how and where they can assist LGBTI persons. Behind the Mask also unmasks the circuits of power through which African LGBTI persons and movement organizations travel and the postcolonial and post-apartheid legacy of racial and sexual politics in South Africa, in southern Africa, and on the continent. Together with LGBTI movement organizations in Namibia and Zimbabwe, Behind the Mask has "spearheaded efforts to organize a pan-African network of LGBT groups … Such a network would aim to respond to human rights crises in Africa with a unified voice" (Epprecht

2004: 316). As a self-appointed monitor and moderator of LGBTI rights and politics in Africa, Behind the Mask may have a larger role guiding development projects and practices in the future.

Notes

1 This material is based on work supported by grants from the National Science Foundation under a Sociology Program Doctoral Dissertation Improvement Grant No. 0601767, the Society for the Scientific Study of Sexuality Student Research Fund, and the University of Pittsburgh International Studies Fund. I thank Kathleen M. Blee, Amy Lind, and Suzanne Bergeron for their helpful suggestions for revising this chapter and the staff at Behind the Mask for granting me access to the organization.

2 In 2000, a Dutch investigative journalist, Bart Luirink (2000), launched Behind the Mask to supplement the paucity of Internet reporting on LGBTI organizing in southern Africa. After confirming that no other Internet magazine fulfilled this purpose, Luirink secured a small grant from a Dutch donor, Hivos, to design a website. Luirink's experience combining anti-apartheid and gay rights activism is reflected in Behind the Mask's commitment to anti-racism, anti-sexism, and anti-homophobia. On the surface, a foreigner's founding of an African LGBTI movement organization smacks of paternalism, and one could claim that Behind the Mask's origins are not African. It is not my goal to prove whether the website and organization are truly African. However, it is necessary to acknowledge debates that encircle foreign funding of African LGBTI movement organizations. Over the years, Luirink has made a concerted effort to ensure that African staff guide Behind the Mask. Though he retained a leadership position throughout the organization's early years, he recruited qualified African staff to fill journalist and director positions. Luirink retired to a role as consultant, occasionally meeting with staff to offer guidance.

3 Racial politics in the South African LGBTI movement are more complicated than a Black–White dichotomy. However, I confine my discussion of racial politics within the movement to Behind the Mask's perpetuation of the Black–White racial dichotomy.

4 This complaint from Black LGBTI activists in Namibia and South Africa that they are little more than window-dressing at public events for donors or other LGBTI organizations surfaced frequently in my fieldwork. In addition to activists feeling that they were not privy to communication within organizations about upcoming activities, there was also tension around activists being visibly reduced to their race. Their visible physical bodies became spectacles and objects of consumption for donors and organizations who congratulated LGBTI movement organizations on how racially diverse the movement was.

5 According to the Swedish International Development Cooperation Agency (SIDA) (2007: 30), Astraea Lesbian Foundation in the US offers "core funding" to LGBTI organizations, Atlantic Philanthropies covers "operational costs for service delivery and capacity development," and Hivos and Mama Cash, Dutch organizations, mainly finance "HIV prevention" and work with men who have sex with men. An organization that supports activist projects that address the lesbian, bisexual, and transgender (LBT) women's issues, Astraea gave Behind the Mask US$7,000 to fund a face-to-face program that trained unemployed LBT women how to use computers (http://www. astraeafoundation.org). A former anti-apartheid organization, Hivos has maintained a financial and political commitment to organizations in southern Africa (http://www. hivos.nl). Atlantic Philanthropies has provided Behind the Mask with "core support" through its "Reconciliation and Human Rights Programme" (http://www.atlantic philanthropies.org). Developed out of the merger of three Dutch anti-apartheid movement organizations, NiZA aids southern African organizations that "promote the

freedom of expression, free media, human rights, peace building and economic justice";
Behind the Mask receives funding from NiZA for the former's dedication to building "[d]iverse, accessible, independent and sustainable media" (http://www.niza.nl).
Another Dutch donor, Mama Cash, financially sustains women's groups in the "Global
South, Central and Eastern Europe, and the former Soviet Union" that fall under one of
their programmatic areas: physical integrity; art, culture, and media; economic justice;
peace and security; and empowerment and participation (http://www.mamacash.nl).

6   In an interview, a Namibian LGBTI activist explained that donors were concerned about
    corruption among LGBTI movement organizations that applied for funding, specifically
    those organizations whose leaders absconded with the funds or did not cater for LGBTI
    persons as they claimed in their applications (Interview, February 22, 2006). The activ-
    ist also noted that it was problematic for Behind the Mask or any other organization to
    play a role in vetting organizations for funding because it placed organizations in an
    unequal power relationship with new or struggling LGBTI organizations and forced
    Behind the Mask to interpret the actions and behavior of other organizations. In other
    words, Behind the Mask had to represent "all of queerdom" in Africa and imagine the
    intentions of suspicious LGBTI organizations by virtue of being an African organiza-
    tion and being reliable (Bacchetta 2002: 951). Competition among LGBTI movement
    organizations from different countries indicates the degree to which the dynamics of a
    regional southern African LGBT movement do not map neatly on to how LGBTI move-
    ment organizations in other countries may behave. Tellingly, the activist admitted that
    no other organization besides Behind the Mask had such extensive, reliable contacts
    among African LGBTI movement organizations.

11 Queer Dominican moves

In the interstices of colonial legacies and global impulses

Maja Horn

The progressiveness (or backwardness) of Latin American countries when it comes to LGBTQ issues and communities tends to be gauged through the presence (or absence) of LGBTQ social movements, political activism and organizing around sexual minority rights, and public expressions of gay and lesbian identities.[1] In recent years some scholars have pointed to the fallacies of this developmental narrative, which transposes the Western public inclusion model and its paradigms to non-Western regions and measures through them a country's "progress" and "development" toward (Western-style) gay and lesbian "liberation" and sexual justice. For example, in their introduction to *Queer Globalizations: Citizenship and the Afterlife of Colonialism*, Arnaldo Cruz-Malavé and Martin F. Manalansan IV critique the predominance of such tropes of "teleogical development" in discourses on non-Western sexualities and note how these tend to render "non-Euro-American queerness" as "premodern" and "prepolitical" vis-à-vis the supposedly more modern Western gay and lesbian identities (2002: 5). Similarly, the cultural critic José Quiroga notes how through these parameters Latin America is not only drawn "as a cartographical dark continent" but, moreover, how thereby the "varied and mobile" ways in which homosexualities are deployed in Latin America – outside dominant notions of gay and lesbian identity – are erased (2000: 15).

In fact, nowadays these "varied and mobile" deployments of homosexualities in Latin America and other regions of the global South are increasingly addressed in scholarship and along with an assertion of their difference from dominant conceptions of gay and lesbian identities in the global North. At the same time scholars also tend to agree in their critique of the socio-cultural and political conditions under which many non-heteronormative subjects' lives unfold in the global South. Yet, as several scholars noted at the International Association for the Study of Sexuality, Culture and Society (IASSCS) conference in Lima, Peru (2007), this leaves us currently in a critical and political cul-de-sac: we agree that much needs to be done for non-heteronormative subjects in the global South to live satisfactorily and to achieve what one might term "sexual justice," but visions for change are invariably inscribed in the paths "modeled" and often also prescribed by societies from the global North.[2]

I argue that it is not sufficient to simply account for the "difference" of non-heteronormative sexualities in the global South and not ask questions about sexual justice. Nor can one simply prescribe paths toward sexual justice that are thoroughly inscribed with Western notions of progress and liberation and which, as some critics have cautioned, either sideline or even tend to erase those non-heteronormative sexualities one might have set out to seek sexual justice for in the first place. As Morris Kaplan, in his book *Sexual Justice*, emphasizes, "both 'Justice in the City' and 'Justice in the Soul' must be realized in specific cultures under specific contingent historical circumstances" (1997: 8). How can sexual justice be achieved in the *city* (society) and in the *soul* (for the individual) – in ways that recognize and build on, rather than erase, the differences of Latin American non-heteronormative sexualities?

Dominant modes of gay and lesbian identity politics in the North are closely tied to a particular notion of the self, a self for which happiness and "Justice in the Soul" are fundamentally dependent on the self-expression of a "true" inner self and on achieving coherence between this true inner self and his/her public identity. The closet, as Eve Kosofsky Sedgwick has convincingly argued, is the principal metaphor for this movement from oppression to liberation, from crossing from the private into the public realm and into "gay personhood." Disclosure, confession, and self-expression, as Michel Foucault has showed (and critiqued), are fundamental in and for modern (Western) gay self-making processes and have profoundly shaped and permeated Western LGBTQ politics.[3]

A few decades ago the Argentine anthropologist and writer Nestor Perlongher was deeply skeptical of the notion of homosexual identity and the sexual minority politics associated with it and sought in turn paths toward sexual justice in Latin America not routed through gay and lesbian identity politics. Perlongher's critique of gay and lesbian identity and his alternative vision of a "devenir homosexual" ("homosexual becoming") are strongly informed, as he himself notes, by Félix Guattari's vision of a "minoritarian micropolitics" and his suspicion of identity.[4] Guattari considered identity "un concepto que es de alguna forma profundamente reaccionario, aun cuando es manejado por movimientos progresistas" ["a concept which is in a way profoundly reactionary, even when handled by progressive movements"] (1991: 89). Guattari's critique of identity was closely tied to his critique of capitalism, the channeling of minority subjectivities into "identities," according to him, "implica un tipo de producción de subjetivad que se ajusta muy bien a los asuntos de las sociedades capitalísticas" ("implies a type of production of subjectivity that adjusts itself very well to the matters of capitalist society," 1991: 89).

Nestor Perlongher's problematization of identity, though clearly indebted to Guattari, is in turn not explained by him solely as a capitalist phenomenon – rather, the problem of identity appears more deep-seated to him; he notes that "la propia noción de identidad" ("the very notion of identity") calls for "una especie de arqueología de la identidad – tarea sin duda necesaria" ("a type of archeology of identity – a task undoubtedly necessary") even if such an archeology, he recognizes, "nos llevaría demasiado lejos (tal vez a la misma esencia del ser) ["would takes us too far (perhaps to the very essence of being)"]. If, as Perlongher senses, the question of sexual justice is deeply wound up with a specific understanding of the self, it is this exploration of the notion of self and its historical formation in the Latin American context from which a vision of sexual justice must emerge: a vision informed specifically by Latin American notions of self, happiness, and justice, all of which, of course, are shaped by the particular history of the region and the legal, political, economic, religious, and educational institutions that have given shape to formations of Latin American subjectivity, including sexual subjectivity.

Colonial legacies[5]

Notably, in Latin America homosexuality and homosexual practices have been legally regulated very differently than in the US. The anthropologist Roberto Strongman has pointed out how "in sharp contrast to the United States' prior prohibition of sodomy, many Latin American states do not have constitutional prohibitions against homosexuality. Thus, whenever homosexuals are arrested, it is usually under charges of public indecency" (2002: 181). Many Latin American penal codes derive from or take as a model the Napoleonic legal code, in which homosexual acts are not criminalized per se. The ramifications of this shared legal foundation of many Latin America countries and how it contrasts with US legislation and its historical and political consequences are yet to be fully outlined and analyzed; however, what stands out at first sight is that while until recently in the US, private sexual acts were subject to legal persecution, in many Latin American countries public acts considered "indecent" and an affront to conventional moral codes were penalized and not explicitly circumscribed or defined as being "homosexual" (or "heterosexual"). One example of how these penal codes derived from or influenced by the Napoleonic code regulated homosexuality is described by James Green in *Beyond Carnival*:

> In 1830, eight years after independence from Portugal, Dom Pedro I signed into law the Imperial Penal Code. Among other provisions, the new law eliminated all references to sodomy. The legislation was influenced by the ideas of Jeremy Bentham, The French Penal Code of 1791, the Neapolitan Code of 1819, and the Napoleonic Code of 1810, which decriminalized sexual relations between consenting adults. However, article 280 of the Brazilian code punished public acts of indecency with ten to forty days' imprisonment and a fine corresponding to one half of the time served. This provision gave the police the discretion to determine what constituted a public act of indecency.
>
> (1999: 21–2)

Prevalent notions of morality and decency thus determined and circumscribed the "legality" or "illegality" of public acts and expressions.

Notions of morality of course change across time and cultures and bear on public life differently in different contexts; this is suggested by the fact that though Brazil and the Dominican Republic have historically regulated homosexuality through a similar legal framework, nowadays Brazil is (arguably) one of the most "progressive" Latin American countries when it comes to LGBTQ issues and expressions, while the Dominican Republic is generally considered a virulently homophobic country. If one takes political organization as an indicator, for example, Brazil's gay pride marches draw millions of national and international participants, contrasting starkly with the Dominican Republic where the first, and so far only, official gay pride march took place in 2001 in the capital Santo Domingo; since then the needed police permit for such an official public demonstration has not been granted. Also, the only officially registered not-for-profit organization directed toward the LGBTQ community is Amigos Siempre Amigos (ASA), whose specific purpose since its founding in 1989 has been creating AIDS prevention programs and care for those living with AIDS; no other officially registered LGBTQ organizations have existed so far. Though unofficial organizations have formed at different times, they have tended to disband after relatively brief periods of activity (Polanco 2004).

Even though the Dominican Republic and Brazil have regulated homosexuality through similar legal frameworks – not through sodomy laws but rather through public (in)decency laws – queer Dominican and Brazilian histories appear to have taken very different turns in the twentieth and twenty-first centuries. The historical and socio-cultural variability of what constitutes "decency" and what is deemed "appropriate" public behavior might account for these divergent trajectories at least in part; notably the church, one of the principal institutions through which public morals are articulated, has played different roles in the supposedly "progressive" Brazil and in the "backward" Dominican Republic. In Brazil, as James Green notes, "the Catholic Church seemed removed" from debates on homosexuality in the late nineteenth and twentieth centuries (1999: 113). "Given the fact that Brazil has long been a Catholic country," Green adds, "one might ask why the church has not played a more aggressive public role in opposing manifestations of homosexuality over most of the twentieth century" (1999: 282). He then explains that:

> [t]he Catholic Church's silence regarding an issue that was hotly debated among certain professionals might have had more to do with the status of church–state relations in the 1920s and the '30s than with any lack of concern for issues related to homosexuality. After the establishment of the Republic in 1889 and the separation of the Catholic Church from the state, Brazil's dominant religious institution went through a process of internal readjustment. Catholicism was no longer the official state religion, and the church lost status, privileges, and benefits from republican disestablishmentarianism.
>
> (1999: 113)

Even when the Catholic Church, after World War I, started a "political and social offensive" to re-establish its pre-eminence and ties with the Brazilian state, it "chose not to attack homosexuality" (Green 1999: 113–14).

In contrast, the relationship between the Dominican State and the Catholic Church has been historically very close. While the establishment of the Brazilian Republic implied the separation of the church and the state, in the Dominican Republic the advent of independence was intrinsically wound up with the Catholic Church and its credo. Luis Martinez-Fernandez, in his essay "The Sword and the Crucifix: Church-State Relations and Nationality in the Nineteenth-Century Dominican Republic," describes how when briefly after the declaration of Dominican independence from Spain Haiti invaded the other half of the island, "the Dominican church survived as the single truly national institution in the sense that it retained influence throughout the Dominican territory" (1995: 69–70). During the Haitian occupation (1822–44), "the church's standing and political influence sunk to their lowest level ... [g]iven these circumstances, it is no surprise that anti-Haitian liberation movements found natural allies among the Catholic clergy and that the Dominican underground independence movement found inspiration within Catholicism" (Martinez-Fernandez 1995: 71). Thus, "[t]he Dominican struggle for independence exhibited many elements of a crusade" and "Dominicans ... defined their nationality in religious terms, juxtaposing it against that of Haiti" (73). The declaration of independence in 1844 "promised that the church would be restored to its earlier splendor and would be declared the official church of the state" (74). As a result, in the Dominican Republic, "[u]nlike the general Latin American experience, in which positions regarding the church and its powers divided liberals and conservatives, liberals as well as conservatives agreed on the centrality of the Catholic Church in the years surrounding Dominican independence" (75). The role of Catholic religion as an essential ideological element of Dominican national identity is reflected in the institutionalized ties between the Catholic Church and the Dominican state up until today. During the Trujillo dictatorship (1930–61) the pre-eminent role of the Church was cemented through the signing of a "Concordato" with the Vatican in 1954, in order "to consecrate Catholicism as the nation's official religion" (Polanco 2004). Now, about 50 years later, "they still sustain the relations between church and state in this non-secularized country" (Polanco 2004). In her article "Rights for Everyone: Media, Religion, and Sexual Orientation in the Dominican Republic" María Filomena González notes that because of how "[t]he Catholic Church and the Dominican State have utilized each other to reinforce their positions of power in society ... the conservative mentality of the traditional Catholic Church marks aspects of social life in a more evident way than in many other countries" (2003).

With much more force than in Brazil the Dominican Catholic Church has vocally and actively condemned homosexuality. As Jacqueline Jímenez Polanco notes, the present Cardinal, Nicolás de Jesús López Rodríguez, "Archbishop of Santo Domingo and top hierarch of the Dominican Catholic Church, plays the main role in the clergy's homophobic discourse and permanent witch-hunt against the gay community" (2004). This "witch-hunt" has been carried out publicly and vociferously. The Cardinal, a figure with high public visibility – in fact, in 2005 a survey determined that he was one of the three most popular Dominican public personas – condemns homosexuality continuously in speeches which are widely broadcast and circulated in radio, television, and print media (Jerez 2005). The Dominican sociologist Denise Paiewonsky has pointed out how precisely through this effective media presence, the Catholic Church's central role in Dominican society is reinforced, strongly influencing public opinion, and consolidating its role as *the* moral watchdog (2002: 249). A public opinion survey by the Dominican weekly newspaper *Clave* appears to attest to the apparent acquiescence of Dominican society with these moral principles; according to the survey, "más del 60% de los dominicanos repudia a los homosexuals y pide castigarlos" ("more than 60 percent of Dominicans repudiate homosexuals and ask for them to be punished," 2006a: 6). Also, according to this survey homosexuality is considered "unnatural" and a "disease" by the majority and more than 80 percent of those surveyed would have a grave problem with their daughter or son having homosexual relationships.

There are undoubtedly palpable pressures and restrictions on public manifestations of same-sex desire and expressions of homosexual identities in Dominican society. Yet, it is all too easy to simply prescribe as a "remedy" a healthy dose of what according to many (but not all) has worked so well in the global North: namely political strategies that rely heavily on increasing gay and lesbian visibility and that strive for public inclusion of sexual minorities. However, I want to pose the following three caveats for this "fix" that gay and lesbian identity politics tend to prescribe. First, such "presentist" prescriptions tend to forestall projects that might lead to a better and broader historical understanding of how these particular prescriptions against public expressions of homosexuality arose in the first place.

One provocative point of departure for thinking in broader historical terms about this question is suggested by the Colombian Víctor Manuel Rodríguez in an essay entitled "De adversidad [] ¡vivimos!: hacia una performatividad *queer* del silencio" ("Of Adversity [] We live!: Toward a Queer Performativity of Silence"): "Uno podría sostener que la diferencia sexual latinoamericana no ha sido construida a través de la proliferación de discursos sino mediante la proliferación de silencio" ("One could sustain that Latin American sexual difference has not been constructed through a proliferation of discourses, but rather through a proliferation of silences," 2006: 262). How might Latin American modernity and its institutions have *not* resulted in the very same proliferation of discourses that, as Foucault showed, arose with Western modernity; or, at the very least, how might Latin American modernity have given rise to different regulatory discourses (i.e. how does the homophobic discourse of the Catholic Church in Latin America and its effects differ from the Protestant variations that have dominated in Western Europe and in the US)?

This proliferation of silence rather than discourses, suggested by Rodríguez, resounds with the extraordinary constraints on, but also reluctance to, publicly professing to a homosexual identity in the Dominican Republic and in many other Latin American countries; it also forces one to pause before ascribing to Latin American non-heteronormative subjects who do not profess a need for coming out or publicly assuming a gay and lesbian identity as simply cases of "false consciousness" and as "a bit behind" on their path towards full (modern) sexual subjectivity. This leads to my second caveat: If one were to take seriously the historical difference of Latin America from Western Europe and the US, then one cannot simply assume the supposed desire for and desirability of disclosure and "coming out" (as if these were universal rather than specific historical constructs), moreover, and perhaps more importantly, one cannot assume that disclosure and expression need to be *the* parameters for measuring gay and lesbian "liberation" or "oppression" in

Latin America, nor that they will necessarily be the best strategies for resistance. In fact, as Rodríguez cogently notes, "si el silencio funciona como una estrategia disciplinaria, también debe ayudarnos a pensar en nuevas estrategias de lucha y resistencia" ("if silence functions as a disciplinary strategy it should also help us to think of new strategies for struggle and resistance", 2006: 265); "Justice of the Soul" and "Justice of the City" might take on very different meanings and expressions in non-Western countries.

Global impulses

Thinking in more historically informed ways about the formation of Latin American sexualities should not only counteract the elision of their differences but also the all too facile and simple assertion of their inherent "difference" vis-à-vis Western sexualities (i.e. by trying to reduce Latin American non-heteronormative sexualities to one particular model – such as the "active/passive" model through which some scholars tried to define and reify the difference of Latin American queer sexual subjectivity); one cannot approach Latin American sexualities (and the institutions that shaped these) as if they had not also been deeply intertwined with Western forces since colonization. Developments in communication and transportation technologies in the past few decades make establishing divisions between the supposedly "autochthonous" (always problematic in the Latin American context) and the "foreign" ever more implausible; yet, the instability and problematic nature of these notions do not warrant a withdrawal from this undertaking but, rather, close attention needs to be paid when their intersection unfolds at a given historical moment.

The increasing presence of global gay and lesbian culture in Dominican society through cable television, print media, and the Internet since the 1990s raises important questions about their effects. Francisco Castillo, in his thesis, "Proceso de expansión de la comunidad homosexual en la sociedad dominicana en los últimos 30 años" ("The expansion process of the homosexual community in dominican society in the past 30 years"), argues that a series of international events related to gay and lesbian lives (the legitimization of homosexual unions in Hawaii, "openly" gay politicians in the US, and the launching of the gay doll "Billy") resulted in positive changes, so that, for example, "para mediados del año 1997, ya los diarios dominicanos se atrevían a presentar informes estadísticos y analíticos, sin ningún pudor sobre las preferencias sexuales íntimas de los homosexuales" ("by the midst of the year 1997, Dominican newspapers dared to present statistic and analytical reports, without any prudishness about the intimate sexual preferences of homosexuals," 2004). In fact the media, particularly television, have become a space for visible expressions of homosexuality as "varios hombres, abiertamente homosexuales se incorporan a los programas de farándula y moda" ("various men, openly homosexuals have become part of yellow press and fashion programs") even though, tellingly, "estas incursiones en la televisión por parte de homosexuales fue severamente criticada por gran parte de la sociedad moralista y por la iglesia, en la persona del Cardenal de la Iglesia Católica, Apostólica y Romana" ("these incursions into television by homosexuals were severely critiqued by a large part of the moralist society and by the church, in the person of the Cardinal of the Apostolic and Roman Catholic Church," Castillo 2004).

These incursions indicate to Castillo that in fact "la existencia de un pluralismo psico-sexual e ideológico" ("the existence of a psycho-sexual and ideological pluralism") was "inminente" ("imminent") in the Dominican Republic (2004). The occurrence of the first public gay and lesbian manifestation in 2001 seemed to confirm this. However, since then no more public official demonstrations have been permitted. Similarly, Francisco Castillo's claim that there are more and more places opening up for gay and lesbians, which he reads as indication of an increasing "expansion" of this community, is questioned by the fact, as the weekly newspaper *Clave* reports, that the number of bars and discos specifically for gays and lesbians has remained relatively stable during the past three decades (though the establishments themselves changed frequently): *Clave* lists six establishments in 1970s, five in the 1980s, six in the 1990s, and seven in the period 2000–05; this includes the now closed *Frito Verde* (2006b). Moreover, though the police had shut down gay and lesbian establishments at different times throughout the years, in 2006 an unprecedented number of bars and clubs were forced to close (*Clave* 2006b). Thus, though there is indeed an increasing presence of mostly international gay and lesbian representations in the media, other factors do not point to an "imminent" new "psycho-sexual and ideological pluralism" in the Dominican Republic.

Yet, trying to determine whether the Dominican Republic is really moving "forward" and is progressing with regards to LGBTQ issues through a lens of teleological development and through parameters from the global North hardly helps to understand what might appear as contradictory impulses (from a Western standpoint) in Dominican society and does little to account for and explain the reality in which non-heteronormative lives unfold there. Increasing visibility and public presence of gays and lesbians – and this is my third caveat with regards to the "visibility/expression fix" – does not straightforwardly nor necessarily translate into "progress" or greater sexual justice for non-heteronormative subjects; as Fernando Blanco in his essay "Erotismo y representación en la modernidad latinoamericana" warns, "los casos en que simplemente se importan los contenidos y su difusión pública se considera un éxito en la visibilización, que, sin embargo, produce exactamente el efecto contrario" ("the cases in which contents are simply imported and their diffusion is considered a successful form of visibilization, which, however, produces exactly the opposite effect," 2007: 61).

The most telling and tangible example of the questionable effects and politics of visibility and representation is perhaps the (first and only) *Antología de la literatura gay en la República Dominicana*, published in 2004 by the Dominican press, Manatí. This unprecedented anthology, compiled by Miguel de Camps and Mélida García, who recently died, reunites 43 texts by Dominican writers and is described by Miguel de Camps as being "una descripción de quienes han abordado el tema" ("a description of those who have touched upon the theme," 2004). The question is what the editors consider "el tema" ("the theme") or what should fall under the title "literatura gay". In this case it includes, for example, several texts that retell the rape and/or brutalizing of a transvestite from the utterly homophobic perspective of the perpetrator. Jimmy Lam, a writer of the Dominican diaspora in the US, in his article "Existe una literatura gay en República Dominicana?" ("Is there a Gay Literature in the Dominican Republic?") notes that though the anthology is "una magnífica recopilación" ("a magnificent compilation") of some Dominican homo-erotic texts, it generally lacks "una necesaria y mínima coherencia … en cuanto al contenido de las obras allí presentada" ("a necessary and minimum coherence … with regards to the content of the works presented.") This lack becomes particularly palpable in the selections or fragments that are included from longer prose texts, from which the supposedly "gay" scenes are cut, that include for example a scene of gang rape as a form of punishment for being "different," the tying up of two soldiers like dogs after they were found having sex, and the rape and beating up of a transvestite. To say the least, the pulling out of such scenes and placing these between the pink, rainbow-adorned cover of the anthology under the title "litera-tura gay" is inappropriate, if not offensive. Quite rightfully, I think, Jimmy Lam thus proposes, "sin modestia" ("without modesty"), that the anthology should be called "Antología de la Literatura Gay y Homofóbica en la R.D" ("Anthology of Gay and Homophobic Literature in the Dominican Republic").

This anthology is the awkward result of literally forcing local expressions into a prefigured framework of global gay and lesbian culture; tellingly, Miguel de Camps explained in an interview that he embarked on this project because he noted that the Dominican Republic was lacking the "anaqueles de literature gay" ("annals of gay literature") that he found in European and US bookstores. After discovering this local market niche, it then took him and his co-editor three years to compile the material that they considered *fitting* – all the while assuring that he, of course, had no doubts about his own sexuality: "Yo conozco mi sexualidad y por eso no tengo que ponerla en cuestionamiento. Yo no tengo la menor duda. Pero todo el que ataca un gay es porque en el fondo teme ser gay" ("I know my sexuality and because of that I do not have to question it. I have not a bit of doubt. But he who attacks a gay person does so because deep down he is afraid to be gay," de Camps 2004). The fact that the editor of this purported anthology of gay Dominican lit-erature feels repeatedly compelled in his public presentations to rectify that he is not gay, points to how the increasing circulation of discourses, images, and prod-ucts associated with global gay and lesbian (consumer) culture in the Dominican Republic coexists alongside the ongoing proscription of publicly identifying as anything other than heterosexual.

This is similarly illustrated by the vast success in 2005 of the comedy *¿Qué sexo prefiere Javier?* (*Which Sex does Javier Prefer?*) aimed at a mainstream audience who received it with sufficient enthusiasm at the Dominican National Theater to extend its run. The play, as the title already suggests, entertained the question of whether Javier, the main character, might be more inclined toward the "wrong" sex, principally because of a lack of evidence to the contrary. Though the play partakes in a discourse of sexual diversity, the main actor, Roberto Salcedo, who played the role of Javier, felt compelled to repeatedly and insistently reas-sure people via the media that "aunque se siente a gusto con la interpretación …

todo lo que hará se debe únicamente al personaje, o sea, a Javier, no a él" ("even though he is pleased with his interpretation of the role ... everything he does corresponds to the character, meaning, to Javier, not to him," Baldera 2005). Similarly, Roberto Salcedo's father, who produced the play and who is now the mayor of Santo Domingo, assured us that in his family they did not have any of "these problems." The success of this play suggests how in fact "playing at" being homosexual has accrued sufficient cultural capital to make it commercially profitable in the Dominican Republic, while "being" homosexual in the public eye remains perilous and unaffordable.

In fact, that same year, in November 2005 newspapers reported the arrest of a group of homosexuals and the closing of the open-air bar *Frito Verde* where they had been gathering regularly on the boulevard of the Avenida 27 de Febrero. The fiscal declared that "aunque no se detectó drogas, encontró una cantidad considerable de homosexuales que se dedicaban a la práctica de actos inmorales, como besarse y acariciarse entre ellos" ("even though they did not find drugs, they found a considerable number of homosexuals who dedicated themselves to immoral acts, like kissing and caressing") which he considered clearly outside of the "normas y éticas que rigen un comportamiento normal" ("the norms and ethics that govern normal behavior," El Nacional 2005). Interestingly, the official who arrested the group of homosexual men and women reflected in his declarations to the press a keen awareness of discrimination based on sexual orientation as something considered "wrong" and insists that these arrests had nothing to do with sexual discrimination:

> El fiscal Hernández Peguero rechazó que con el apresamiento se haya producido una discriminación de sexo, dado de que se trata de una actividad de inmoralidad social. "No discriminamos por razones de sexo, pero requerimos que el ciudadano que pretenda divertirse lo haga dentro de las normas y éticas que rigen un comportamiento normal."
>
> (The prosecutor Hernández Peguero rejected that the arrests were based on discrimination based on sexuality, given that these were socially immoral activities. "We do not discriminate because of sexuality, but we do require that citizens enjoy themselves within the norms and ethics that govern normal behavior.")
>
> (El Nacional 2005)

The more than curious logic of this statement reflects an embedded belief in the amorality of homosexuality, the conviction that the public expression of homosexuality transgresses Dominican social norms, and that this should be punishable and needs to be regulated. As an open letter to the newspaper, which reported what happened and (illegally) published the names of those arrested, pointed out, the laws regulating public decency in fact do no longer exist as such in the Dominican legal code. The prosecutor's statement, however, reflects the ingrained belief in (and ongoing practice of) the judicial policing and penalizing of public manifestations of same-sex desire, following what are considered "proper" moral codes. At the same time, though, this statement reflects the prosecutor's keen awareness of such a thing as "discrimination based on sexual preference" and the need to avoid such a charge for his actions.

These different incidents point to an increasing circulation of the terms and discourses associated with global gay and lesbian culture and the sexual rights movement in the Dominican Republic, but also they highlight how these global discourses can sit awkwardly on top of local practices and beliefs, leading to some perplexing and not necessarily "liberatory" results. It is not a matter of simply doing without the goals of public visibility and inclusion nor to question the gains these have brought for (some) gays and lesbians throughout the world. Rather, it is a matter of leaving open a space of interrogation of these goals and to not with-hold from accounting for Dominican (and other non-Western) queer lives and their strategies and cultures on their own terms – which do and do not intersect with global gay and lesbian culture and politics. We have to ask, as the editors in the recently published online book *SexPolitics* urge us to do:

> How are emerging gay and lesbian communities in relatively peripheral social and economic settings creating and re-creating their own understandings of citizenship and empowerment that may or may not have the same terms of reference as LGBT and queer activism as it evolved in the centers of economic and political power ... ?
>
> (Parker, *et al.*, 2007: 409)

The many fissures between and negotiations of visibility and invisibility, between speaking out and silence, between public presence and withdrawal, are much more representative and telling of queer lives not only in the Dominican Republic but in many other places, including the US. What a *political* strategy that responds to these fissures and emerges from them might look like was demonstrated during recent gay and lesbian pride celebrations in Santo Domingo. These celebrations included a series of activities in 2005 but not an official gay and lesbian pride march that in many other countries constitutes the principal event. Rather, because of the ongoing difficulty of securing a permit for such a political march since the first and only official march in 2001, the organizers decided "por eso hacer una convocato-ria informal en un lugar público de encuentro, y como no existe ninguna ley que prohíba la realización de una reunión festiva en un lugar público, no consideramos necesario solicitar permiso a las autoridades" ("because [we were having] an infor-mal meeting in a public space, and since there is no law prohibiting the undertaking of a festive reunion in a public space, we did not consider it necessary to ask for per-mission from the authorities" (Nota de prensa 2005). Though police and officials were present in large numbers as more and more gays and lesbians began to gather on the Boulevard of the Avenida 27 de Febrero, they did not ultimately intervene. Not only did the convocation of an informal party circumvent its prohibition, but also the fact that this event took place at night allowed each participant to control his/her amount of exposure. The area provided dark spaces, semi-lit spaces, and an open area inhabited by the media, photographers, and camera crews. While some decided to be filmed and interviewed, one could just as easily remain almost invisible in other areas; and, yes, public exposure did have a negative backlash: at least two of those whose pictures appeared in the newspaper the next day lost their employment as a direct consequence of their public "outing."

Pride celebrations in 2006 followed the two very different strategies but both avoided catering to sensationalist media coverage. The "official" and carefully planned event on June 23, 2006 took the form of a forum on human rights with various presentations and work-group sessions organized by Amigos Siempre Amigos and partially government-funded by the Presidential AIDS Council (COPRESIDA) with a focus on the theme of "Expresión de la diversidad" ("Expression of Diversity"). Briefly thereafter an unofficial *public* pride celebration took place, which was solely organized through text messages and e-mails sent briefly before the event among members of the Dominican queer community. This event again took the form of a social get-together and celebration at night in a public space, this time without official proclamations or press releases to the media, and with ample room for exchanges among the participants. Undoubtedly, these celebrations were shaped by the specific pressures and limitations on expressing queer identities and desires publicly in Dominican society; yet, one might at least want to pause between recognizing these pressures and proscribing the forms that public expressions of same-sex desires must take, which assumedly all must long for, and be achieved on the supposedly only path toward greater sexual justice.

Notes

1 As the editor Amy Lind in the introduction to this anthology notes, "gayness and queerness have been used as barometers of national progress and development."
2 In the recently published anthology *SexPolitics* (Parker, *et al.*, 2007), which includes reports on the state of "sex politics" in various countries (Brazil, Egypt, India, Peru, Poland, South Africa, Turkey, Vietnam), the editors' telling remark on this tendency: "none of these authors is ideologically neutral with respect to the material she or he represents. All are committed to so-called 'modern' ideologies of sexuality and reproduction" (2007: 384).
3 In a more recent elaboration, the legal scholar Sonia Katyal highlights how the US legal context influenced the emergence of gay and lesbian identity politics. She points out how in the US "gay civil rights … have become inextricably permeated with an expressive, identity-based rhetoric," which she describes as being principally a response to: "the unavailability of privacy-based strategies of liberation"; sodomy laws in the US effectively "forced individuals out of the closet, into the streets, and ultimately forged a visible, unitary view of gay community. Under this visage, public, expressive identity becomes everything" (2006: 1439). This stark emphasis on expression in US gay and lesbian politics is thus in part a specific response to the juridical constrictions that this community has faced by US legal codes.
4 Guattari extensively broached his notion of "minoritarian micropolitics" in talks and conversations during a 1982 stay in Brazil, which would later be transcribed and published first in Brazil and later in Argentina under the title "Micropolítica: Cartografías del deseo". This suggestive text is only now being translated into English and will be published in October 2007 by MIT Press under the title *Molecular Revolution in Brazil*.
5 Portions of this section were previously published in Horn 2008.

6 This apparent "progressiveness" is deduced on one hand from the visibility of queer expressions in the Brazilian carnival and, on the other hand, from "the emergence of a new gay identity among urban, middle-class Brazilians in the 1960s" (Green 1999: 8). As James Green describes:

> [f]or many foreign observers, from Buenos Aires to San Francisco and Paris, ... varied images of uninhibited and licentious Brazilian homosexuals who express sensuality, sexuality, or camp during Carnival festivities have come to be equated with an alleged cultural and social toleration for homosexuality and bisexuality in that country.
>
> (3)

Green, however, warns that over-interpreting the "apparent permissiveness during Carnival" erases the complexities of Brazilian homosexual expressions and obscures the violence experienced by queer Brazilian subjects, "the indiscriminate murder of homosexual men, lesbians, and transvestites in Brazil" (1999: 3).

Bibliography

Aarmo, M. (1999) "How homosexuality became 'un-African': the case of Zimbabwe." *In* E. Blackwood & S. Wieringa (eds.) *Female Desires: same-sex relations and transgender practices across cultures*, New York: Columbia University Press, pp. 255–80.

Abelove, H., Barale, M. A. & Halperin, D. M. (eds.) (1993) *The Lesbian and Gay Studies Reader*, New York: Routledge.

AbuKhalil, A. (1993) "A note on the study of homosexuality in the Arab/Islamic civilization," *The Arab Studies Journal*, 1: 32–34.

—— (1997) "Gender boundaries and sexual categories in the Arab world," *Feminist Issues*, 15: 91–104.

Achmat, Z. (1995) "My childhood as an adult molester." *In* M. Gevisser & E. Cameron (eds.) *Defiant Desire*, New York: Routledge.

Adam, B. D., Duyvendak, J. W. & Krouwel, A. (eds.) (1999) *The Global Emergence of Gay and Lesbian Politics: national imprints of a worldwide movement*, Philadelphia: Temple University Press.

Adams, V. & Pigg, S. L. (2005) "Introduction: the moral object of sex." *In* V. Adams & S. L. Pigg (eds.) *Sex in Development: science, sexuality, and morality in global perspective*, Durham: Duke University Press, pp. 1–38.

Adams, V. & Pigg, S. L. (eds.) (2005) *Sex in Development: science, sexuality, and morality in global perspective*, Durham: Duke University Press.

ADEIM-Simbiosis, Artemisa, Cattrachas, Criola, IGLHRC, Red Nosotras LBT. (2006) *"Unnatural," "Unsuitable," Unemployed!: lesbians and workplace discrimination in Bolivia, Brazil, Colombia, Honduras, Mexico*, New York: IGLHRC.

Afary, J. (2004) "The human rights of Middle Eastern & Muslim women: a project for the 21st century," *Human Rights Quarterly*, 26: 106–25.

Agamben, G. (1998) *Homo Sacer: sovereign power and bare life*, Stanford, CA: Stanford University Press.

Agarwal, B. (1994) *A Field of One's Own: gender and land rights in South Asia*, Cambridge, England; New York, NY, USA: Cambridge University Press.

—— (1997) "Bargaining and gender relations: within and beyond the household," *Feminist Economics*, 3: 1–51.

Albro, R. (2007) "Indigenous politics in Bolivia's Evo era: clientelism, llunkerio, and the problem of stigma," *Urban Anthropology and Studies of Cultural Systems and World Economic Development*, 36: 281.

Alexander, M. J. (2005) *Pedagogies of Crossing: meditations on feminism, sexual politics, memory, and the sacred*, Durham: Duke University Press.

Al-Ghafari, I. (2002) "Is there a lesbian identity in the Arab culture?," *Al-Raida*, XX: 86–90.

Altman, D. (1996) "On global queering," *Australian Humanities Review*, July.

—— (2001) *Global Sex*, Chicago, IL: University of Chicago Press.

—— (2004) "Sexuality and globalization," *Sexuality and Social Research Policy*, 1, 1: 63–8.

Alvarez, S. E. (1990) *Engendering Democracy in Brazil: women's movements in transition politics*, Princeton, NJ: Princeton University Press.

—— (1998) "Latin American Feminisms 'Go Global': Trends of the 1990s and challenges for the new millennium." *In* S. E. Alvarez, E. Dagnino & A. Escobar (eds.) *Cultures of Politics/Politics of Cultures: re-visioning Latin American social movements*, Boulder, CO: Westview Press.

Appadurai, A. (1996) *Modernity at Large: cultural dimensions of globalization*, Minneapolis, MN: University of Minnesota Press.

Arnold, D. Y. (ed.) (1998) *Gente De Carne Y Hueso: las tramas de parentesco en Los Andes*, La Paz; St. Andrews: ILCA, Instituto de Lengua y Cultura Aymara; CIASE, Centre for Indigenous American Studies and Exchange.

Arrizón, A. (2006). *Queering Mestizaje: transculturation and performance*, Ann Arbor: University of Michigan Press.

Assfar, A. (1996) "Lesbians in Jordan: yet we exist." In R. Rosenbloom (ed.) *Unspoken Rules: sexual orientation and women's human rights*, New York: International Gay and Lesbian Human Rights Commission/Cassell.

Astraea Lesbian Foundation (2006) *Behind the Mask* [online]. Available from: http://www.astraeafoundation.org/PHP/Grants/BehindTheMask.php4

Atamer, Y. M. (2005) "The legal status of transsexuals in Turkey," *International Journal of Transgenderism*, 8: 65–71.

Atkinson, D. (2005) *La Familia Galan, Bolivia's Leading Troupe of Drag Queens* [online]. BBC. Available at: http://news.bbc.co.uk/2/shared/spl/hi/picture_gallery/05/americas_bolivia_gay_pride/html/5.stm [accessed May 1, 2006].

Atlantic Philanthropies (2006) *Reconciliation and Human Rights Programme* [online]. Atlantic Philanthropies. Available at: http://www.atlanticphilanthropies.org/rights [accessed May 6, 2008].

Atton, C. (2003) "Reshaping social movement media for a new millennium," *Social Movement Studies*, 2: 3–16.

Bacchetta, P. (2002) "Rescaling transnational 'Queerdom': lesbian and 'lesbian' identitary-positionalities in Delhi in the 1980s," *Antipode*, 34: 947–73.

Badgett, L. & Hyman, P. (1998) "Introduction: Toward Lesbian, Gay and Bisexual Perspectives on Economics: why and how they may make a difference," *Feminist Economics* 4(2): 49–54.

Bahgat, H. (2001) *Explaining Egypt's Targeting of Gays*, International Gay and Lesbian Rights Commission.

Baldera, E. (2005) "Qué Sexo Prefiere Javier? Se estrena mañana en el tn," *HOY Daily Newspaper*, February 21.

Barker, D. K. (2005) "Beyond women and economics: rereading 'women's work'," *Signs*, 30: 2189–210.

Barker, G. (2005) *Dying to be Men: youth, masculinity and social exclusion*, London: Routledge.

Barndt, D. (ed.) (1999) *Women Working the Nafta Food Chain: women, food & globalization*, Toronto: Second Story Press.

Barrow, C. (1986) "Anthropology, the family and women in the Caribbean." *In* P. Mohammed & C. Shepherd (eds.) *Gender in Caribbean Development: papers presented at the inaugural seminar of the University of the West Indies, women and development studies project.* Mona, Kingston, Jamaica: Institute of Social and Economic Research, pp. 156–69.

BBC (2002) "Egyptian rights group 'cannot protect gays'," BBC Online News Service. February 11, 2002. Available at: http://news.bbc.co.uk/2/hi/middle_east/1813926.stm [accessed May 23, 2006].

Becker, G. S. (1991) *A Treatise on the Family*, 2nd enlarged ed., Cambridge, MA: Harvard University Press.

Beckerman, P. E. & Solimano, A. (eds.) (2002) *Crisis and Dollarization in Ecuador: stability, growth, and social equity*, Washington, DC: World Bank.

Bedford, K. (2005a) *Empowering Women, Domesticating Men, and Resolving the Social Reproduction Dilemma: the World Bank's employment policies in Ecuador and beyond*, dissertation, New Brunswick, NJ: Rutgers University.

—— (2005b) "Loving to straighten out development: sexuality and ethnodevelopment in the World Bank's Ecuadorian lending," *Feminist Legal Studies*, 13: 295–322.

—— (2007) "The imperative of male inclusion: how institutional context influences World Bank gender policy," *International Feminist Journal of Politics*, 9: 289–311.

Bell, D. and Valentine, G. (eds.) (1995) *Mapping Desire: Geographies of Sexualitiies*, London: Routledge.

Benería, L. (2003) *Gender, Development, and Globalization: economics as if all people mattered*, New York: Routledge.

Benería, L. & Feldman, S. (eds.) (1992) *Unequal Burden: economic crises, persistent poverty, and women's work*, Boulder, CO: Westview Press.

Berer, M. & Ravindran, T. K. S. (1996) "Fundamentalism, women's empowerment and reproductive rights," *Reproductive Health Matters*, 4 (8): 7–10.

Berger, J. (1981) *Ways of Seeing*, London; New York: British Broadcasting Corporation; Penguin Books.

—— (2004) "Re-sexualising the epidemic: desire, risk and HIV prevention," *Development Update: from disaster to development: HIV and AIDS in southern Africa*, 5: 45–67.

Bergeron, S. (2004) *Fragments of Development: nation, gender, and the space of modernity*, Ann Arbor: University of Michigan Press.

Berkins, L., Sarda, A. & Long, S. (2001) *The Rights of Transvestites in Argentina: a report to United Nations at the 57th meeting of the UN commission on human rights*. New York: International Gay and Lesbian Human Rights Commission (IGLHRC).

Berlant, L. & Freeman, E. (1998) "Queer nationality." *In* S. Mariniello & P. A. Bové (eds.) *Gendered Agents: women & institutional knowledge*, Durham, NC: Duke University Press, 245–78.

Berlant, L. & Warner, M. (1998) "Sex in public," *Critical Inquiry*, 24: 547–66.

Bhabha, H. K. (1994) *The Location of Culture*, London; New York: Routledge.

—— (1997) "Of mimicry and man: the ambivalence of colonial discourse," *In* F. Cooper & A. L. Stoler (eds.) *Tensions of Empire: colonial cultures in a bourgeois world*, Berkeley, CA: University of California Press.

Bhaskaran, S. (2004) *Made in India: decolonizations, queer sexualities, trans/national projects*, New York: Palgrave Macmillan.

Binnie, J. (1997) "Coming out of geography: towards a queer epistemology?" *Environment and Planning D: society & space*, 15: 223–37.

Binnie, J. & Valentine, G. (1999) "Geographies of sexuality," *Progress in Human Geography*, 23: 175–88.

Binswanger, H. (2005 & 2006) Personal interviews & e-mail correspondence. Washington.

Blackden, C. M. & Bhanu, C. (1999) *Gender, Growth and Poverty Reduction Special Program of Assistance for Africa, 1998 Status Report on Poverty in Sub-Saharan Africa*, Washington, DC: World Bank.

Blackwood, E. (2005) "Wedding bell blues: marriage, missing men, and matrifocal follies," *American Ethnologist*, 32: 3–19.

Blanco, F. (2007) "Erotismo y representación en la modernidad Latinoamericana." *In* K. Araujo (ed.) *Cruce De Lenguas: sexualidades, diversidad y ciudadanía*, Chile: LOM Ediciones.

Bob, C. (2002) "Political process theory and transnational movements: dialectics of protest among Nigeria's Ogoni minority," *Social Problems*, 49: 395–415.

—— (2005) *The Marketing of Rebellion: insurgents, media, and international activism*, Cambridge; New York: Cambridge University Press.

Boli, J. & Thomas, G. M. (1999) *Constructing World Culture: international nongovernmental organizations since 1875*, Stanford, CA: Stanford University Press.

Bolles, A. L. (1996) *Sister Jamaica: a study of women, work, and households in Kingston*, Lanham: University Press of America.

Bondi, L. & Laurie, N. (2005) "Working the spaces of neoliberalism: activism, professionalisation and incorporation papers: Introduction," *Antipode*, 37: 393–401.

Bondyopadhay, A. (2002) *Statement to UN Commission on Human Rights* [online]. International Gay and Lesbian Human Rights Commission. Available from: http://www. iglhrc.org

Booth, K. M. (1998) "National mother, global whore, and transnational femocrats: the politics of aids and the construction of women at the World Health Organization," *Feminist Studies*, 24: 115–40.

Born into Brothels (2004). Directed by Kauffman, R., Briski, Z., Dreyfous, G.W., Boll, P.T., Baker, N. & McDowell, J. [New York]: Thinkfilm, LLC. HBO/Cinemax Documentary Films.

Borneman, J. (1996) "Until death do us part: marriage/death in anthropological discourse," *American Ethnologist*, 23: 215–34.

Bornstein, K. (1994) *Gender Outlaw: on men, women, and the rest of us*, New York: Routledge.

Braziel, J. E. & Mannur, A. (2003). *Theorizing Diaspora: a reader*, Malden, MA: Blackwell.

Breilh, J. & Beltrán, J. (2003) *Manejo Clínico y Monitoreo de la Salud en Empresas Floriculturas*, Quito: EcoHealth CEAS/CIID Project.

Browne, K. (2004) "Genderism and the bathroom problem: (re)materialising sexed sites, (re)creating sexed bodies," *Gender, Place and Culture*, 11: 331–46.

Bullough, V. L. & Bullough, B. (1993) *Cross Dressing, Sex, and Gender*, Philadelphia: University of Pennsylvania Press.

Buss, D. & Herman, D. (2003) *Globalizing Family Values: the Christian right in international politics*, Minneapolis, MN: University of Minnesota Press.

Butler, J. (1990) *Gender Trouble: feminism and the subversion of identity*, New York: Routledge.

—— (2002) "Is kinship always already heterosexual?," *Differences: a journal of feminist cultural studies*, 13: 14–44.

—— (2006) *Born Again: the Christian right globalized*, London; Ann Arbor, MI: Pluto Press.

Cabral, M. (2005a) Public Lecture, New York, NY: Human Rights Watch.

—— (2005b) Staff in-Service Meeting Led by Mauro Cabral. IGLHRC.

Cameron, J. (2000) "Domesticating class: femininity, heterosexuality, and household poli-tics." *In* J. K. Gibson-Graham, S. A. Resnick & R. D. Wolff (eds.) *Class and its Others*, Minneapolis: University of Minnesota Press, pp. 47–68.

Campuzano, G. (2008) "Building Identity While Managing Disadvantage: Peruvian Transgender Issue," Institute of Development Studies (IDS) Working Paper 310, Brighton, England: IDS.

Canessa, A. (ed.) (2005) *Natives Making Nation: gender, indigeneity, and the state in the Andes*, Tucson: University of Arizona Press.

—— (2007) "Who is indigenous? Self-identification, indigeneity, and claims to justice in contemporary Bolivia," *Urban Anthropology*, 36: 195–238.

Carabine, J. (1996) "A straight playing field or queering the pitch? Centering sexuality in social policy," *Feminist Review*, 54: 31–64.

Carriére, J. (2001) "Neoliberalism, economic crisis and popular mobilization in Ecuador." *In* J. Demmers, A. E. Fernãndez Jilberto & B. Hogenboom (eds.) *Miraculous Metamorphoses: The neoliberalisation of Latin American populism*. London; New York: Zed Books; Distributed exclusively in the USA by Palgrave, pp. 132–49.

Castells, M. (1989) *The Informational City: information technology, economic restructur-ing, and the urban-regional process*, Cambridge, MA: Blackwell.

—— (1997) *The Power of Identity*, Malden, MA: Blackwell.

Castillo, F. (2004) *Proceso De Expansión De La Comunidad Homosexual En La Sociedad Dominicana En Los Últimos 30 Años.*

Centre for Media and Alternative Communication (2005) *Kaaya, Beyond Gender: a window into the lives of a transgender community*, New Delhi: Centre for Media and Alternative Communication.

Chabot, S. & Duyvendak, J. W. (2002) "Globalization and transnational diffusion between social movements: reconceptualizing the dissemination of the Gandhian repertoire and the 'coming out' routine," *Theory and Society*, 31: 697–740.

Chant, S. (1999) "Women-headed households: global orthodoxies and grassroots reali-ties." *In* H. Afshar & S. Barrientos (eds.) *Women, Globalization and Fragmentation in the Developing World*, Houndmills, Basingstoke, Hampshire; New York: Palgrave Macmillan, pp. 91–130.

Charusheela, S. (2003) "Empowering work: bargaining models reconsidered." *In* D. K. Barker & E. Kuiper (eds.) *Toward a Feminist Philosophy of Economics*, London; New York: Routledge.

Chasin, A. (2001) *Selling Out: the gay and lesbian movement goes to market*, London: Palgrave-Macmillan.

Chen, M. A. (1996) "Engendering world conferences: the international women's movement and the United Nations." *In* T. G. Weiss and L. Gordenker (eds.) *NGOs, the UN, and Global Governance: emerging global issues*, Boulder, CO: Lynne Rienner.

Choy, T. K. (2005) "Articulated knowledges: environmental forms after universality's demise," *American Anthropologist*, 107: 5–18.

Clave (2006a) "Encuesta Clave-CIES," *Clave* (weekly newspaper), Santo Domingo, Dominican Republic: March 16.

—— (2006b) "La Zona Colonial entre velos rosa," *Clave* (weekly newspaper), Santo Domingo, Dominican Republic: June 15.

Cleaver, F. (2002) "Men and masculinities: new directions in gender and development." *In* F. Cleaver (ed.) *Masculinities Matter!: men, gender, and development*, London; New York: Zed Books.

Cock, J. (2003) "Engendering gay and lesbian rights: the equality clause in the South African constitution," *Women's Studies International Forum*, 26: 35–45.

Cohen, C. (1997) "Punks, bulldaggers, and welfare queens: the radical potential of queer politics?" *GLQ*, 3: 437–66.

—— (2006) "African American youth: Broadening our understanding of politics, civic engagement and activism," *Youth Activism*, New York: Social Science Research Council. Available at: http://ya.ssrc.org/african/Cohen/ [accessed August 26, 2009].

Cohen, C. J. (2004) Interview with Cathy Cohen. Ann Arbor, MI: University of Michigan Global Feminisms Project.

Cohen, L. (1995) "The pleasures of castration." *In* P. R. Abramson & S. D. Pinkerton (eds.) *Sexual Nature, Sexual Culture*, Chicago: University of Chicago Press.

Collins, J. (2004) "Linking movement and electoral politics: Ecuador's indigenous movement and the rise of Pachakutik." *In* J.-M. Burt & P. Mauceri (eds.) *Politics in the Andes: identity, conflict, reform*, Pittsburgh, PA: University of Pittsburgh Press, pp. 38–57.

Colloredo-Mansfeld, R. J. (1999) *The Native Leisure Class: consumption and cultural creativity in the Andes*, Chicago: University of Chicago Press.

CONAMU (Consejo Nacional de la Mujer) (2003) *Pea Ocupada, Según Sectores Del Mercado Laboral*. Available at: http://www.conamu.gov.ec/CONAMU/files/sectores. pdf [accessed June 30, 2006].

Cooper, D. (1995) *Power in Struggle: feminism, sexuality and the state*, New York: New York University Press.

CORPEI (Corporación de Promoción de Exportaciones e Inversiones) (2004) *Ecuador Exports*, Ministerio de Relaciones Exteriories del Ecuador/CORPEI.

Corrêa, S. (2002) "Sexual rights: much has been said, much remains to be resolved." Lecture, *The Sexuality Health and Gender Seminar, Department of Social Sciences*, Public Health School, Columbia University.

—— (2006) "Why feminists should engage in the queer theory," *Women in Action*, Manila: ISIS International.

Corrêa, S. & Parker, R. (2004) "Sexuality, human rights, and demographic thinking: connections and disjunctions in a changing world," *Sexuality Research and Social Policy*, 1(1): 15–38.

Correia, M. (2000) *Ecuador Gender Review: issues and recommendations. A World Bank country study*, Washington, DC: World Bank.

Corteen, K. (2002) "Lesbian safety talk: problematizing definitions and experiences of violence, sexuality and space," *Sexualities*, 5: 259–80.

Crago, A.-L. (2003) *Unholy Alliance – some feminists are in bed with the Christian right*. Alternet. Available from: http://www.walnet.org/csis/news/usa_2003/alternet-030521. html [accessed October 20, 2009].

Crisafulli, D. (2005 & 2006) Personal interviews and e-mail correspondence, Washington.

Crossette, B. (2003) "Equal rights for homosexuals contentious at U.N.," *U.N. Wire*, August 6.

Croucher, S. (2002) "South Africa's democratisation and the politics of gay liberation," *Journal of Southern African Studies*, 28: 315–30.

CRR (Center for Reproductive Rights) (2005) "Pregnant women living with HIV/AIDS: protecting human rights in programs to prevent mother-to-child transmission of HIV," *CRR Briefing Paper*, New York: CRR. Available at: http://reproductiverights.org/en/ resources/publications/Briefing-Papers [accessed May 6, 2008].

Cruz-Malavé, A. & Manalansan, M. F. (eds.) (2002) *Queer Globalizations: citizenship and the afterlife of colonialism*, New York: New York University Press.

Currah, P. (2006) "Gender pluralisms under the transgender umbrella." *In* P. Currah, R. M.

Juang & S. Minter (eds.) *Transgender Rights*, Minneapolis: University of Minnesota Press, pp. 3–31.

D'Emilio, J. (1983) "Capitalism and gay identity." *In* A. B. Snitow, C. Stansell & S. Thompson (eds.) *Powers of Desire: the politics of sexuality*, New York: Monthly Review Press, pp. 100–13.

Davison, E. L. & Rouse, J. (2004) "Exploring domestic partnership benefits policies in corporate America," *Journal of Homosexuality*, 48: 21–44.

Dayanita, S. & Ahmed, M. (2001) *Myself Mona Ahmed*, Zurich; New York: Scalo.

De Camps, M. (2004) Interview with Mabel Caballero in El Caribe. Santo Domingo.

Deen, T. (2003) "Human rights: U.N. in debt to gays and lesbians," Inter Press Service News Agency, October 14.

Delgado, G. (1983) "Evo Morales en el contexto de los más recientes movimientos sociales," *LASA Forum*, 37: 18–21.

—— (2006) "Evo Morales en el contexto de los más recientes movimientos sociales," *LASA Forum*, *37*(1): 18–21.

Demir, D. (1995) "Stonewall-Ülkerwall" *Lambdaistanbul Bulletin*, June–July 2005. Available at: http://www.lambdaistanbul.org/php/main.php?menuID=26&altMenuID= 56&icerikID=713 [accessed August 25, 2009].

—— (1997) Acceptance speech given by Demir at the International Gay and Lesbian Human Rights Award Ceremony and posted on the Lambda Istanbul website, http://www.lambdaistanbul.org/php/main.php.

Derman, B. (2003) "Cultures of development and indigenous knowledge: the erosion of traditional boundaries," *Africa Today*, 50: 67–86.

Doan, P. L. (2001) "Are the transgendered the mine shaft canaries of urban areas?," *Progressive Planning Magazine: special issue on queers and planning*.

—— (2006) "Violence and transgendered people," *Progressive Planning Magazine: special issue on gender and violence*, Spring.

—— (2007) "Queers in the American city: transgendered perceptions of urban space," *Gender, Place, and Culture*, 14: 57–74.

Dowsett, G. W., Grierson, J. W. & McNally, S. P. (2006) *A Review of Knowledge About the Sexual Networks and Behaviours of Men Who Have Sex with Men in Asia*. Melbourne, Australia: La Trobe University.

Dowuona, S. (2005) *Women, Sexual Rights and HIV/Aids*. Ghana Home Page. Available at: http://www.ghanaweb.com/GhanaHomePage/NewsArchive/artikel.php?ID = 72731 [accessed October 20, 2009].

Drake, J. (1992) "'Le Vice' in Turkey." *In* W. R. Dynes & S. Donaldson (eds.) *Asian Homosexuality*, New York: Garland Publishing.

Duggan, L. (2003) *The Twilight of Equality?: neoliberalism, cultural politics, and the attack on democracy*, Boston: Beacon Press.

Dunne, B. (1990) "Homosexuality in the Middle East: an agenda for historical research," *Arab Studies Quarterly*, 12: 55–82.

—— (1998) "Power and sexuality in the Middle East," *Middle East Report*, 28: 8.

Dynes, W. R. & Donaldson, S. (1992) *Asian Homosexuality*, New York: Garland Publishing.

Edelman, M. (2003) "Transnational peasant and farmer movements and networks." *In* M. Kaldor, H. Anheier & M. Glasius (eds.) *Global Civil Society*, Oxford: Oxford University Press.

Edwards, M. & Hulme, D. (eds.) (1996) *Beyond the Magic Bullet: NGO performance and accountability in the post-Cold War world*, West Hartford, CN: Kumarian Press.

"Egyptian Rights Group 'Cannot Protect Gays'" (2002) *BBC*, February 11.

El Nacional (2005) "Cierran bar por prácticas inmorales," *El Nacional* (daily newspaper), Santo Domingo, Dominican Republic, November 19.

Elson, D. (1995) *Male Bias in the Development Process*, 2nd ed., Manchester, England: Manchester University Press.

—— (1996) "Gender-aware analysis and development economics." *In* C. K. Wilber & K. P. Jameson (eds.) *The Political Economy of Development and Underdevelopment*, New York; London: McGraw-Hill.

England, P. & Kilbourne, B. (1990) "Markets, marriages and other mates: the problem of power." *In* R. Friedland & A. F. Robertson (eds.) *Beyond the Marketplace: rethinking economy and society*, New York: Aldine de Gruyter.

Epprecht, M. (2001) "'Unnatural vice' in South Africa: the 1907 Commission of Inquiry," *International Journal of African Historical Studies*, 34: 121–40.

—— (2004) *Hungochani: the history of a dissident sexuality in southern Africa*, Montreal; Ithaca: McGill-Queen's University Press.

—— (2005) "Black skin, 'cowboy' masculinity: a genealogy of homophobia in the African Nationalist Movement in Zimbabwe to 1983," *Culture, Health & Sexuality*, 7: 253–66.

Escobar, A. (1995) *Encountering Development: the making and unmaking of the Third World*, Princeton, NJ: Princeton University Press.

Fathi, N. (2004) "As repression lifts, more Iranians change their sex," *The New York Times*, August 2.

—— (2005) "Rights advocates condemn Iran for executing 2 young men," *New York Times*, July 29.

Fausto-Sterling, A. (1992) *Myths of Gender: biological theories about women and men*, 2nd ed., New York, NY: Basic Books.

Featherstone, M. (ed.) (1990) *Global Culture: nationalism, globalization and modernity*, London: Sage.

Feinberg, L. (1996) *Transgender Warriors: making history from Joan of Arc to Rupaul*, Boston: Beacon Press.

Feldman, R. & Clark, K. (1996) "Women, religious fundamentalism and reproductive rights," *Reproductive Health Matters*, 8: 12–20.

Ferguson, J. (1994) [1990] *The Anti-Politics Machine: "development," depoliticization, and bureaucratic power in Lesotho*, Minneapolis: University of Minnesota Press.

—— (1999) "Expectations of domesticity." *In* J. Ferguson (ed.) *Expectations of Modernity: myths and meanings of urban life on the Zambian copperbelt*, Berkeley: University of California Press.

—— (2006) *Global Shadows: Africa in the neoliberal world order*, Durham, NC: Duke University Press.

Fernandes, S. (2007) "Everyday wars of position: media, social movements, and the state in Chavez' Venezuela," *Annual Meetings of the Latin American Studies Association*, Montreal, Canada.

Fernández-Alemany, M. (2000) "Negotiating gay identities: the neoliberalization of sexual politics in Honduras," *Congress of the Latin American Studies Association*, Miami, Florida.

Ferraro, E. (2000) "Las políticas agrarias y el discurso del neoliberalismo." *In* M. Cuvi Sánchez, E. Ferraro & F. A. Martínez (eds.) *Discursos Sobre Género Y Ruralidad En El Ecuador: la década de 1990*, Quito, Ecuador: Consejo Nacional de las Mujeres, pp. 27–48.

Ferree, M. M. & Martin, P. Y. (eds.) (1995) *Feminist Organizations: harvest of the new women's movement*, Philadelphia: Temple University Press.

Fisher, J. (1998) *Nongovernments: NGOS and the political development of the Third World*, West Hartford, CT: Kumarian Press.

Fisher, W. F. (1997) "Doing good? The politics and anti-politics of NGO practices," *Annual Review of Anthropology*, 26: 439–64.

Fleishman, J. (2000) "A quiet rebel turns to sexual issue," *The Philadelphia Inquirer*, December 18.

Folbre, N. (1994) *Who Pays for the Kids?: gender and the structures of constraint*, London; New York: Routledge.

Franco, J. (1989) *Plotting Women: gender and representation in Mexico*, New York: Columbia University Press.

Fraser, N. (1997) *Justice Interruptus: Critical Reflections on the Post-Socialist Condition*, London: Routledge.

Fretes-Cibils, V. & López-Cálix, J. R. (2003) "Synthesis." *In* V. Fretes Cibils, M. Giugale & J. R. López-Cálix (eds.) *Ecuador: an economic and social agenda in the new millennium*, Washington, DC: World Bank, pp. xxxiii–lxvii.

Fried, S., Miller, A. & Rothschild, C. (2007) *Stop Violence Against Women: lesbians, gender and human rights violations*. Amnesty International.

Friedemann-Sánchez, G. (2006) "Assets in intrahousehold bargaining among women workers in Colombia's cut-flower industry," *Feminist Economics*, 12: 247–69.

Galindo, M. & Paredes, J. (2002) *Machos, Varones Y Maricones: manual para conocer tu sexualidad por ti mismo*, La Paz, Bolivia: Ediciones Mujeres Creando.

Gamson, J. (1995) "Must identity movements self-destruct? A queer dilemma," *Social Problems*, 42: 390.

Gamson, J. & Moon, D. (2004) "The sociology of sexualities: queer and beyond," *Annual Review of Sociology*, 30: 47–64.

Garber, M. (1991) "The chic of Araby: transvestism, transsexualism, and the erotics of cultural appropriation." *In* J. Epstein & K. Straub (eds.) *Body Guards: the cultural politics of gender ambiguity*, New York: Routledge, pp. 223–47.

García Linera, Á. (2004) "The multitude." *In* O. Olivera & T. Lewis (eds.) *"Cochabamba": water war in Bolivia*, Cambridge, MA: South End Press, pp. 65–86.

García, M. L. & De Camps JiméNez, M. (2004) *Antología De La Literatura Gay En La República Dominicana*, República Dominicana Editora Manatí.

Gavanas, A. (2004) *Fatherhood Politics in the United States: masculinity, sexuality, race and marriage*, Urbana: University of Illinois Press.

Gay and Lesbian Arab Society (2006) "Gay teen shot in Iraq," Available at: http://glas.org/ahbab/ [accessed May 19 2006].

Gevisser, M. (1995) "A different fight for freedom: a history of South African lesbian and gay organisation from the 1950s to the 1990s." *In* M. Gevisser & E. Cameron (eds.) *Defiant Desire*, New York: Routledge, pp. 14–88.

Gibson-Graham, J. K. (1996–97) "Querying globalization," *Rethinking Marxism*, 9: 1–27.

Gill, L. (1997) "Creating citizens, making men: the military and masculinity in Bolivia," *Cultural Anthropology*, 12: 527–50.

Giovarelli, R. E. (2005) *Gender Issues and Best Practices in Land Administration Projects*, Washington, DC: Agriculture & Rural Development Dept., World Bank.

Global Policy Forum (1999) *NGOs and the United Nations: comments for the report of the Secretary General*. New York: Global Policy Forum.

Goetz, A. M. (1997) *Getting Institutions Right for Women in Development*, New York: Zed Books.

González, M. F. (2003) "Rights for everyone: media, religion, and sexual orientation in the Dominican Republic," *Lesbigay SIGnals*, NAFSA Rainbow SIGnals Newsletter. Available at: http://www.indiana.edu/~overseas/lesbigay/vol9_2/92domrep.html [accessed August 26, 2009].

González, N. L. (1984) "Rethinking the consanguineal household and matrifocality," *Ethnology*, 23: 1–12.

Gosine, A. (2005a) "Sex for pleasure, rights to participation, and alternatives to AIDS: placing sexual minorities and/or dissidents in development," *IDS Working Paper 228*, February ed., Brighton, England: Institute for Development Studies.

—— (2005b) "Stumbling into sexualities: international discourse discovers dissident desire," *Canadian Woman Studies Journal*, 24: 59–64.

Green, J. N. (1999) *Beyond Carnival: male homosexuality in twentieth-century Brazil*, Chicago: University of Chicago Press.

—— (2001) *Beyond Carnival: male homosexuality in twentieth-century Brazil*, Chicago, Ill.; London: University of Chicago Press.

Grimson, A. & Kessler, G. (2005) *On Argentina and the Southern Cone: neoliberalism and national imaginations*, New York: Routledge.

Guidry, J. A. (2003) "The struggle to be seen: social movements and the public sphere in Brazil," *International Journal of Politics, Culture, and Society*, 16: 493–524.

Guilland, R. (1943) "Les eunuques dans l'empire Byzantin: étude de titulature et de prosopographie Byzantines," *Études Byzantines*, I: 197–238.

Gutmann, M. C. (ed.) (2003) *Changing Men and Masculinities in Latin America*, Durham & London: Duke University Press.

Hachette, D. (2003). "Trade policy and competition." *In* V. Fretes-Cibils, M. M. Giugale & J. R. López-Cálix (eds.) *Ecuador: an economic and social agenda in the new millennium*, Washington, DC: World Bank, pp. 163–94.

Haddad, L. J., Hoddinott, J. & Alderman, H. (1997) *Intrahousehold Resource Allocation in Developing Countries: models, methods, and policy*, Baltimore: Johns Hopkins University Press.

Hamdar, A. (2002) "A young Lebanese woman talks about her lesbian identity, her relationships, and her perspective on homosexuality," *Al-Raida: Quarterly Journal of the Institute for Women's Studies in the Arab World*, Chouran, Beirut: Lebanese American University: 91–94.

Hardt, M. and Negri, A. (2000) *Empire*, Cambridge, MA: Harvard University Press.

—— (2004) *Multitude: war and democracy in the age of empire*, New York: Penguin.

Harrison, F. (2005) "Iran's sex-change operations," *BBC News*.

Hart, G. (1997) "From 'rotten wives to good mothers': household models and the limits of economism," *IDS Bulletin*, 28: 14–25.

Hartmann, B. (1995) *Reproductive Rights and Wrongs: the global politics of population control*, rev. ed., Boston, MA: South End Press.

Hatem, M. (1986) "The politics of sexuality and gender in segregated patriarchal systems: the case of eighteenth- and nineteenth-century Egypt," *Feminist Studies*, 12: 251–74.

Hazra, A. (2005) "Can introducing 'elements of sensuousness' in the way male-to-male sex is perceived and experienced in India make it safer?:preliminary findings from a study in Calcutta, West Bengal State, India, solidarity and action against the HIV infection in India (Saathii)," *Realising Sexual Rights – International Workshop*, Institute of Development Studies, Sussex University, Brighton, UK.

Hélie, A. (2006) "Threats and survival: the religious right and LGBT strategies in Muslim contexts," *Women in Action*, 1: 19–31.

Hennessy, R. (2000) *Profit and Pleasure: sexual identities in late capitalism*, New York: Routledge.

Hewitson, G. (2003) "Domestic labor and gender identity." *In* D. K. Barker & E. Kuiper (eds.) *Toward a Feminist Philosophy of Economics*, New York: Routledge, pp. 266–83.

Hirsch, M. (1997) *Family Frames: photography, narrative, and postmemory*, Cambridge, MA: Harvard University Press.

Hoad, N.W. (2007) *African Intimacies: race, homosexuality, and globalization*, Minneapolis MN: University of Minnesota Press.

Horn, M. (2008) "Queer Caribbean Homecomings: the collaborative art exhibits of Nelson Ricart-Guerrero and Christian Vauzelle," *GLQ*, special issue on Queer/Migration, 14: 2–3, 361–81.

HRW (Human Rights Watch) (2004) "Egypt: crackdown on homosexual conduct exposes torture crisis," *Human Rights News*. March 1 ed. Cairo: HRW.

—— (2005) "Saudi Arabia: men 'behaving like women' face flogging: sentences imposed for alleged homosexual conduct violate basic rights," *Human Rights News*, April 7 ed. Geneva: HRW.

HRW (Human Rights Watch) and IGLHRC (International Gay and Lesbian Human Rights Commission) (2005) *Sexual Orientation, Gender Identity and the Human Rights Mechanisms of the United Nations: examples and approaches*, New York: HRW/IGLHRC.

Hubbard, P. (2001) "Sex zones: intimacy, citizenship and public space," *Sexualities*, 4: 51.

Hulme, D. & Edwards, M. (1997) "NGOs, states and donors: an overview." *In* D. Hulme & M. Edwards (eds.) *NGOs, States and Donors: too close for comfort?*, New York: St. Martin's Press, pp. xvii.

ICW (International Community of Women Living with HIV/AIDS) (n.d.) "HIV positive young women," ICW Vision Paper 1. London: ICW.

IGLHRC (International Gay and Lesbian Human Rights Organization) (2004) *"Unnatural," "Unsuitable," Unemployed!: lesbians and workplace discrimination in Bolivia, Brazil, Colombia, Honduras, and Mexico*.

Ilkkaracan, I. & Seral, G. (2000) "Sexual pleasure as a women's human right: experiences from a grassroots training program in Turkey." *In* P. Ilkkaracan (ed.) *Women and Sexuality in Muslim Societies*, Istanbul: Women for Women's Human Rights (WWHR), pp. 187–96.

Ilkkaracan, P. & Mack, A. (2002) "Women, sexuality, and social change in the Middle East and the Maghreb," *Social Research*, 69: 753–79.

ILO (International Labour Organization) (2000) *Gender! A Partnership of Equals*, Geneva: International Labour Office: ILO.

INE (Instituto Nacional de Estadística de Bolivia) (n.d.) "Carencias, déficit habitacional y acceso a servicios básicos." Available at: http://www.ine.gov.bo/PDF/SerBas/SerBas0.pdf [accessed 1 November 2007].

Ingham, R. (2005) "'We didn't cover that at school': education against pleasure or education for pleasure?," *Sex Education*, 5: 375–88.

IPPF/ICW, (2004) *Dreams and Desires: sexual and reproductive health experiences of HIV positive women*, London: International Planned Parenthood Federation (IPPF) and International Community of Women Living with HIV/AIDS (ICW).

Jackson, C. (2001) *Men at Work: labour, masculinities, development*, Portland, OR: F. Cass/European Association of Development Research and Training Institutes.

Jackson, C. & Pearson, R. (eds.) (1998) *Feminist Visions of Development: gender, analysis and policy*, London; New York: Routledge.

Jackson, J. T. (2005) *The Globalizers: development workers in action*, Baltimore: Johns Hopkins University Press.

Jami, H. (2005) *Condition and Status of Hijras (Transgender, Transvestites Etc.) in Pakistan (Country Report)*, Islamabad, Pakistan: National Institute of Psychology, Quaid-i-Azam University.

Janssen, T. (1992) "Transvestites and transsexuals in Turkey." *In* A. Schmitt & J. Sofer (eds.) *Sexuality and Eroticism Among Males in Moslem Societies*, New York: Haworth Press, pp. 83–91.

Jaquette, J. S. & Staudt, K. (2006) "Women, gender and development." *In* J. S. Jaquette & G. Summerfield (eds.) *Women and Gender Equity in Development Theory and Practice: institutions, resources, and mobilization*, Durham, NC: Duke University Press, pp. 17–52.

Jassey, K. (2006) *Report from Expert Group on Development Issues (EGDI) Conference: making the linkages – sexuality, rights and development*, Stockholm: Ministry of Foreign Affairs.

Jay, M. (1996) "Vision in context: reflections and refractions." *In* T. Brennan & M. Jay (eds.) *Vision in Context: historical and contemporary perspectives on sight*, New York: Routledge, pp. 16–28.

Jeffreys, S. (1991) *Anticlimax: a feminist perspective on the sexual revolution*, Washington Square, NY: New York University Press.

Jerez, R. (2005) "Doña Margarita, El Cardenal y Roberto, Mejor Evaluados," *Listín Diario*, November 17 ed. Santo Domingo: Section 'La República.

Jolly, S. (2007) *Why the Development Industry Should Get Over Its Obsession with Bad Sex and Start to Think About Pleasure*, Brighton, England: Institute of Development Studies at the University of Sussex.

—— (2000a) "'Queering' development: exploring the links between same-sex sexualities, gender, and development," *Gender and Development*, 8: 78–88.

—— (2000b) "What use is queer theory to development?," *Queering Development Seminar Series – Session 3*, Sussex University: Institute for Development Studies.

—— (2006a) "Not so strange bedfellows: sexuality and international development," *Women's Rights and Development*, special issue with AWID, Development, 49: 77–80.

—— (2006b) "Sexuality and development," *IDS Policy Brief*, Sussex: Institute of Development Studies.

Jolly, S. & Wang, W. (2003) *Gender Mainstreaming Strategy for the China-UK HIV/Aids Prevention and Care Project*, London: Department for International Development (DFID).

Jones, C. (1983) "The mobilization of women's labor for cash crop production: a game theoretic approach," *American Journal of Agricultural Economics*, 65: 1049–54.

Jonsson, H. (2001) "Serious fun: minority cultural dynamics and national integration in Thailand," *American Ethnologist*, 28: 151–78.

Joseph, M. (2002) *Against the Romance of Community*, Minneapolis, MN: University of Minnesota Press.

Julien, I. & Mercer, K. (1991) "True confessions." *In* E. Hemphill (ed.) *Brother to Brother: new writings by Black gay men*, 1st ed. Boston: Alyson Publications.

Kabeer, N. (1994) *Reversed Realities: gender hierarchies in development thought*, London; New York: Verso.

Kaddour, A. (2005) "Turning a blind eye: health care for women with non-conforming sexual lifestyles." Speech given at the Tenth International Women's Health Meeting, New Delhi, September 21–25, 2005. Available at: http://www.wwhr.org/id_919.

Kandiyoti, D. & Robert, M. (1998) "Photo Essay: transsexuals and the urban landscape in Istanbul," *Middle East Report*, No. 206, 20–25.

Kaplan, M. B. (1997) *Sexual Justice: democratic citizenship and the politics of desire*, New York: Routledge.

Kapur, R. (2002) "The tragedy of victimization rhetoric: resurrecting the native subject in international/postcolonial feminist legal politics," *Harvard Human Rights Law Journal*, 15: 1.

Katyal, S. K. (2006) "Sexuality and sovereignty: the global limits and possibilities of Lawrence," *The William and Mary Bill of Rights Journal: a student publication of the Marshall-Wythe School of Law*, 14: 1429–92.

Katz, E. (1997) "The intra-household economics of voice and exit," *Feminist Economics*, 3: 25–46.

Keck, M. E. & Sikkink, K. (1998) *Activists Beyond Borders: advocacy networks in international politics*, Ithaca, NY: Cornell University Press.

Khan, S. & Khilji, T. (2002) "Pakistan Enhanced HIV/AIDS Program: social assessment and mapping of men who have sex with men (MSM) in Lahore, Pakistan," *Short Report for The World Bank, Pakistan*, Naz Foundations.

Khattab, A. (2004) "Sally's Story," *Egypt Today*, July ed.

Kleitz, G. (2000) "Why is development work so straight?" Queering Development seminar series at the Institute for Development Studies, Sussex, England.

Klugman, B. (2000) "Sexual rights in southern Africa: a Beijing discourse or a strategic necessity?," *Health and Human Rights*, 4: 144–73.

—— (2006) "Gazing into the crystal ball: prophecies for the field, 10 years hence," *States of Sexuality: a "generative" meeting of networking and discussion*. The Capstone Event and Closure Meeting of the Sexuality Research Fellowship Program, Santa Ana Pueblo, New Mexico.

Kuiper, E. & Barker, D. K. (2006) *Feminist Economics and the World Bank: history, theory, and policy*, London; New York: Routledge.

Kulick, D. (1997) "A man in the house: the boyfriends of Brazilian travesti prostitutes," *Social Text*, 52/53: 133–60.

Kyle, D. (2000) *Transnational Peasants: migrations, networks, and ethnicity in Andean Ecuador*, Baltimore: Johns Hopkins University Press.

Lackard, J. (2005) "Hegemonic democracy in the Middle East," *Tikkun*, 20: 26–8.

Lam, J. *Existe Una Literatura Gay En República Dominicana?* Available online at: http://www.cielonaranja.com/jimmylanantologia.htm [accessed October 8, 2009].

Lancaster, R. N. (2005) "Text, subtext, and context: strategies for reading alliance theory," *American Ethnologist*, 32: 22–7.

Larson, B. (2005) "Capturing Indian bodies, hearths, and minds: the gendered politics of rural school reform in Bolivia 1920s–1940s." *In* A. Canessa (ed.) *Natives Making Nation: gender, indigeneity, and the state in the Andes*, Tucson: University of Arizona Press, pp. 32–59.

Leatt, A. & Hendricks, G. (2005) "Beyond identity politics: homosexuality and gayness in South Africa." *In* M. Van Zyl & M. E. Steyn (eds.) *Performing Queer: shaping sexualities 1994–2004 Volume One*, 1st ed. Roggebaai, South Africa: Kwela Books, pp. 302–21.

León Trujillo, M. (2001) "Políticas neoliberales frente al trabajo femenino, Ecuador 1984–8." *In* Herrera Mosquera, G (ed.) *Estudios de género*, 211–58. Quito: FLACSO-Ecuador/ILDIS.

Lewin, E. (1993) *Lesbian Mothers: accounts of gender in American culture*, Ithaca, NY: Cornell University Press.

—— (1998) *Recognizing Ourselves: ceremonies of lesbian and gay commitment*, New York: Columbia University Press.

Lewis, J. & Gordon, G. (2005) "Terms of contact and touching change: investigating pleasure in an HIV epidemic," *Realising Sexual Rights – International workshop*, Institute of Development Studies, Sussex University, Brighton, UK.

Lim, S., Smith, L. E. & Dissanayake, W. (1999) *Transnational Asia Pacific: gender, culture, and the public sphere*, Urbana: University of Illinois Press.

Lind, A. (2005) *Gendered Paradoxes: women's movements, state restructuring, and global development in Ecuador*, University Park, PA: Pennsylvania State University Press.

—— (1997) "Gay rights: out of the closet and into La Calle," *NACLA Report on the Americas*, 30: 6–9.

—— (2007) "Becoming a sexual citizen: constitutional reform and sexual politics in (post-) neoliberal Ecuador," *The Annual Meetings of the Latin American Studies Association*, Montreal, Canada.

—— (Forthcoming) "Development, sexual subjectivities, and the global governance of intimacy." *In* M. H. Marchand & A. S. Runyan (eds.) *Gender and International Political Economy*, New York: Routledge.

Lind, A. & Share, J. (2003) "Queering development: institutionalized heterosexuality in development theory, practice and politics in Latin America." *In* K.-K. Bhavnani, J. Foran & P. A. Kurian (eds.) *Feminist Futures: re-imagining women, culture and development*, New York: Zed Books, pp. 55–73.

Lockard, J. (2005) "Hegemonic Democracy in the Middle East," *Tikkun*, 20, 3: 26–28.

Long, S. (2005) *Anatomy of a Backlash: sexuality and the "cultural" war on human rights*, New York: Human Rights Watch.

Luirink, B. (2000) *Moffies: gay life in southern Africa*, Cape Town: David Philip.

Mãndez, J. B. (2005) *From the Revolution to the Maquiladoras: gender, labor, and globalization in Nicaragua*, Durham: Duke University Press.

Magdalena, L. T. (2001) "Políticas neoliberales frente al trabajo femenino." *In* G. Herrera (ed.) *Antología De Estudios De Género*, Quito, Ecuador: FLACSO-Ecuador: ILDIS [Instituto Latinoamericano de Investigaciones Sociales].

Maletta, H. (2005) *Vulnerabilidad De La Niñez Y La Familia En Bolivia*, La Paz: MS PNUD.

Malimabe, L. (2005) *Soweto Holds a Historic Mini-Pride Parade*.

Mallaby, S. (2004) *The World's Banker: a story of failed states, financial crises, and the wealth and poverty of nations*, New York: Penguin Press.

Mama Cash (2006) *Who Is She* [online]. Mama Cash. Available online at: http://www.mamacash.org/page.php?id = 1 [Accessed: May 6, 2008].

Mamdani, M. (1996) *Citizen and Subject: contemporary Africa and the legacy of late colonialism*, Princeton, NJ: Princeton University Press.

Manalansan Iv, M. F. (1997) "In the shadows of stonewall: examining gay transnational politics and the diasporic dilemma." *In* L. Lowe & D. Lloyd (eds.) *The Politics of Culture in the Shadow of Capital*, Durham, NC: Duke University Press, pp. 485–505.

Marchand, M. H. & Parpart, J. L. (1995) *Feminism/Postmodernism/Development*, London; New York: Routledge.

Marcus, S. (2005) "Queer theory for everyone: a review essay," *Signs-Chicago*, 31: 191–218.

Mark, M. E. (1981) *Falkland Road: prostitutes of Bombay: photographs and text*, New York: Knopf.

Martin, S. (2003) *A City Comes Out*, St. Petersburg Times.

Martinez-Fernandez, L. (1995) "The sword and the crucifix: church–state relations and nationality in the nineteenth-century Dominican Republic," *Latin American Research Review*, 30: 69–93.

Massad, J. A. (2002) "Re-orienting desire: the gay international and the Arab world," *Public Culture*, 14: 361–85.

Mathope, E. (2005) *Leave the Boardroom Politics to the Experts and the Toyi-Toying to the Masses*.

Mathuray, M. (2000) "On the (African) national question: sexuality and tradition," *Queering Development Seminar Series*, Sussex University: Institute for Development Studies.

McCrate, E. (1987) "Trade, merger and employment: economic theory on marriage, review of radical political economics," *International Library of Critical Writings in Economics*, 64: 154–70.

McDonough, M. (2006) "Gay Iraqis fear for their lives," *BBC News website*.

McElroy, M. B. & Horney, M. J. (1981) "Nash-bargained household decisions: toward a generalization of the theory of demand," *International Economic Review*, 22(2): 333–49.

McFadden, P. (2003) "Sexual pleasure as feminist choice," *Feminist Africa*, 2: 50–60.

McIlwaine, C. & Datta, K. (2003) "From feminising to engendering development," *Gender Place and Culture*, 10: 369–82.

Mena, N. (1999) *Impacto De La Floricultura En Los Campesinos De Cayambe*, Ecuador: Instituto de Ecologa y Desarrollo de las Comunidades Andinas.

Méndez, J. B. (2002) "Organizing a space of their own? Global/local processes in a Nicaraguan women's organization," *Journal of Developing Societies*, 18: 196–227.

Merabet, S. (2004) "Disavowed homosexualities in Beirut," *MERIP Middle East Report*, 34: 30–3.

Mercer, C. (2002) "NGOs, civil society and democratization: a critical review of the literature," *Progress in Development Studies*, 2: 5–22.

Merry, S. E. (2006) *Human Rights and Gender Violence: translating international law into local justice*, Chicago: University of Chicago Press.

Meyer, M.K. & Prügl, E. (1999) *Gender Politics in Global Governance*, Lanham, MD: Rowman & Littlefield Publishers.

Miller, A. M. (2000) "Sexual but not reproductive: exploring the junction and disjunction of sexual and reproductive rights," *Health and Human Rights*, 4: 68–109.

—— (2006) Public Lecture. New York: Columbia University School of International and Public Affairs.

—— (2004) "Sexuality, violence against women, and human rights: Women make demands and ladies get protection," *Health and Human Rights*, 7: 2, 16–47.

Mills, M. B. (2005) "Consuming desires, contested selves, rural women and labor migration in Thailand." *In* C. Brettell & C. F. Sargent (eds.) *Gender in Cross-Cultural Perspective*, 4th ed., Upper Saddle River, NJ: Pearson Prentice Hall, pp. 536–47.

—— (2005). "Women and labor activism: struggle, power, and pleasure," *Ninth International Conference on Thai Studies*. Northern Illinois University, DeKalb IL.

Ministerio de Relaciones Exteriories del Ecuador/CORPEI. (2004) Ecuador Exports. Quito: Ministerio de Relaciones Exteriories del Ecuador/CORPEI.

Mirzoeff, N. (1998) "What is visual culture." *In* N. Mirzoeff (ed.) *The Visual Culture Reader*, London; New York: Routledge.

Moghadam, V. M. (2005) *Globalizing Women: transnational feminist networks*, Baltimore: Johns Hopkins University Press.

Mohanty, C. T. (1991) "Under Western eyes: feminist scholarship and colonial discourse." *In* C. T. Mohanty, A. Russo & L. Torres (eds.) *Third World Women and the Politics of Feminism*, Bloomington: Indiana University Press, pp. 51–80.

—— (1997) "Women workers and capitalist scripts: ideologies of domination, common interests, and the politics of solidarity." *In* M. J. Alexander & C. T. Mohanty (eds.) *Feminist Genealogies, Colonial Legacies, Democratic Futures*, New York: Routledge.

Molyneux, M. (2006) "Mothers at the service of the new poverty agenda: progresa/oportunidades, Mexico's conditional transfer programme," *Social Policy and Administration*, 40: 425–49.

Mona. (2002) "Secrets in Tehran," tr. Niloufar, *The Gully*. Available at: http://www.the gully.com/essays/gaymundo/020922_mona_iran_lesbian.html [accessed August 25, 2009].

Monagan, A. P. (1985) "Rethinking 'Matrifocality'," *Phylon (1960–)*, 46: 353–62.

Monro, S. (2005) *Gender Politics*, London; Ann Arbor, MI: Pluto Press.

Morgan, R. & Wieringa, S. (eds.) (2005) *Tommy Boys, Lesbian Men and Ancestral Wives*, Johannesburg; London: Jacana; Global [distributor].

Moriel, L. (1999) "Dana international: a self-made Jewish diva," *Gender, Race, & Class*, 6: 110–18.

Morris-Suzuki, T. (2000) "For and against NGOs," *New Left Review*, 2: 63–84.

Morton, D. E. (ed.) (1996) *The Material Queer: a lesbigay cultural studies reader*, Boulder, CO: Westview Press.

Moser, C. (2003) *Gender Planning and Development: theory, practice and training*. London: Routledge.

Mosse, D. (2005) *Cultivating Development: an ethnography of aid policy and practice*, London; Ann Arbor, MI: Pluto Press.

Muholi, Z. (2004) "Thinking through lesbian rape," *Agenda*, 61: 116–25.

Murdock, D. (2003) "That stubborn 'doing good?' question: ethical/epistemological concerns in the study of NGOs," *Ethnos*, 68: 507–32.

Murray, S. O. (ed.) (1995) *Latin American Male Homosexualities*, Albuquerque: University of New Mexico Press.

Murray, S.O. & Roscoe, W. (1997) *Islamic Homosexualities: culture, history, and literature*, New York: New York University Press.

Nagel, J. (2003) *Race, Ethnicity, and Sexuality: intimate intersections, forbidden frontiers*, New York: Oxford University Press.

Nanda, S. (1990) *Neither Man nor Woman: the hijras of India*, Belmont, CA: Wadsworth Publishing Co.

—— (2000) *Gender Diversity: crosscultural variations*, Prospect Heights, IL: Waveland Press.

Nestle, J., Howell, C. & Wilchins, R. A. (eds.) (2002) *Genderqueer: voices from beyond the sexual binary*, Los Angeles: Alyson Books.

Newman, C. (2002) "Gender, time use, and change: the impact of the cut flower industry in Ecuador," *World Bank Economic Review*, 16: 375–96.

Newman, C. (World Bank. Development Research Group, World Bank Poverty Reduction & Economic Management Network) (2001) *Gender, Time Use, and Change: impacts of agricultural export employment in Ecuador*, Washington, DC: World Bank, Development Research Group/ Poverty Reduction and Economic Management Network.

Newman, C., Larreamendy, P. & Maldonado, A. M. A. (2001) *Mujeres Y Floricultura: cambios y consecuencias en El Hogar*, Quito, Ecuador: Abya-Yala: Banco Mundial: CONAMU.

Ngubane, M. (2005) "Confusion as SMUG doesn't understand why the police are being 'nice' towards them." Available at: http://www.mask.org.za/SECTIONS/AfricaPerCountry/ABC/uganda/uganda_107.htm [accessed January 13, 2006].

Nguyen, V. K. (2005) "Uses and pleasures: sexual modernity, HIV/Aids, and confessional technologies in a West African metropolis." *In* V. Adams & S. L. Pigg (eds.) *Sex in Development: science, sexuality, and morality in global perspective*, Durham: Duke University Press.

NiZA (Netherlands Institute for Southern Africa) (2006) Mission Statement. Amsterdam: NiZA. Available at: http://www.aluka.org/action/showCompilationPage?doi = 10.5555/AL.SFF.COMPILATION.COLLECTION-MAJOR.NIZA&cookieSet = 1 [accessed May 6, 2008].

North, L. (2004) "State building, state dismantling, and financial crises in Ecuador." *In* J.-M. Burt & P. Mauceri (eds.) *Politics in the Andes: identity, conflict, reform*, Pittsburgh, PA: University of Pittsburgh Press, pp. 186–206.

Nota de prensa (2005) "A la comunidad dominicana e internacional," Santo Domingo, Dominican Republic, July 2.

Olcott, J. (2007) "'You only talk about lesbians and prostitutes': the sexual politics of transnational feminism at the 1975 United Nations International Women's Year Conference in Mexico City," *Conference on Lesbian and Gay History and the American Historical Association*, Atlanta, GA.

Olds, K. 2001. *Globalization and Urban Change: capital, culture and pacific rim megaprojects*, Oxford: Oxford University Press.

One World Action (2005). *Glossary*, London: One World Action. Available at: http://www.oneworldaction.org/papers_documents_archives/glossary.htm [accessed May 6, 2008].

Ong, A. (1991) "The gender and labor politics of postmodernity," in Lowe, L. and Lloyd, D. (eds.) *The Politics of Culture in the Shadow of Capital*, Durham NC: Duke University Press, pp. 61–97.

—— (1997) "The Gender and Labor Politics of Postmodernity," in Lowe, L. and Lloyd, D. (eds.) *The Politics of Culture in the Shadow of Capital*, Durham, N.C.: Duke University Press.

—— (2006) *Neoliberalism as Exception: mutations in citizenship and sovereignty*, Durham, NC: Duke University Press.

Ong, A. & Collier, S. J. (eds.) (2005) *Global Assemblages: technology, politics, and ethics as anthropological problems*, Malden, MA: Blackwell.

Online Discussion on "Sexual Pleasure, Sexuality and Rights" (2005), The South and South East Asia Resource Centre on Sexuality.

Oswin, N. (2005) "Researching 'Gay Cape Town' finding value-added queerness," *Social and Cultural Geography*, 6: 567–86.

—— (2007a) "The end of queer (as we knew it): globalization and the making of a gay-friendly South Africa," *Gender Place and Culture*, 14: 93–110.

—— (2007b) "Producing homonormativity in neoliberal South Africa: recognition, redistribution, and the Equality Project," *Signs: Journal of Women in Culture and Society*, 32: 649–70.

Otto, D. (1996) "Nongovernmental organizations in the United Nations system: the emerging role of international civil society," *Human Rights Quarterly*, 18: 107–41.

—— (1999) "Everything is dangerous: some poststructural tools for rethinking the universal knowledge claims of human rights law," *Australian Journal of Human Rights*, 5: 17.

Ouzgane, L. & Morrell, R. (2005) *African Masculinities: men in Africa from the late nineteenth century to the present*, New York: Palgrave Macmillan.

Oyegun, J. (2005) Personal interview.

Paiewonsky, D. (2002) *El GéNero En La Agenda PúBlica Dominicana: estudios de caso y análisis comparativo*, Santo Domingo, RD: Centro de Estudios de Género, Instituto Tecnológico de Santo Domingo.

Palán, Z. & Palán, C. (1999) *Employment and Working Conditions in the Ecuadorian Flower Industry*, Geneva: International Labour Office.

Palmberg, M. (1999) "Emerging visibility of gays and lesbians in southern Africa." *In* B. D. Adam, J. W. Duyvendak & A. Krouwel (eds.) *The Global Emergence of Gay and Lesbian Politics: national imprints of a worldwide movement*. Philadelphia: Temple University Press, pp. 266–92.

Parker, R., Petchesky, R. & Sember, R. (2007) *Sex Politics: reports from the front lines*, Rio de Janeiro, RJ: Sexuality Policy Watch.

Parker, R. G. (1999) *Beneath the Equator: cultures of desire, male homosexuality, and emerging gay communities in Brazil*, New York: Routledge.

Parpart, J. L. (2003) "Rethinking particpatory empowerment, gender and development: the PRA approach." *In* J. L. Parpart, S. Rai & K. A. Staudt (eds.) *Rethinking Empowerment: gender and development in a global/local world*, London; New York: Routledge, pp. 165–81.

Parpart, J. L., Rai, S. & Staudt, K. A. (2003) "Rethinking em(power)ment, gender and development: an introduction," *In* J. L. Parpart, S. Rai & K. A. Staudt (eds.) *Rethinking Empowerment: gender and development in a global/local world*, London; New York: Routledge, pp. 3–21.

Patel, G. (1997) "Home, homo, hybrid: translating gender," *College Literature*, 24: 133–51.

Paulson, S. (1996) "Familias que no conyugan e identidades que no conjugan: la vida en mizque desafía nuestras categorías," *In* S. Rivera Cusicanqui & D. Y. Arnold (eds.) *Ser Mujer IndíGena, Chola O Birlocha En La Bolivia Postcolonial De Los años 90*, La Paz, Bolivia: Ministerio de Desarrollo Humano, pp. 84–154.

——— (2000) "Cultural bodies in Bolivia's gendered environment," *International Journal of Sexuality and Gender Studies*, 5: 125–40.

——— (2004) "Gendered practices and landscapes in the Andes: the shape of asymmetrical exchanges." *In* S. Paulson & L. L. Gezon (eds.) *Political Ecology across Spaces, Scales, and Social Groups*, New Brunswick, NJ: Rutgers University Press, pp. 174–195.

——— (2006) "Connecting queer studies of men who desire men with feminist analysis of unmarried women in Bolivia," *LASA Forum*, XXXVII: 12–15.

——— (2007) "Model families of modern development cede to alternative bonds in Bolivia's social movements," *Urban Anthropology and Studies of Cultural Systems and World Economic Development*, 36: 239–80.

Paulson, S. & Bailey, P. (2003) "Culturally constructed relationships shape sexual and reproductive health in Bolivia," *Culture Health and Sexuality*, 5: 483–98.

Pellegrini, A. (2002) "Consuming lifestyle: commodity capitalism and transformations in gay identity." *In* A. Cruz-Malavé & M. F. Manalansan (eds.) *Queer Globalizations: citizenship and the afterlife of colonialism*, New York: New York University Press, pp. 134–45.

People's Union for Civil Liberties (2003) *Human Rights Violations Against the Transgender Community: a study of kothi and hijra sex workers in Bangalore, India*, Karnataka: People's Union for Civil Liberties.

Pereira, C. (2003) "Where angels fear to tread?" Some thoughts on Patricia McFadden's 'Sexual Pleasure as Feminist Choice', *Feminist Africa*, 2: 61–5.

Pérez, G. & Jesús, M. D. (2005) "Marcha del orgullo por la diversidad sexual. Manifestación colectiva que desafía las políticas del cuerpo," *El Cotidiano*, 20.

Perlongher, N. (1991) "Los devenires minoritarios," *Revista de Critica Cultural*, 4.

Petchesky, R. P. (2005). "Rights of the body and perversions of war: sexual rights and wrongs ten years past Beijing," *UNESCO's International Social Science Journal*, 57: 301–18.

Peterson, V. S. (2003) *A Critical Rewriting of Global Political Economy: integrating reproductive, productive, and virtual economies*, London; New York: Routledge.

Phelan, S. (2000) "Queer liberalism?," *American Political Science Review*, 94: 431–42.

Phillips, H. (2001) "Gender – why two sexes are not enough," *New Scientist*, 2290: 28–42.

Phillips, O. (2000) "Constituting the global gay: issues of individual subjectivity and sexuality in southern Africa," *Challenging Dominant Models of Sexuality in Development seminar series at the Institute for Development Studies*, Sussex, England.

Philpott, A. Knerr, W. & Maher, D. (2006) "Promoting protection and pleasure: amplifying the effectiveness of barriers against sexually transmitted infections and pregnancy," *The Lancet*, 368: 2028–31.

Pigg, S. L. & Adams., V. (2005) "Introduction: The Moral Object of Sex," in V. Adams & S. L. Pigg, (eds.) *Sex in Development: Science, Sexuality, and Morality in Global Perspective*, Durham, NC: Duke University Press, pp. 1–38.

Pleasure Project (2005) "Global mapping of pleasure focused projects," The Pleasure Project. Available online at: http://thepleasureproject.org [Accessed: May 2008].

Plummer, K. (2001) "The square of intimate citizenship: some preliminary proposals," *Citizenship Studies*, 5: 237–53.

Polanco, J. J. (2004) "The lesbian, gay, bisexual, trans, and queer (LGBTQ) movement in the Dominican Republic: a sociopolitical and cultural approach," Available at: http://www.globalgayz.com/domrep-JP-news.html [accessed April 27, 2009].

Porter, F. & Sweetman, C. (eds.) (2005) *Mainstreaming Gender in Development: a critical review*, Oxford: Oxfam GB.

Prügl, E. & Lustgarten, A. (2006) "Mainstreaming gender in international organizations." *In* J. S. Jaquette & G. Summerfield (eds.) *Women and Gender Equity in Development Theory and Practice: institutions, resources, and mobilization*, Durham, NC: Duke University Press, pp. 53–70.

Puar, J. K. (2007) *Terrorist Assemblages: homonationalism in queer times*, Durham: Duke University Press.

Puri, J. (2006) "Sexuality, state and nation." *In* S. Seidman, N. Fischer & C. Meeks (eds.) *Handbook of the New Sexuality Studies*, London; New York: Routledge, pp. 317–24.

—— (2008) "Sexualizing the state: sodomy, civil liberties, and the Indian penal code." *In* A. P. Chatterji & L. N. Chaudhry (eds.) *Contesting Nation: gendered violence in South Asia. Notes on the postcolonial present*, New Delhi: Zubaan Books/Kali for Women.

Quiroga, J. (2000). *Tropics of Desire: interventions from queer Latino America*, New York: New York University Press.

Quisumbing, M. A. R. & McClafferty, B. F. (2006) *Food Security in Practice: using gender research in development*, Washington, DC: International Food Policy Research Institute.

Raeburn, N.C. (2004) *Changing Corporate America from Inside Out: lesbian and gay workplace rights*, Minneapolis: University of Minnesota Press.

Rao, A., Stuart, R. & Kelleher, D. (eds.) (1999) *Gender at Work: organizational change for equality*, West Hartford, CN: Kumarian Press.

Ratele, K. (2004) "Kinky politics." *In* S. Arnfred (ed.) *Re-Thinking Sexualities in Africa*, Uppsala, Sweden: Nordiska Afrikainstitutet.

Rathgeber, E. M. (1990) "WID, WAD, GAD: trends in research and practice," *Journal of Developing Areas*, 24: 489–502.

Rattansi, A. (1994) "Western racisms, ethnicities and identities in a 'postmodern' frame." *In* A. Rattansi & S. Westwood (eds.) *Racism, Modernity and Identity: on the western front*, Cambridge, UK; Cambridge, MA: Polity Press, pp. 15–86.

Reddy, G. (2005) *With Respect to Sex: negotiating hijra identity in South India*, Chicago: University of Chicago Press.

Reddy, V. (2005) "Subversive pleasures, spaces of agency: some reflections on lesbian and gay service-delivery work in Ethekwini," *Feminist Africa*, 5.

Reid, G. & Dirsuweit, T. (2002) "Understanding systemic violence: homophobic attacks in Johannesburg and its surrounds," *Urban Forum*, 13: 99–126.

Richardson, D. (1996) "Heterosexuality and social theory." *In* D. Richardson (ed.) *Theorising Heterosexuality: telling it straight*, Buckingham; Philadelphia, PA: Open University Press, pp. 1–20.

—— (2005) "Desiring sameness? The rise of a neoliberal politics of normalization," *Antipode*, 37: 515–35.

Riles, A. (2000) *The Network Inside Out*, Ann Arbor: University of Michigan Press.

Ringrose, K. (1994) "Living in the shadows: eunuchs and gender in Byzantium." *In* G. H. Herdt (ed.) *Third Sex, Third Gender: beyond sexual dimorphism in culture and history*, New York: Zone Books, pp. 85–109.

Robert, M. & Kandiyoti, D. (1998) "Photo essay: transsexuals and the urban landscape in Istanbul," *Middle East Report*, 206: 20–25.

Rockefeller, S. A. (2007) "Dual power in Bolivia: movement and government since the election of 2005," *Urban Anthropology*, 36: 161–94.

Rodríguez, V. M. (2006) "De Adversidad [] 'Vivimos': hacia una performatividad queer del silencio." *In* M. Viveros (ed.) *Saberes, Culturas Y Derechos Sexuales*, Colombia, Colombia: Tercer Mundo Editores.

Rogoff, I. (1996) "'Other's Others': spectatorship and difference." *In* T. Brennan & M. Jay (eds.) *Vision in Context: historical and contemporary perspectives on sight*, New York: Routledge.

Roseneil, S. (2004) "Why we should care about friends: an argument for queering the care imaginary in social policy," *Social Policy and Society*, 3: 409–19.

Rothschild, C. (2000) *Written Out: how sexuality is used to attack women's organizing*, San Francisco: IGLHRC.

Rothschild, C., Long, S. & Fried, S. T. (eds.) (2005) *Written Out: how sexuality is used to attack women's organizing*, New York; New Brunswick, NJ: International Gay and Lesbian Human Rights Commission (IGLHRC); Center for Women's Global Leadership (CWGL).

Rowson, E. (1991) "The categorization of gender and sexual irregularity in medieval Arabic vice lists." *In* J. Epstein & K. Straub (eds.) *Body Guards: the cultural politics of gender ambiguity*, New York: Routledge, pp. 50–79.

Rubin, G. (1984) "Thinking sex: notes for a radical theory of politics of sexuality." *In* C. S. Vance (ed.) *Pleasure and Danger: exploring female sexuality*. Boston: Routledge & Kegan Paul.

Rupp, L. (1997a) *World of Women: the making of an international women's movement*, Princeton, NJ: Princeton University Press.

—— (1997b) "Sexuality and politics in the early twentieth century: the case of the international women's movement," *Feminist Studies*, 23: 577–606.

Rutter, E. (1928) *The Holy Cities of Arabia*, London; New York: G.P. Putnam's Sons.

Said, E. W. (1978) *Orientalism*, New York: Pantheon Books.

Samuelson, P. A. (1956) "Social indifference curves," *The Quarterly Journal of Economics*, 70: 1–22.

Sandoval, C. (2002) "Dissident globalizations, emancipatory methods, social erotics." *In* A. Cruz & M. F. Manalansan (eds.) *Queer Globalizations: citizenship and the afterlife of colonialism*, New York: New York University Press, pp. 20–32.

Schimdt, P. (2005) "Ohio lawmaker sues university to end benefits for domestic partners," *The Chronicle of Higher Education*, December 9, Washington DC.

Schmitt, A. & Sofer, J. (eds.) (1992) *Sexuality and Eroticism among Males in Moslem Societies*, Binghamton, NY: Harrington Park Press.

Schmitt, E. (2001) "For first time, nuclear families drop below 25% of households," *New York Times*, May 15.

Scott, J. C. (1998) *Seeing Like a State: how certain schemes to improve the human condition have failed*, New Haven: Yale University Press.

Sedgwick, E. K. (1990) *Epistemology of the Closet*, Berkeley: University of California Press.

Seidman, S. (2001) "From identity to queer politics: shifts in normative heterosexuality and the meaning of citizenship," *Citizenship Studies*, 5: 321–28.

Seiz, J. (2000) "Game theory and bargaining models." *In* J. Peterson & M. Lewis (eds.) *The Elgar Companion to Feminist Economics*, Northampton, MA: Edward Elgar Pub.

Sen, A. K. (1999) *Development as Freedom*, Oxford; New York: Oxford University Press.

Sen, G. & Grown, C. (1987) *Development, Crises, and Alternative Visions: Third World women's perspectives*, New York: Monthly Review Press.

Shah, P. (2005) *"Imaging self," Kaaya, Beyond Gender: a window into the lives of a transgender community*, New Delhi: Centre for Media and Alternative Communication.

Shah, S. P. (2005) "Born into saving brothel children," *Samar*, February 1.

Shepherd, G. (1978) "Transsexualism in Oman?" *Man*, 13: 133–4.

Shoffman, M. (2006a) "Iraqi Ayatollah Removes Gay Fatwa," May 15 ed.: Pink News Service.

—— (2006b) "Iraqi Ayatollah Sparks Outrage after Decreeing Death to Gays," March 17 ed.: Pink News Service.

—— (2006c) "The UAE Condemned for Jailing Gay People," International Gay and Lesbian Association News Website.

Shore, C. & Wright, S. (1997) "Policy: a new field of anthropology." *In* C. Shore & S. Wright (eds.) *Anthropology of Policy: critical perspectives on governance and power*, London; New York: Routledge, pp. 3–39.

Shukri, S. J. A. (1996) *Arab Women: unequal partners in development*, Brookfield, VT: Avebury Publishing Co.

SICA, (2006) *Ecuador: Main Agricultural Export Commodities*, Ecuador: SICA-IBRD/ MAG Project.

SIDA (Swedish International Development Cooperation Agency) (2007) *Sexual Orientation and Gender Identity Issues in Development*, Stockholm: SIDA.

Simmons, P. J. (1998) "Learning to Live with NGOs," *Foreign Policy Washington*, pp. 82–96.

Sinfield, A. (1998) *Gay and After*, London: Serpent's Tail.

—— (2004) *On Sexuality and Power*, New York: Columbia University Press.

—— (2006) "Rape and rights: measure for measure and the limits of cultural imperialism." *In* A. Sinfield (ed.) *Shakespeare, Authority, Sexuality: unfinished business in cultural materialism*, New York: Routledge.

Sinnott, M. (2004) *Toms and Dees: transgender identity and female same-sex relationships in Thailand*, Honolulu: University of Hawaii Press.

Sontag, S. (1977) *On Photography*, New York: Farrar, Straus and Giroux.

Sparr, P. (ed.) (1994) *Mortgaging Women's Lives: feminist critiques of structural adjustment*, London; Atlantic Highlands, NJ: Zed Books.

Spivak, G. (1988) "Can the subaltern speak?." *In* C. Nelson & L. Grossberg (eds.) *Marxism and the Interpretation of Culture*, Urbana: University of Illinois Press.

—— (1996) "'Woman' as theatre: Beijing 1995," *Radical Philosophy*, 75: 2–4.

Spruill, J. (2004) "Ad/Dressing the nation: drag and authenticity in post-apartheid South Africa," *Journal of Homosexuality*, 46: 91–112.

Sreberny, A. (1998) "Feminist internationalism: imagining and building global civil society." *In* D. K. Thussu (ed.) *Electronic Empires: global media and local resistance*, London; New York: Arnold, pp. 209–22.

Srinivas, M. N. (1965) *Religion and Society Among the Coorgs of South India*, New York: Asia Pub. House.

Standing, G. (2004) "Globalization: eight crises of social protection." *In* L. Benería & S. Bisnath (eds.) *Global Tensions: challenges and opportunities in the world economy*, New York: Routledge, pp. 111–33.

Steinbugler, A. C. (2005) "Visibility as privilege and danger: heterosexual and same-sex interracial intimacy in the 21st century," *Sexualities*, 8: 425–44.

Stevens, J. (2004) "The politics of LGBTQ scholarship," *GLQ: A Journal of Lesbian and Gay Studies*, 10: 220–6.

Stevenson, M. R. (1995) "Searching for a gay identity in Indonesia," *The Journal of Men's Studies*, 4: 93–108.

Strongman, R. (2002) "Syncretic religion and dissident sexualities." *In* A. Cruz & M. F. Manalansan (eds.) *Queer Gobalizations: citizenship and the afterlife of colonialism*, New York: New York University Press.

Stryker, S. & Whittle, S. (eds.) (2006) *The Transgender Studies Reader*, New York: Routledge.

Swarr, A. L. (2003) *South African Transgendered Subjectivities: exploring the boundaries of sex, gender, and race*, Minneapolis, MN: University of Minnesota.

Swarr, A. L. & Nagar, R. (2004) "Dismantling assumptions: interrogating 'lesbian' struggles for identity and survival in India and South Africa," *Signs*, 29: 491–516.

Swedenburg, T. (1997) "Saida Sultan/Dana International: transgender pop and polysemiotics of sex, nation, and ethnicity on the Israeli-Egyptian border," *The Musical Quarterly*, 81:1, 81–108.

Sylvester, C. (2006) "Bare life as a development/postcolonial problematic," *Geographical Journal*, 172: 66–77.

Tait, R. (2005) "A Fatwa for Transsexuals," *Salon*, July 27, 2005. Available at: http://dir.salon.com/story/news/feature/2005/07/28/iran_transsexuals/index.html. [accessed June 26, 2006].

Talcott, M. (2004) "Gendered webs of development and resistance: women, children, and flowers in Bogota," *Signs*, 29: 465–90.

Tamale, S. (2005) "Eroticism, sensuality and 'women's secrets' among the Baganda: a critical analysis," *Feminist Africa*, 5: 9–36.

Tellería, J. M. & Pers López, H. (1996) *Investigacion Sobre Masculinidades*, La Paz Bolivia Centro de Investigacion Social, Tecnologia Apropiada y Capacitacion (CISTAC).

Thomsen, S., Stalker, M. & Toroitich-Ruto, C. (2004) "Fifty ways to leave your rubber: how men in Mombasa rationalise unsafe sex," *Sexually Transmitted Infections*, 80: 430–4.

Tolman, D. L. (2002) *Dilemmas of Desire: teenage girls talk about sexuality*, Cambridge, MA: Harvard University Press.

Torbey, C. (2005) "Lebanon's gays struggle with law," *BBC News*.

Towle, E. B. & Morgan, L. M. (2002) "Romancing the transgender native: rethinking the use of the "third gender" concept," *GLQ*, 8: 469–98.

Treakle, K. (1998) "Ecuador: structural adjustment and indigenous and environmentalist resistance." *In* J. A. Fox, L. D. Brown & I. Netlibrary (eds.) *The Struggle for Accountability the World Bank, NGOs, and Grassroots Movements*, Cambridge, MA: MIT Press.

Tsing, A. L. (2005) *Friction: an ethnography of global connection*, Princeton, NJ: Princeton University Press.

Udry, C. (1996) "Gender, agricultural production, and the theory of the household," *Journal of Political Economy*, 104: 1010–46.

Urgent Action Fund (2006) *LGBTI Organizing in East Africa: the true test for human rights defenders*, Urgent Action Fund.

USAID (United States Agency for International Development) (2000) *The USAID Commitment: Women 2000, Beijing Plus Five*, Washington, DC: USAID, Office of Women in Development.

Vance, C. S. (1984) *Pleasure and Danger: exploring female sexuality*, Boston: Routledge & Kegan Paul.

Vargas, V. (2003) "Feminism, Globalization and the Global Justice and Solidarity Movement," *Cultural Studies 17*(6): 905–20.

Wagner, J. (2005) *Kaaya – the process. Kaaya, beyond gender: a window into the lives of a transgender community*, New Delhi: Centre for Media and Alternative Communication.

Waite, J. (2005) Personal Interview.

Wallace-Lorencová, V. (2003) "Queering civil society in postsocialist Slovakia," *Anthropology of East Europe Review*, Amherst: University of Massachusetts.

Waring, M. (1988) *If Women Counted: a new feminist economics*, San Francisco: Harper & Row.

Warner, M. (1993) "Introduction," in M. Warner (ed.) *Fear of a Queer Planet: Queer Politics and Social Theory*, Minneapolis: University of Minnesota Press.

Wassersug, R. (2004) "Eunuch power in old Byzantium: their bisexuality was emblematic of eunuchs' varied social roles," *Gay and Lesbian Review*, 11: 18–20.

Weston, K. (1991) *Families We Choose: lesbians, gays, kinship*, New York: Columbia University Press.

Westphal-Hellbusch, S. (1997) "Institutionalized gender-crossing in southern Iraq." *In* S.O. Murray & W. Roscoe (eds.) *Islamic Homosexualities: culture, history, and literature*, New York: New York University Press.

WHO (World Health Organization) (2002) "Gender and Human Rights: sexual health." Available at: http://www.who.int/reproductivehealth/topics/gender_rights/sexual_health/en/ [accessed August 26, 2009].

—— (n.d.) *Technical Consultation on Sexual Health: working definitions*, Geneva: WHO.

Wieringa, S. & Morgan, R. (2005) *Tommy Boys, Lesbian Men and Ancestral Wives*, Johannesburg; London: Jacana; Global [distributor].

Wikan, U. (1977) "Man becomes woman: transsexualism in Oman as a key to gender roles," *Man*, 12: 304–19.

Wilchins, R. A. (1997) *Read My Lips: sexual subversion and the end of gender*, Ithaca, NY: Firebrand Books.

—— (2002) "A continuous nonverbal communication." *In* J. Nestle, C. Howell & R. A. Wilchins (eds.) *Genderqueer: voices from beyond the sexual binary*, Los Angeles: Alyson Books.

—— (2004) *Queer Theory, Gender Theory: an instant primer*, Los Angeles: Alyson Books.

Wilson, A. (1996) "Lesbian visibility and sexual rights at Beijing," *Signs*, 22: 214.

—— (2002) "The transnational geography of sexual rights." *In* M. Bradley & P. Petro (eds.) *Truth Claims: representation and human rights*, New Brunswick, NJ: Rutgers University Press.

—— (2004) *The Intimate Economies of Bangkok: tomboys, tycoons, and Avon ladies in the global city*, Berkeley: University of California Press.

Wood, C. (2003) "Economic marginalia: postcolonial readings of unpaid domestic labor and development." *In* D. K. Barker & E. Kuiper (eds.) *Toward a Feminist Philosophy of Economics*, London; New York: Routledge.

World Bank (1996) *Ecuador Poverty Report: a World Bank country study*, Washington D.C.: World Bank.

—— (1997a) *Ecuador International Trade and Integration Project: project appraisal document*, Report Number 17882, Washington DC: World Bank.

—— (1997b) *Ecuador: Export Development Project: project information document*, Report Number PIC 2564, Washington DC: World Bank.

—— (2001a) *Building a Positive Work Environment: working with respect in the World Bank Group*, Working Paper, Report Number 23944, Washington DC: World Bank.

—— (2001b) *Engendering Development through Gender Equality in Rights, Resources, and Voice*, Washington DC: World Bank/Oxford University Press.

—— (2003a) *Ecuador – International Trade and Integration Project: implementation completion report*. Report Number 27376, Washington DC: World Bank.

—— (2003b) *Ecuador – International Trade and Integration Project: implementation completion report*, Report Number 27376, Washington DC: World Bank.

—— (2003c) *Indigenous and Afro-Ecuadorian People's Development Project: implementation completion report*. Report Number 25361, Washington DC: World Bank.

——(2003d) *Indigenous and Afro-Ecuadorian People's Development Project: implementation completion report*. Report Number 25361, Washington DC: World Bank.

—— (2004a) *Ecuador Poverty Assessment*. PREM Sector Unit, LAC Region, April, Report number 27061-EC, Washington DC: World Bank.

—— (2004b) "Integration of gender issues in selected HIV/AIDS projects in the Africa region: a baseline assessment," *ARHD Report No. 67*, Washington DC: Prepared by The Gender and Development Group (PREM), The World Bank.

—— (2004c) "Targeting vulnerable groups in national HIV/AIDS programs: the case of men who have sex with men – Senegal, Burkina Faso, the Gambia," *ARHD Working Paper 82*, Human Development Sector, Africa Region: World Bank Group.

World Bank, Gender and Rural Development Thematic Group and the Land Policy and Administration Thematic Group of the World Bank (2005) "Gender Issues and Best Practices in Land Administration Projects, A Synthesis Report," Washington DC: World Bank.

Wright, T. (2000) "Gay organizations, NGOs and the globalization of sexual identity: the case of Bolivia," *Journal of Latin American Anthropology*, 5: 89–111.

Wright, T. R. (2006) *Bolivia, Making Gays in a Queer Place: AIDS, modernization, and the politics of sexual identity*. Berkeley: University of California Press.

Wynne-Jones, R. (1999) "Princess who wants to live happily ever after as a boy," *Express on Sunday*, June 13. Available at: http://www.pfc.org.uk/node/850 [accessed October 20, 2009].

Xerox World: news for active and retired employees of The Document Company (1995) Issue No. 1. Available at: http://www.galaxe.org [accessed May 2008].

Yenicioğlu, Y. (1997) *Gay Identities, Communities and Places in the 1990s in Istanbul*, Ýstanbul University, Department of Theatre Criticism.

Young, R. (1995) *Colonial Desire: Hybridity in Theory, Culture, and Race*, London; New York: Routledge.

Zein-Elabdin, E. (2003) The Difficulty of a Feminist Economics. *In* D. K. Barker & E. Kuiper (eds.) *Toward a Feminist Philosophy of Economics*, London; New York: Routledge.

Zuhur, S. (2005) *Gender, Sexuality and the Criminal Laws in the Middle East and North Africa: A Comparative Study*, Istanbul, Turkey: Women for Women's Human Rights (WWHR).

—— (2003) Women and Empowerment in the Arab World. *Arab Studies Quarterly*, 25, 17–38.

Index

Dana International 148
de Camps, M. 176–7
Demir, D. 148, 153
Deutsche Gesellschaft für Technische Zusammenarbeit (GTZ) 41, 42, 45
development: attitudes to 7–10, 23–4; queer practitioners in 10–12
Dominican Republic: "Anthology of Gay and Homophobic Literature in the Dominican Republic" 176–7; arrests 178–9; Catholic Church 172–4; colonial legacies 171–5; comedy (*Which Sex does Javier Prefer?*) 177–8; global impulses 175–80; identity politics 170–1; legal framework 171–2; media 175–6, 179; pride celebrations 179–80; queer visibility/invisibility 174, 176, 179–80
Dowsett, G. *et al.* 134
Dowuona, S. 24–5

economics: dependency of women 24–5; households models 56–63
Ecuador 13–14, 61, 62, 134; World Bank floriculture and gender roles study 100–9
Egypt 147–8, 149, 153
empowerment 34–6
Epprecht, M. 166–7
Equality Project (EP), South Africa 13
Ersoy, Bülent 147

Familia Galan 124–5
family: heteronormative constructions of 7–8, 9–10, 113–14; impact of employment 103–5; *see also* households; marriage
Featherstone, M. 94
female-headed households 59–60, 109, 115, 119, 120–1
feminist economics: households models 56–63
Ferguson, J. 45, 54, 57, 89, 91–2, 96
Fiji 134
Fisher, W.F. 91
flower industry: Colombia 60; Ecuador 100–9
Folbre, N. 59–60
Friedemann-Sánchez, G. 60

Galan, D. 125
game-theoretical models of households 58
Gamson, J. 133, 136; and Moon, D. 157–8

Gay, Lesbian or Bisexual Employees (GLOBE), World Bank 67–8; achievements 69–70; as gay-friendly organization 70, 71, 72; goals 69; HIV/AIDS issue 76, 77–8, 80–2; limitations 81–2; membership 67–8, 72; queering development 75–81, 82–3; race, gender and class issues 72–5; related developments 68–9; and UNGLOBE 10–12; visibility 70–1
gays and lesbians: community 35; rights 3; *see also entries beginning* lesbian
Gays and Lesbians of Zimbabwe (GALZ) 78
gender inequality *see* power relations
gender justice *see* sexual rights and gender justice
gender roles 27; Ecuadorian floriculture study 100–9
Global Emergency AIDS Act (2003), US 26
González, M.F. 173
Gosine, A. 7, 8, 9, 54, 81
Green, J. 158, 171, 172
Guattari, F. 170

Hardt, M. and Negri, A. 89, 90, 94
Hart, G. 62
Hazra, A. 32–3
Hélie, A. 152, 153–4
Hennessy, R. 158
heteronormativity 2; constructions of family 7–8, 9–10, 113–14; and development policy 61–3, 99, 109, 110, 117–22; and non-normative framework 5–6
heterosexual matrix 15, 55, 60, 63
heterosexuality: adolescent girls, US 34–5; and gender inequality 29–30; reproductive 9, 10
hijras 27, 28, 39–41; *see also Kaaya: Beyond Gender* photographic series
HIV/AIDS 8, 9, 23, 134; GLOBE 76, 77–8, 80–2; prevention programs, Bolivia 114, 117–18, 122, 123; transgender people 28; women 23, 24–5
homosexuality; Latin America 171–5; Middle East 149, 150; *see also* men who have sex with men (MSM)
households: female-headed 59–60, 109, 115, 119, 120–1; models 56–63
housework 106–7, 108, 109
Hubbard, P. 92–3

eBooks – at www.eBookstore.tandf.co.uk

A library at your fingertips!

eBooks are electronic versions of printed books. You can store them on your PC/laptop or browse them online.

They have advantages for anyone needing rapid access to a wide variety of published, copyright information.

eBooks can help your research by enabling you to bookmark chapters, annotate text and use instant searches to find specific words or phrases. Several eBook files would fit on even a small laptop or PDA.

NEW: Save money by eSubscribing: cheap, online access to any eBook for as long as you need it.

Annual subscription packages

We now offer special low-cost bulk subscriptions to packages of eBooks in certain subject areas. These are available to libraries or to individuals.

For more information please contact webmaster.ebooks@tandf.co.uk

We're continually developing the eBook concept, so keep up to date by visiting the website.

www.eBookstore.tandf.co.uk